AFTER LIMBANG

A Royal Marines Anthology of Experiences of the Confrontation with Indonesia December 1962 to September 1966

Compiled by

Lt Col Brian Edwards RM

Series Editor

Captain Derek Oakley MBE RM

ROYAL MARINES HISTORICAL SOCIETY
SPECIAL PUBLICATION NO 36

AFTER LIMBANG

978 0 9536163 8 1

First published 2010 by the
ROYAL MARINES HISTORICAL SOCIETY
Royal Marines Museum
Eastney
Southsea
Hants PO4 9PX
United Kingdom

Printed and bound in Great Britain by
CPI Antony Rowe Ltd, Chippenham and Eastbourne

Contents

Foreword

By Major General Julian Thompson CB, OBE

Denis Healey, Secretary of State for Defence during the last two years of Confrontation, commenting in his memoirs on the highly successful campaign, said that it was a 'textbook demonstration of how to use economy of force, under political guidance for political ends'. The passage of time has not produced any evidence to refute this assertion. In his book *Brushfire Wars*, Michael Dewar, himself a Greenjacket, remarks that although some fifteen British Regiments served in Borneo, 'the brunt [of the campaign] undoubtedly had been borne by the eight Gurkha battalions and the two Royal Marine Commandos'.

Greenjackets are not given to handing out plaudits, and what Dewar says is nothing less than the truth. However, as is the way of our Corps, we do not go about shooting things like this from the housetops. It is therefore timely that Lieutenant Colonel Brian Edwards has compiled this Royal Marines Historical Society Special Publication. Although he calls it *After Limbang*, it includes a chapter on that remarkable operation by L Company, 42 Commando on December 1962, led by the then Captain Jeremy Moore. From then on until the end of Confrontation in August 1966, there was a period of only six weeks when there was no Royal Marine unit or sub-unit in Borneo. Even then there were several individuals serving there as helicopter pilots, staff officers or on special tasks.

There is still some doubt in some circles about how much of a hand the Indonesians under President Soekarno had in the Brunei revolt of December 1962, which is usually depicted as kickstarting the campaign, which became to be known as 'Confrontation', a word coined by the Indonesians. But there is no doubt that the revolt acted as a catalyst for what followed. The Indonesian Foreign Minister announced in January 1963, 'We cannot but adopt a policy of Confrontation against Malaya because at present they present themselves as accomplices of the neo-imperialist pursuing a hostile policy towards Indonesia'.

Confrontation was divided into roughly three phases. From April 1963 to February 1964, the Indonesians pursued a combination of subversion and guerrilla war. The next phase involved the Indonesian Army, employing deep penetration raids to set up guerrilla bases, and shallow incursions to intimidate the local population. Indonesian regular soldiers accompanied the raiding parties. From time to time these raiding sub-units not only stood their ground, but occasionally counter-attacked. The Indonesian units on the border at this time probably numbered no more than 2,500, one third of them regulars. In January 1965, the Indonesians turned up the pressure, and committed regular army units to cross-border attacks on British bases in Borneo. Accordingly, the Indonesian strength in the border areas increased to possibly as high as 30,000.

The accounts in After Limbang give a very good feel for the way in which the campaign escalated. After the initial operations to suppress the Brunei revolt, the tempo slackened for a while, before picking up. The effect this had on the Troops taking part comes across clearly. Confrontation started as a Section Commander's war, soon becoming a Troop Commander's war. By the end it was a Company Commander's war, with occasionally two companies taking part in the same operation.

The outcome of Confrontation was by no means inevitable, as it might seem with the benefit of hindsight. The picture in the early 1960s looked quite different. After kicking out the Dutch from most of their Far East possessions by 1949, Soekarno, with UN support, finally ejected them from their last foothold, Netherlands New Guinea, as late as 1963. He had a 300,000 strong army, and had recently received a billion dollar arms loan from the USA. He might have turned the campaign into the kind of open sore that eventually persuaded a number of European powers to quit involvement in their colonies or former colonies.

The British fortunately had plenty of experience of fighting in the jungle. The more senior had fought in Burma and many of the middle rank in the Malayan Emergency. Those with experience in Malaya found that campaigning in Borneo was even more difficult. Operations took place over a wider area, and included coastal regions. The jungle was more extensive, the country was more challenging in every way: more mountainous, bigger rivers, extensive swamps, mangrove on the coast, and violent tropical storms, all present in Malaya yes, but in a vastly greater scale in Borneo. The enemy in Borneo was far more formidable than the Communist terrorists encountered in Malaya: better trained and equipped, considerably more numerous, and operating from secure bases inside their own country.

Without the support of helicopters the British would not have succeeded in covering the nearly 1,000 miles of border, and reacting to incursions across it, let along being able to operate across it themselves. So it is good to see two accounts by helicopter pilots in *After Limbang*.

There are some excellent accounts of cross border operations, codenamed Claret, in *After Limbang*. To this day, an aura of secrecy surrounds these operations. Quite why remains a mystery, since the Indonesians make no secrecy of their operations in the opposite direction. It had been argued that Soekarno was complicit if keeping Claret operations under wraps, not wishing to publicize the British intrusions and so revealing his own weaknesses, and the folly of his own policy. Claret operations contributed to British success by forcing the Indonesians back from the frontier, and making their own incursion more difficult.

Confrontation in Borneo is a good example of a campaign where low, mid and high intensity war can all be taking place in the same theatre of operations simultaneously. At the tactical level the rules of engagement were those of conventional war; in a nutshell kill the enemy. At the operational and strategic levels, soldiers and politicians were very careful to use force selectively and take into account the political implications of every move. For this reason, I believe that this publication is of as much interest to the serving Corps as it is to the retired. I congratulate the contributors, the editor Derek Oakley and the compiler Brian Edwards; both of whom took part in the campaign, on an excellent publication.

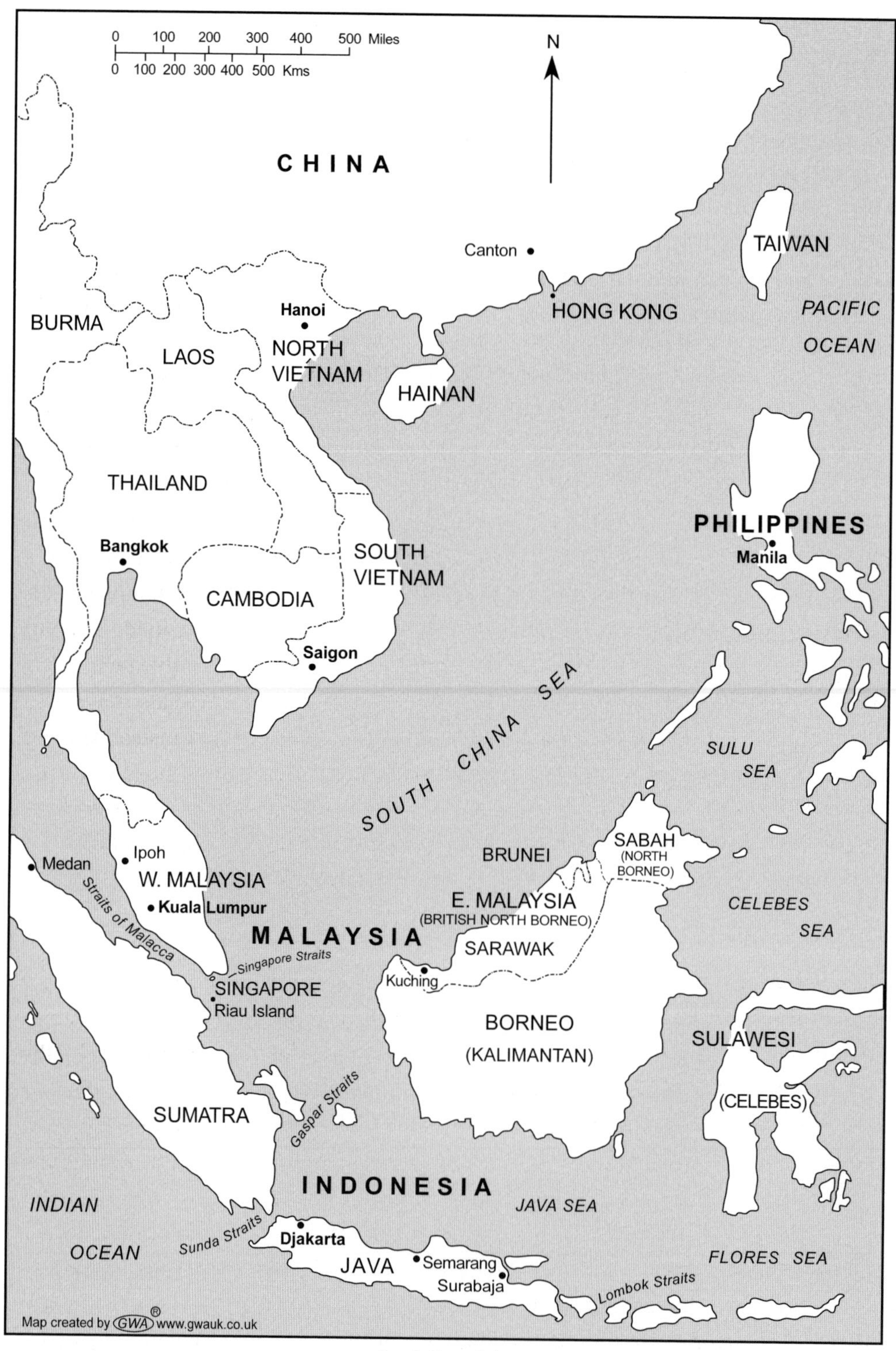

South East Asia

Introduction
'An Impossible Task'

From time to time the Council of the Royal Marines Historical Society seeks to identify significant gaps in published coverage of the history of the Corps. For the past few years two specific areas have been noted as having priority among those that are in need of tackling. First and alone among the RM Commando units, 42 Commando has no recorded history. In recent years two attempts to fill the gap have been initiated but these have proved abortive. Second and arguably the more immediate priority task, as the surviving participants' ages increase, is the Corps' four-year involvement in the Confrontation with Indonesia, between 1962 and 1966. Somewhat as a hostage to fortune, I therefore undertook to compile an account for publication by the Society.

One colleague has referred to the project as an 'Impossible Task'. Certainly it would be impossible to attempt to write a definitive account of the Campaign, made complex by the political fluctuations and by the Royal Marines' piecemeal involvement, under a system by which units did not necessarily relieve each other; it would also have been outside the normal scope of the Society's publications. I have sought instead to piece together a number of personal accounts obtained from a selection of those who took part and to place them in some sort of sequence in time and location. In doing so I have had recourse to relevant contemporary articles published in the Corps journal, *The Globe & Laurel*, and to the relevant 'war diaries' in the National Archives.

Confrontation

The insurrection sponsored by Indonesia in Brunei in December 1962 spilt over into the neighbouring area of Sarawak, the fifth of its five administrative divisions, with a capital at the small town of Limbang. When the rebellion was crushed by the quick response of Gurkha and British troops, Indonesia began a process described as 'Confrontation', a political and military offensive which 'allowed' cross border terrorist attacks and encouraged internal subversion, while stopping short of a declaration of war. Indonesia's immediate aim was to derail the arrangements for the transfer to a Malaysian Federation of the former British territories along its northern border in Borneo (Kalimantan). Over the next three and a half years, Indonesian initiatives were frustrated by the successful defence and the sustained but graduated military response provided by British and Commonwealth troops. This eventually allowed a political solution which saw the establishment of Malaysia as the viable federation that it remains to this day.

For an understanding of the complex political aspects and the various stages of 'Confrontation' I have relied largely on the book under that title by Nick van der Bijl, published by Pen and Sword in 2007. The book is an excellent reference for this purpose; however, while the author acknowledges the extent of the Corps' involvement in the campaign, it is hoped that this publication will go some way complement his story.

3 Commando Brigade

HQ 3 Commando Brigade, 40 Commando and 42 Commando were deployed to the Far East in the early sixties, when HQ and 42 Commando were based in Singapore and 40 Commando in Johore on the Malayan mainland. This was the last such overseas deployment in which those married could be accompanied by their family. Posting to the HQ and to units was for two years on the 'trickle draft' system; there was therefore continuous turnover, ensuring that there was always at least a leavening of seasoned jungle operators; conversely there were always some novices and the number of men in the pipeline each way meant that units were never at full strength.

During the period of Confrontation, between April '63 and September '66, one Commando was always deployed somewhere in Borneo, give or take a few days. As might be expected in an undeclared war, there were twilight periods, when operations continued but individuals were withdrawn from their border posts to play in inter-service sporting competitions back in Singapore or to take part in a ceremonial occasion. There were even times when some of those deployed in Sarawak might have felt that they were in less danger than their families, exposed to racial riots in Singapore or Indonesian incursions into mainland Malaya.

Those joining units were randomly prepared, depending on previous experience, the availability of courses and the pressure of operations. During much of 1963 and 64 the tasks to be covered by a unit deployed to Borneo dictated the provision of a maximum number of four man patrols. This and periodic shortages of Junior NCOs meant that a young Marine on the list of candidates for promotion was quickly required to prove his leadership qualities; few failed. Likewise the young officer arriving for his year's attachment to a Commando, in the middle of his training courses, quickly found himself in command of a front line patrol base, with miles of jungle between him and his Company Commander, a Troop of NCOs and men among whom he was possibly the youngest and with the responsibility for protecting a number of tribal villages from incursions across an extensive stretch of border. It was a heady introduction to operational soldiering and a prime school for aspiring junior leaders.

Deployments

Beginning at the other end of the scale, the Brigade Headquarters deployed to Sarawak three times; twice to Kuching, as HQ West Brigade in '62/'63, and once to Sibu for a brief period in early '65, as HQ of the newly formed Mid-West Brigade. The Brigade Commander changed twice during the period of Confrontation.

Both 40 and 42 Commandos were involved in the operations that immediately followed the Brunei insurrection; 42 Commando in Brunei and Sarawak's Fifth Division between December '62 and the end of March' 63; 40 Commando in various areas of Sarawak and North Borneo, beginning in December '62 and ending in January '63.

In March '63, B Company of 40 Commando returned to Kuching to provide a military presence in Sarawak's First Division, where, following a raid on a border police station during the second week of April, they were joined by Brigade Headquarters and the rest of the Commando. During the first six weeks of this deployment 40 Commando also had 'L' Company of 42 Commando under command. In July '63, 42 Commando relieved 40 and began a system of roulement that would continue until the end of Confrontation.

By April '65 each unit had served two tours in Sarawak's First Division, followed by one each in Sabah (North Borneo). 40 Commando's so-called fourth tour began in May '65 in the Serian District of Sarawak's First D division, while 42 Commando's followed in December '65 in the Lundu District and ended in May '66. With Confrontation drawing to a close in May '66, 40 Commando began a fifth and final tour in the Second Division of Sarawak.

During the whole period from December '62 to September '66, each unit twice changed Commanding Officer. Locations differed but each CO found himself rich in responsibility – military, territorial and political – but could sometimes be limited in resources, freedom to respond or means to control. This potentially 'no win' situation is perhaps typified by the CO who was a passenger in the back of a helicopter, navigated off a near featureless map across an unmarked border, to touch down briefly in Indonesia and initiate ripples that reached 10 Downing Street. The Society's recent publication, *The Long Summer* by Colonel 'Paddy' Stevens, told the experiences of a Commanding Officer of 45 Commando during the 'Radfan' campaign; this publication sets out to capture the experiences of those at lower or sub-unit level during 'Confrontation'

Coverage

Each Commando normally had three rifle companies, though 40 Commando twice cobbled together a fourth (D Company); L Company, which I commanded during three deployments to Borneo, is probably typical in having four Company Commanders during the campaign; this suggests that across both units some two dozen or more officers enjoyed this responsibility at some stage. A similar simplistic estimate for the total of eighteen rifle troops within the two Commandos suggests that some eighty subalterns served in this capacity. To these must be added the succession of Recce Troop

Commanders, as well as Heavy Weapons Troop Commanders who often operated as additional rifle troops. The spread of operations and the nature of the country meant that sub-unit Commanders at company and/or Troop level were the most closely involved and it is they that have provided the majority of contributions to this account.

The importance and difficulties of radio communications is frequently mentioned and specifically addressed in contributions at each level of the Signals hierarchy. In this context specific mention is due to Captain Ray Frost, 42 Commando Signals Officer and instigator of the 'Yagi' Aerial; Ray Frost died in 1996 but had already provided accounts of his experiences in contemporary editions of the Corps Journal, from which we are privileged to quote in appropriate detail.

In whatever location the units found themselves, mobility of men and supplies was a problem. Roads were few, rivers difficult and distances great. Aircraft were therefore essential, both fixed wing and rotor. Fixed wing aircraft moved men to, from and, to a lesser extent, within the theatre of operations. The principal provider of fixed wing aircraft was of course the Royal Air Force, but the RASC also provided a Beaver communication flight and the gunners Auster air OPs, while civilian Twin Pioneer aircraft played a crucial part in suppressing the original rebellion in Brunei and Sarawak. The RAF and the RNZAF provided regular supply drops to forward bases and patrols; if close to the border, they were escorted by RAF Javelin fighters. All these operators receive appropriate reference but the Corps had no fixed wing pilots and no direct involvement in fixed wing provision other than as users.

In an area in which steep contours and forests predominated, the work horse of the campaign was bound to be the helicopter. Every account refers to movement or supply by helicopter, or 'chopper'. The RAF operated twin rotor Belvedere and single rotor Whirlwind 10 aircraft; in Sabah the Malaysian forces operated Alouette light helicopters; the Naval Air Squadrons from *Albion* and *Bulwark* operated Wessex (845 and 848 Squadrons) and Whirlwind 7 aircraft (846 Squadron). Finally, in their last tours each Commando deployed with its own integral Air Troop, equipped with the Sioux light helicopter. The Naval Air Squadrons included Royal Marines among the pilots and both they and the Air Troops are represented among the contributors. This is in no way detracts from the skilled support given by RAF and RN pilots and specifically acknowledged in various accounts.

Apart from two short periods in the early stages of the campaign, *Albion* and *Bulwark* operated outside the 'Commando ship' tactical concept, simply deploying and withdrawing units and supporting the helicopter detachments ashore; arguably the most complex move was that involving the three way rotation of both Commandos and a battalion of Malaysian Rangers in December '65. Amphibious training with a Commando embarked was, therefore, an important task to be fitted into a very full calendar in a unit's period of rehabilitation, once back in Singapore or Johore.

This aspect is outside the general scope of this account but receives some coverage from the 'Company Signaller' (Chapter 10) who also tells of 42 Commando's very limited involvement in Indonesia's mainland venture of mid to late '64.

Last among the RM participants to be considered are Nos 1 and 2 Special Boat Section. Always a grey area by design, the SBS coverage has not been straight forward; an apparently arbitrary ruling provides a degree of censorship on related subject matter after 1959. In particular this has meant that specific targets and dates have been omitted but we are left with a clear picture of the scale and nature of SBS involvement and of their contemporary procedures.

There are of course areas that could receive greater attention if space permitted. Foremost among these might be the Commando Batteries, Royal Artillery. They and other batteries feature in relevant accounts, but space has limited more specific coverage to Royal Marines or those serving in their units. In no way is this intended to detract from the importance of the contribution made by gunners throughout the campaign; nor should it be interpreted as lessening the perceived affinity between the Commando units and the Batteries of the Commando Light Regiment.

The breadth of experience covered by several accounts has meant that relevant sections have been placed in different Chapters – or appropriate appendices – to match the time, subject or locations involved and to introduce a degree of continuity into the publication. Two examples will perhaps suffice. Keith Wilkins served in 42 Commando between '62 and '64, during which he deployed to Borneo three times; in one he commanded the Recce Troop, in the next the Mortar Troop and, after a brief interlude with anti-tank weapons, in the third he was Second-in-Command of K Company. Ian Uzzell went to and from the Commando Brigade three times; in '62/'63 he was serving his training attachment as a Troop Commander in 40 Commando; on completion of training he came back in '64 as a Troop Commander in 42 Commando; in '66, after flying training, he joined the Air Troop of 40 Command in time for the final tour in Sarawak's Second Division.

Acknowledgements

However they have been fitted into the narrative, the substance and honesty of the contributions have turned a so called 'impossible task' into what I believe to be a comprehensive portrayal of the involvement of the Royal Marines and their units in the various stages of Confrontation. For this the contributors listed below have my special gratitude; each input has been attributed in the text and shown with quotation marks at the beginning of each paragraph. Where appropriate I have introduced one or more paragraphs to lend continuity or fill gaps in the overall narrative; occasionally, where I was directly involved, I have lapsed into the first person; these paragraphs should be self evident to the reader if only because of the absence of quotation marks.

I am grateful for the substantial help and support given by colleagues in the Society – in addition to those members who have provided a significant percentage of the contributions. Particular thanks are also due to the Editor of *The Globe & Laurel* for permission to quote extensively from contemporary editions and to John Ambler for his assistance in providing illustrations from the archives of the Royal Marines Museum.

Many of the photographs have come from the contributors while others are from collections of individuals where the sources are not known. We thank all of them and note that, as these are now all over forty years old and taken on personal cameras, the quality varies occasionally.

I am indebted to Nick van der Byl for allowing us to use the excellent maps previously published in his book *'Confrontation' – the War with Indonesia 1962–66*; and to his illustrator Peter Wood.

I have also quoted briefly from Lord Ashdown's recent autobiography in respect of one operation in Lundu District in March/April '64

The views of the compiler and contributors are of course their own and not necessarily those of the Society; likewise, though I have endeavoured to check accuracy of general facts, such as dates, names and locations, and to make appropriate amendments, we are each custodian of our own errors for which I apologise collectively in advance.

Contributors – in order of first appearance

Derek Oakley	Capt	GSO 3 (Int)	HQ 3 Cdo Bde	Ch 1,2,3,4 and 8; Appx D
Terry Clarke	SBA	L and M Coy	42 Cdo	Ch 1, 2, 3 and 4
Keith Wilkins	Lt	OC Recce Tp	42 Cdo	Ch 2
		OC Mortar Tp		Ch 4
	Capt	2I/C K Coy		Ch 6
Ian Uzzell	2nd Lt	OC 7 Tp	40 Cdo	Ch 2
	Lt	OC 9 Tp	42 Cdo	Ch 6
	Lt	Air Tp	40 Cdo	Ch 14
Pat Gardner	Capt	OC B Coy	40 Cdo	Ch 3 and 6; Appx A and D
Ian Moore	Lt	OC 5 Tp	42 Cdo	Ch 3 and 4
Alan Hooper	Lt	IO and OC 4 Tp	42 Cdo	Ch 4
D Christie-Miller	2nd Lt	OC 5 Tp	42 Cdo	Ch 7
Martin Read	2nd Lt	OC 6 Tp	42 Cdo	Ch 8 and 9; Appx B and D
Dick Sidwell	Capt	Adjt	40 Cdo	Ch 9
		OC B Coy		Ch 11; Appx D
R A M Seeger	Lt	OC 6 Tp	40 Cdo	Ch 9
		OC D Coy		Ch 11; Appx B
Andrew Jackson	S3	Signal Troop	42 Cdo	Ch 9 and 10; Appx D
Sam Pope	Lt	Asst BSO	HQ 3 Cdo Bde	Ch 11

John Weston	Major	OC C Coy	40 Cdo.	Ch 11
Mick Reece	Capt	Det Comd	845 NAS Sqn.	Ch 12; Appx D
Tom Seccombe	Capt	OC M Coy	42 Cdo	Ch13
David Mitchell	Capt	OC	2 SBS	Ch 15

Attributed extracts from The Globe & Laurel

Ray Frost	Capt	Signals Offr	42 Cdo	Ch 1, 2 and 5
Peter Darling	Maj	SOO	42 Cdo	Ch 2
R Van der Horst	Lt	‘Rupertforce’	42 Cdo	Ch 2
Edwards	Sgt	Recce Tp	42 Cdo	Ch 9
Phillips	LCpl	HQ Coy	42 Cdo	Appx E

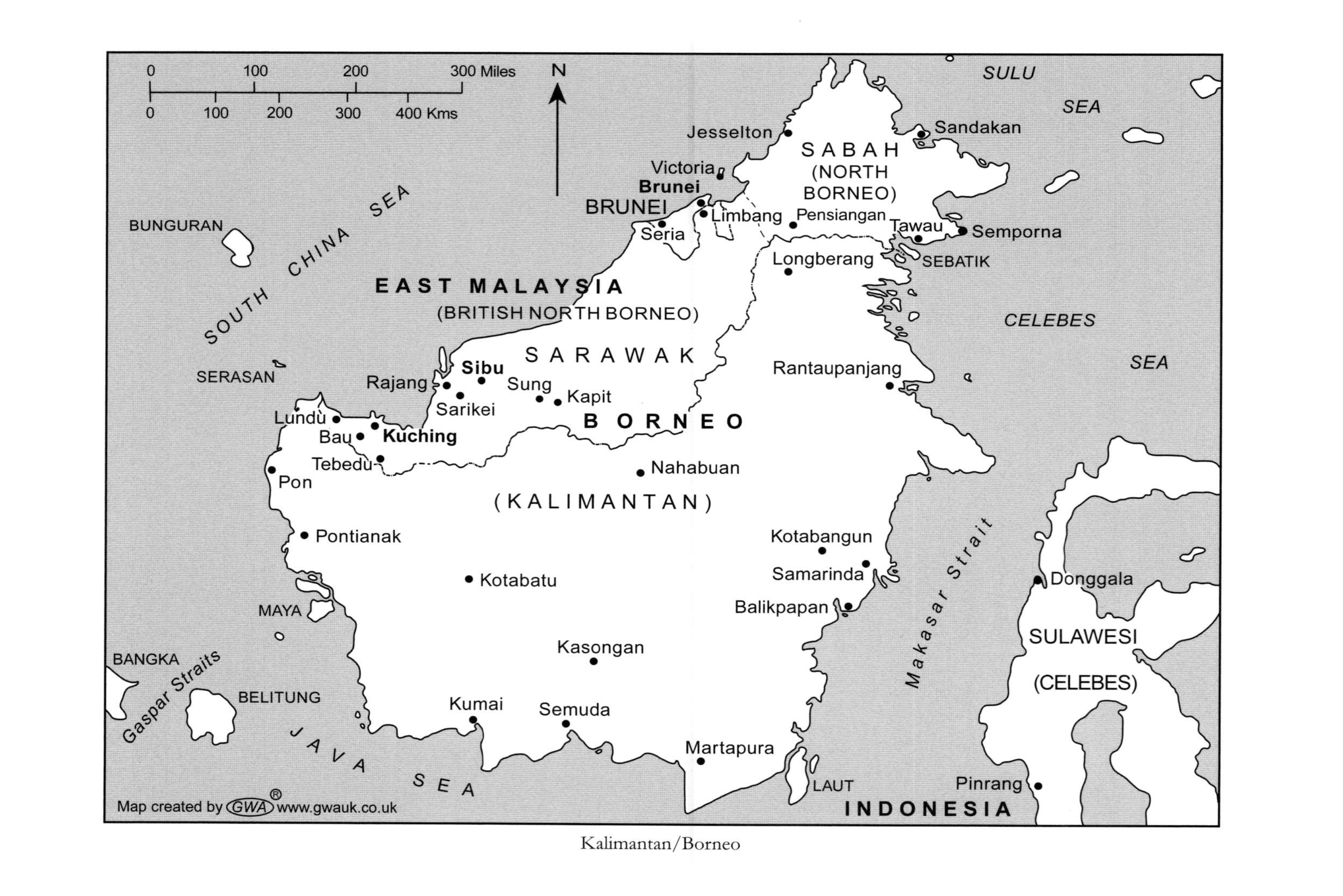

Kalimantan/Borneo

Chapter 1

Brunei Insurrection

Prelude to Confrontation

December 1962

Brunei Insurrection

The Beginning

Captain Derek Oakley was 3 Commando Brigade's GSO3 Intelligence (G3 Int) at the time of the Brunei Insurrection in December '62. For the next thirteen months he spent nearly all of his overseas tour in Borneo, either fulfilling his duties as Brigade Intelligence Officer or acting as the Brigade's liaison officer with other Headquarters. He probably saw less of his family in Singapore than did any other member of the Brigade on an accompanied tour; conversely he was uniquely involved and well informed on the development of the Campaign in its first year,

Derek Oakley, Captain – G3 Int

'Until 1962 the island of Borneo, the second largest island in the world, was divided into the vast southern area under Indonesian rule and three British dependencies, Sarawak (the largest), North Borneo and, sandwiched between them, the tiny but very rich protectorate of Brunei. With British interests gradually declining in this part of the Far East, a federation of these three Borneo states with Malaya and Singapore was emerging. Although the indigenous tribes of the Borneo jungle were basically hard working and distant from political and territorial ideals, many, including the Kedayans were of Indonesian origin. Through such tribes, the Indonesian Army had infiltrated and trained some in the use of arms, so that when the time was right, they could rebel against the Sultan of Brunei.

'Such in simplest terms was the background to a revolt which was sparked off in early December 1962, when several towns were occupied by rebels – including Brunei town and Limbang – a small community twelve miles up river and across the border in Sarawak, where lived the British Resident of the colony's 5th Division. Although the revolt had been planned for 5 December, seizure of hostages at Limbang, Seria, Miri and other towns took place on the morning of the 8th.

'On the evening of Saturday 8 December, my wife Pam and I, along with many of the officers of Brigade Headquarters, had been invited to a supper with our DAA and QMG, Alec Horsfall and his wife. I do not remember anyone saying that there was a flap on but then Singapore parties were often like that and it was something of a rarity for Alec to 'push the boat out'. We arrived home in our usual inebriated, hot and sticky state and went to bed at some unearthly hour of the morning.

'Because the children were always up at crack of dawn, even on a Sunday, and were being given breakfast by our amah, there was not much need for us to make an early appearance. Admittedly Philip was only three months old so needed attention. About 1030 hrs the telephone rang and Pam said it was the Brigade Major, Roger Ephraums, on the phone and I was to report to Sembawang, our HQ up in the north of the Island, immediately as there was an emergency. I clambered into some form of uniform and jumped into the car. I was not feeling at all good and not only was my stomach churning but I also felt sick. Too much booze and maybe something wrong with the food last night.

'I arrived up at the 'Birdcage' – as the HQ block was called – to be met by Roger Ephraums and Brigadier Billy Barton, both looking unusually pale but otherwise calmly unflustered. Their pallidity was likewise due to the party the previous evening. They said there was a revolt in the town of Brunei on the mainland of Borneo and some hostages had been taken in the nearby village of Limbang in Sarawak, the residency of the 5th Division. These were places of which I was unaware at the time but have been engraved on my heart ever since. Almost as soon as I arrived I was asked whether I could remember the top secret code word we had been given (and swallowed!) when being briefed in the UK by the Intelligence authorities. Neither of them could remember and we needed it to confirm that we could open some top secret documents and orders. Naturally I had also forgotten it so we decided to open the documents anyway.

'I was given a quick briefing on the situation, told that 42 Commando were already on their way and to go to the Army's GHQ (Far East Land Forces) to see what I could glean, get intelligence reports on the area and draw maps. My driver had been alerted and I drove home to King's Road to return my car and get myself better kitted up, then we went to GHQ. I suppose I spent an hour or so there and was fairly well briefed, though no one had much idea of what the situation was.

'On my arrival back at the Birdcage, I briefed the Brigadier and Brigade Major on what I had gleaned and after a brief discussion, Billy Barton said to me "Right, I want you to join up with this ad hoc Brigade Headquarters that is going to Brunei as our representative and liaison officer with 42 Commando". On enquiring how I should get there he said, "There are plenty of Royal Navy ships going – catch the first one you can find" and he promptly disappeared into more planning. I collected a few more maps and some Confidential Books that dealt with Brunei and Sarawak, stuffed them into my already full equipment and was driven up to the Dockyard all ready to go to war!'

A Rough Trip to War

'I enquired which ships were going and was told that the destroyer HMS *Cavalier*, purportedly the fastest ship in the fleet though showing her age a bit, was sailing that afternoon carrying a company of Queen's Own Highlanders and a Company of

Gurkhas to Labuan, the port for Brunei. As I had met the First Lieutenant a week or so earlier and discovered he had been in HMS *Newcastle* with me some years previously, I had a ready-made contact. He welcomed me aboard what was a very crowded ship indeed – there were over 200 troops embarked in a 2,500 ton destroyer, rather more than the ship's complement of about 180. I was quickly introduced to the Captain and discovered that I knew rather more about what was happening in the revolt than he did, He had just been ordered to take two companies of military to Labuan.

'As I was on my own and had a friend on board, I was given a comfortable bunk in the sick bay, while the troops had to find anywhere to kip down on the upper deck. I then discovered that *Cavalier* had been due to sail anyway to the west coast of the USA on a good will trip and then home. She was certainly not prepared for 'war' though we expected no seaborne opposition. The skipper had a problem – because they were leaving the Far East Station, they had returned all their Confidential Books on the area and had drawn a new set for the eastern Pacific. Consequently he had nothing to refer to regarding docking facilities and tide conditions in Labuan; these were just the books I had taken with me. He then asked me to broadcast over the ship's SRE system to all on board on the military situation (as I knew it). What a way to go to war!

'The weather forecast was foul with a typhoon blowing up in the South China Sea, but his orders were to get the troops there as fast as possible. With a maximum speed of about forty knots, the fastest in the Navy, we must have made a bee-line for our destination in north-west Borneo 750 miles away and we had a very rough passage all the way. Highlanders and Gurkhas, the latter renowned for their allergy to sea sickness, suffered rather more than I did in my comfort, though my stomach churned over more than once during the night. It was a memorable and sleepless trip like no other. The troops were certainly not fit to go into immediate action.

'We arrived at Labuan in the dark; the date must have been 10 December. Just before going ashore I realised that, here I was going into unknown action and I hadn't even drawn a weapon. I went down to the Gunner's Store on board and managed to persuade a reluctant Gunner that I urgently needed a pistol at least. I drew a 9mm Browning and some ammunition. This was to have amusing repercussions when, four months later, I tried to return the weapon to store. I was back in Singapore for a short stay and went to the Dockyard to hand it in. In no way would any storeman accept it, as it was 'not one of theirs'. I would have to return it to the ship from whence it came. I explained to him that *Cavalier* was now back in UK and was no doubt being re-commissioned. After some argument I saw the armaments officer who very reluctantly accepted it against seemingly reams of paperwork. I never found out what *Cavalier* did when they realised they were a pistol short – a court martial offence?'

Air Photo of Limbang, the only guide Captain Jeremy Moore had of his objective

Riposte

'On our arrival, we found Labuan was in chaos – troops of all types were arriving by sea and air and there were sleeping bodies strewn everywhere. I sought out 42 Commando who were at the airport. I reported to the CO, Robin Bridges, and the Adjutant and told them why I had been sent. I was quickly swallowed into the planning melee and went down into Brunei Town where there were still pockets of resistance.

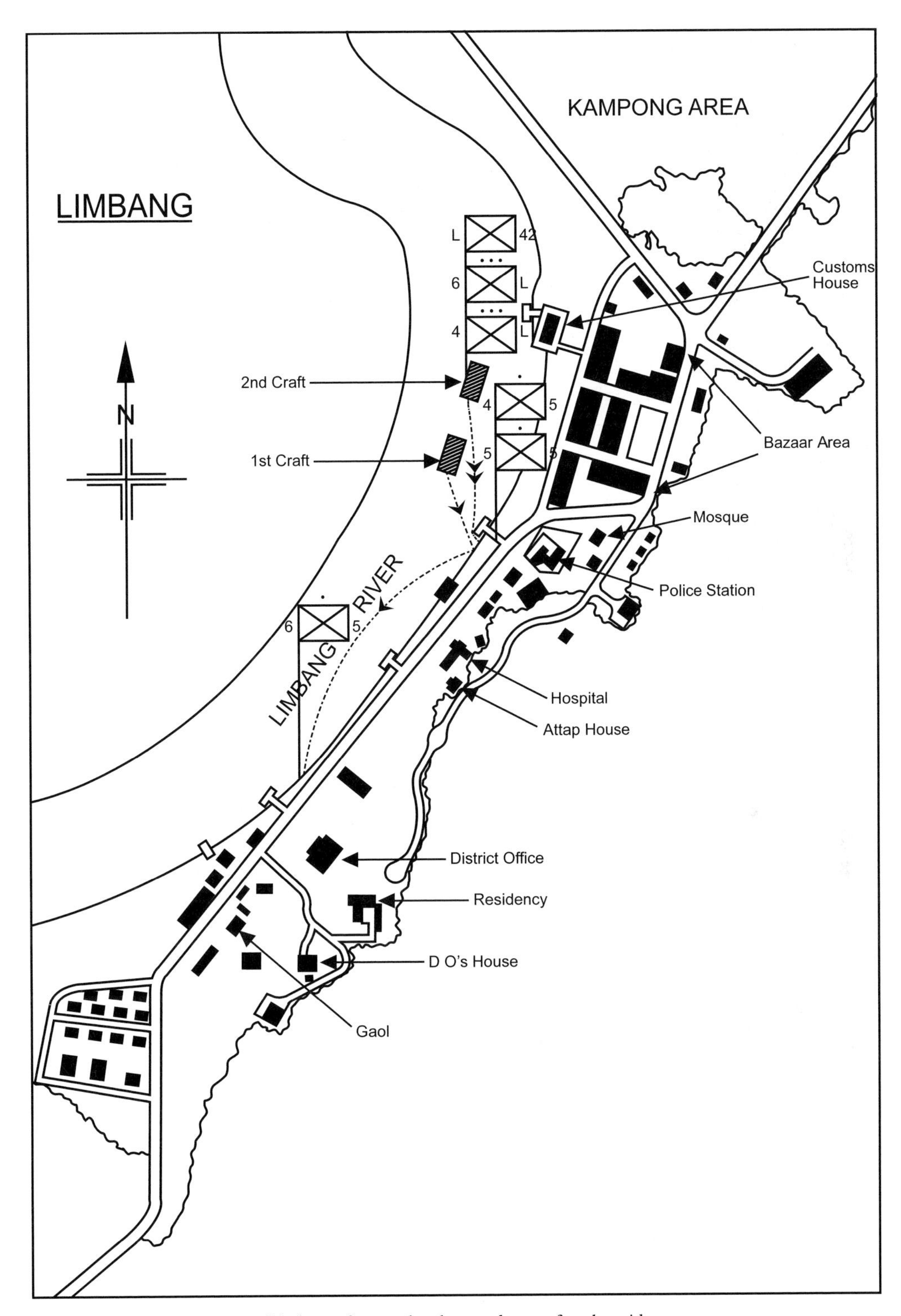

Limbang, from a sketch map drawn after the raid.
From 42 Commando's article in *The Globe & Laurel.*

As I crossed the main square towards the police station, I got a timely warning that bullets were still flying about and, as the Navy would put it, 'made speed'.

'Entering the police station I was astounded to meet a young looking Corporal grinning at me from ear to ear – a face that I had last seen eleven years ago in Malaya. It was my old friend the Iban tracker, whose name instantly sprang into my head 'Kayan'. He now spoke very reasonable English and I learnt that he had joined the Brunei police force soon after returning from Malaya. We barely spoke again as the situation was rather more important – but what a small world it is. What happened next can be explained in the edited article that I subsequently wrote. It runs as follows:

> "3 Commando Brigade Royal Marines at this time consisted of 42 Commando, awaiting Christmas in Singapore after an extremely busy year of exercises, and 40 Commando who were embarked in HMS *Albion* off Mombassa. Brigade Headquarters had only recently returned from controlling exercises in the Aden protectorate. 45 Commando were under independent operational command in Aden.
>
> "On 8 December 42 Commando was put at short notice to move to Brunei and two days later were on their way, with Commando Headquarters and L Company flying firstly into Labuan and then into Brunei town where the Gurkhas had restored order.
>
> "It was 0600 hrs on 11 December 1962 when Brigadier Pat Patterson, commander of 99 Gurkha Infantry Brigade and now in command of operations greeted the newly arrived Company Commander of L Company, 42 Commando Royal Marines, Captain Jeremy Moore, who had already won a Military Cross in the Malayan jungle ten years earlier. The Brigadier made his directive quite clear "Your Company will rescue the hostages at Limbang". At that time only fifty-six men of his company had reached Brunei plus a section of medium machine gunners, although the final number on the raid was eighty-nine. It was believed that about a dozen hostages were held in Limbang, including the Resident Dick Morris and his wife, another woman, and a US Peace Corps Officer Fritz Klattenhof.
>
> "As Captain Moore, his Second-in-Command, Lieutenant Peter Waters, and his Company Sergeant Major, QMS Scoins, took stock of the situation, the Marines prepared themselves for the ordeal to come. Some three hours later, the CO of 42 Commando, Lieutenant Colonel Robin Bridges and his Intelligence Officer, Lieutenant Benjy Walden arrived to take over the difficult responsibility for obtaining information and intelligence on the operation. It was clear in everyone's mind that speed and surprise were essential. The decision was soon made that the rescue attempt would have to take place at dawn the following morning.
>
> "Of prime importance was the need to find some river craft in which to mount the operation. Paddy Davis and I set about this task inspecting the myriad of small boats along the Brunei waterfront. There were hundreds of them but none particularly suitable for transporting 100 men up river for twelve miles and then carrying out a frontal

assault. Just as we reached the north end of the extensive waterfront, we came across two old Z Craft belonging to the Brunei government that appeared to be in working order. But there were no signs of any crew. Dick Morris, then Commissioner of Development in Brunei and now one of the hostages in Limbang, had ordered these craft in 1958.

"Just after midday – and subsequently providing the only reliable communications between Brunei and Singapore – into the harbour sailed the two coastal minesweepers, HMS *Fiskerton* and HMS *Chawton*. The Royal Navy immediately took command of the situation providing their two First Lieutenants to command the craft and engine room staff to ensure that they were both in working order.

"The minesweeper Captains, Lieutenant Harry Mucklow and Lieutenant Jeremy Black came ashore and with Captain Moore helped in the detailed planning. By late afternoon, both craft were ready, with large packs acting as sandbags, a few earth filled oil drums and the crafts' own one and a half inch wooden planking being the only protection.

There was very little reliable intelligence and only small-scale maps and an out of date air photograph. Moore knew that a small police launch, which had approached Limbang town two days earlier, had been driven off by heavy small arms fire. It was known that the rebels were there in some numbers and had captured police weapons in addition to their own.

"He anticipated that he might be able, by a show of force, to bluff the rebels into surrendering, but if that failed or if the operation was prolonged, the rebels would either shoot the hostages out of hand or threaten to do so in order to make him withdraw. His prime concern was the safety of the hostages, but he did not know where they were being held. Several possible locations presented themselves, the police station, the gaol, the hospital and the British Residency, which were all separated by about 300 yards. His simple plan was to overwhelm their likely positions as fast as possible, each Marine holding his fire until the rebels opened up..."

42 Commando's Signals Officer had his own problems and wrote in the Corps Journal of this period of briefing and final preparation...

Ray Frost, Captain – OC Signals Troop

L Company had already been briefed for the recapture of Limbang and it was only as I was giving the company signallers their final instructions that I realised that this was no exercise but the real thing. How tough it was going to be no one knew. As I looked at the 62 set which I had so often and loudly decried and thought of the batteries and charging engine that were heaven knows where, between Singapore and Brunei, I crossed my fingers. They were to stay crossed for a long time. This time there would be no wash-up for me to blame out-of-date equipment if communication failed – no detailed investigation in two days time into the failure of essential equipment to arrive by air – no calm official or unofficial criticism of the exercise planning. The 62 set just had to work; so did the set going to Lawas; so did all the other sets which had not even arrived in Brunei yet. If they did not work we would never get anywhere in this road-less, trackless country, or at the best we would grind slowly on from point to point, never taking bold leaps, never getting the rebels off balance…'

Derek Oakley's narrative describes the sequel…

Limbang Assault

"…That afternoon, ammunition and equipment were checked, the medium machine guns were mounted forward on the Z craft where they would be most effective, while food and rest were hastily taken during what was left of the day. In order to arrive off Limbang at dawn, it was decided to sail about midnight, guided by Captain Muton, the Brunei Director of Marine who admitted that he had never sailed the Limbang River before. Casting off about midnight their route lay along a series of complicated winding channels between thirty and 100 yards wide flanked by the hideous Nipa swamp. The Marines on board, already exhausted from nearly two days without proper sleep since they left Singapore, snatched whatever catnaps they could.

"The two craft, keeping just within visual distance, slowly edged their way down the narrow channels as silently as they could, no lights or noise emanating from those on deck, leaving only the grinding engines to announce their presence to any waiting ambushers. By 0200 hrs, both craft reached the main Limbang River some five miles from the town where they laid up hidden in the shadows of the jungle edges until 0430 hrs.

"As the engines started up, last minute checks were made as the craft rounded the final bend before the town. Dimly they saw the lights of the town in the distance. Somehow they were reassuring to the waiting Marines, and then to their surprise, the lights suddenly went out. Later they learnt that it was just a routine, as dawn approached. As silently as their engines allowed and with three cables between them, they came level with the northern edge of the town. Captain Moore, with his Malay speaking Intelligence Sergeant David Smith alongside him, suddenly saw movements everywhere. The bazaar area seemed alive and they could just make out the police station. Full ahead was ordered and the leading craft surged towards the bank. Sergeant Smith through his loud hailer informed the enemy that the rebellion was over and that they should lay down their arms and surrender. At this a hail of fire greeted the approaching craft The response from each craft was instantaneous and by the time the leading craft had beached about thirty yards from the police station, some twenty seconds later, it was clear that L Company had the fire initiative thanks largely to their Vickers medium machine guns.

"Two Marines of the leading Troop were killed even before they got to the bank and Lieutenant Peter Waters was hit in the leg as he jumped ashore. The coxswain of the leading craft was also hit, as were Lieutenant Paddy Davis and a seaman in the second craft, which was still standing off and giving covering fire. No 5 Troop stormed ashore clearing the police station in its stride, Corporal Bill Lester taking his section across the road, mopping up and providing a cut off to the rear. Sergeant Johnny Bickford, a Corps footballer and PTI, with his Section Commander Corporal Bob Rawlinson pressed home the attack, though Rawlinson was wounded in the back.

"Meanwhile, with the coxswain wounded, the leading craft had drifted off the bank, but Lieutenant David Willis managed to beach it half way between the Residency and the hospital, some 150 yards from the initial landing. Captain Moore now reassessed the situation and ordered Troop Sergeant, Sergeant Wally Macfarlane, ashore with the reserve section. By this time there was only spasmodic fire, and Macfarlane moved stealthily north, clearing the enemy from the jungle edges that came right down to the bank in places. They reached the hospital without incident and he decided to press on to join up with the initial landing force near the police station. Suddenly a group of determined enemy opened fire, killing the Troop Sergeant and two Marines.

"Through the sounds of battle, Sergeant Smith heard some inharmonious singing from within the hospital. Recognising the tune as a version of *Coming round the Mountain*, he called out to them in English and identified the Resident, Dick Morris, and his wife Dorothy, along with several other hostages, unharmed but severely shocked. Their guards had fled. Captain Moore, his main task achieved, that of freeing the hostages, checked with Dick Morris that there were no more held elsewhere.

"During the whole of this time, the second craft had been manoeuvring in the fast flowing river to give the best supporting fire possible. The Company Sergeant Major had taken command of the situation when Lieutenant Davis had been severely wounded. At this juncture the reserve sections on the second craft came ashore, the craft itself once again taking up a position in mid-stream covering any eventuality with its MMGs.

"A number of enemy were soon routed by 5 Troop, whilst 6 Troop cleared the police station and 4 Troop moved north, past the Mosque to the back of the bazaar, where one of the rebels engaged them from a room full of women and children. He was soon dislodged with no further casualties. From this time on most of the enemy resistance collapsed although a number of dissidents held out in the town and the jungle, and there was considerable movement and sniping during the next twenty-four hours.

"As soon as the second craft beached, SBA Terry Clarke made his way to the hospital and set up a dressing station, treating the casualties while the released hostages helped him to prepare dressings. Four of the six cases of gunshot wounds were in the legs. Sergeant Smith set about interrogating the hostages and other prisoners, discovering that some more were held in the gaol and the southern area of the town. By late afternoon this area had been systematically cleared and a total of fourteen hostages had been rescued. Later in the morning, the Z craft returned to Brunei, this time rather more quickly and triumphantly, bringing the hostages and the casualties with them. L Company had lost five dead and five wounded, plus one sailor. The wounded were quickly flown to Labuan and thence evacuated to Singapore.

"As L Company consolidated the next day, fifteen rebel bodies were found and about fifty prisoners were taken. It was subsequently learned that many others died of wounds in the jungle. It transpired that nearly 350 rebels had held Limbang initially, many later discarding their uniforms and melting anonymously into the bazaar areas of the town. Much later Captain Jeremy Moore made the following observations:

"It is perhaps interesting to note that, though my assessment of where the enemy headquarters might be was right, I was quite wrong about the hostages. Furthermore it was chance that the second beaching happened where it did that resulted in us taking the hospital from the direction we did. It could be that this saved us heavier casualties, though I assess the most important factor in the success of the operation as first class leadership by junior NCOs. Their section battle craft was a joy to watch, and the credit for this belongs to the Troop and Section Commanders"

"This action, along with others by the Queen's Own Highlanders at Seria and 1/2 Gurkhas at Tutong crushed the revolt within five days of it breaking out. For the action at Limbang, Captain J J Moore was awarded a bar to his MC, Corporals R C Rawlinson and W J Lester MMs, Lieutenant David Willis RN a DSC and PO D J D Kirwin a DSM. Marine Barry Underwood was mentioned in despatches and SBA Terry Clarke received a commendation."

The last named tells his own story of the event and of how he came to be there in the first place…

Terry Clarke, Sick Berth Attendant – L Company Medic

'On 6 September 1960 I qualified as a Sick Berth Attendant (SBA) at the Royal Naval Hospital, Haslar and then was put to work on various wards to gain nursing experience. This was normal procedure, but as I had joined the Navy, 'to go to sea and see the world,' my first response was to enquire as to when I might leave the hospital and go on draft. I was keen to be a 'proper' Sickbay man and not a nurse. The reply to my request was that there was little likelihood of me being drafted to a sea/shore billet in the foreseeable future and, I should therefore get on with the business in hand!

'Working on the wards not only brought me into contact with many of the branches of the Navy, but also with personnel from the other Armed Forces. I particularly remember however, a Royal Marine patient on one of the orthopaedic wards. He had been injured, in Malta, whilst climbing into the back of a Land Rover, by another vehicle reversing and trapping his legs between both vehicles. Following evacuation and further surgery in Haslar, it had not been possible to grant him any leave. In a desperate attempt to get home, he had crawled, during the night, from his hospital bed and into the hospital grounds before being detected and brought back to the ward. As a result of this incident I became quite friendly with him and so gained my first insight into service with the Royal Marines.

'The next episode I recall, which increased my curiosity further, was meeting an SBA dressed in Battledress with shoulder flashes bearing the insignia 'Royal Navy Commando'. In the short time available, (he was only passing through Haslar prior to joining his new RM unit) I was able to gain information of his personal experience as to the work and life of an SBA serving with the Corps.

'Being a sportsman and therefore quite fit, were values, I was told, that were an integral part of service with the Royal Marines, so my interest became more acute. Finally, several of my colleagues returned to Haslar after completing the Commando course at CTCRM, Lympstone. They were keen to impart their experiences (but not the harrowing ones) and having successfully passed the course, were now awaiting drafts to RM units. Without further ado, I immediately requested to volunteer for Commando training. It was not until October 1961 that I received my draft order to CTCRM, but at last I was on my way!'

Commando Training

'Arriving at CTCRM, I have vivid memories of meetings with several other SBAs who were already undergoing training. They were sat around a pot-bellied stove looking glum, dirty and feeling thoroughly demoralised. It appeared that they had commenced training, but part way through had been given seasonal leave. On their return, following two weeks of drinking, eating and other pleasures at Blackpool and various resorts, they had found it extremely difficult to get back into the rigours of training.

'Their advice to me was not to unpack, but leave immediately and return to civilisation as quickly as possible. I obviously ignored their advice (though at times later on wondered if I had made the correct decision), and within several days they were back into the swing of things. All of them were subsequently awarded their 'Green Beret'. For myself, even though I believed that I was quite fit, I found the course very testing. The weather was at times appalling, very wet and windy and not the ideal time of the year to spend on Dartmoor. However, I had volunteered for the course. I never ceased being amazed, during my time with the Corps, by the fortitude and resilience demonstrated on many occasions by SBAs and other medical staff, who were not sporting or physical types. They were and are a credit to their Service.

'On completion of Commando training, it was back to Haslar to await, hopefully, a draft to foreign part; it was May of 1961 when I received my draft order to join 42 Commando RM on 17 May 1962. Getting to Singapore from Brize Norton proved a slight problem as I was bumped off several flights before being allocated a seat. It was explained to me by a rather officious RAF Sergeant that seating was sometimes a question of priority and as an SBA I did not have any!

'On arrival at Singapore I was collected by Land Rover and taken to Nee-Soon Garrison. It soon became apparent that I was in transit to 40 Commando RM by a mistake and so I was off on my travels yet again, this time to my correct unit. With hindsight, I might have realised then that this was going to prove an interesting tour.'

42 Commando

'I settled into the routine of working in a Sick Bay and more importantly, learning how to recognise and treat the various illnesses (rashes and fevers) and injuries, associated with conditions in the Far East. It soon became apparent how ill prepared I was both in knowledge and experience of tropical medicine and the general practice of working in a unit Sick Bay. It would have been of immense value to have worked in Accident and Emergency and been given some insight as to the general conditions which existed in the Far East, prior to draft to a front line unit!

'Thankfully the Sick Berth staff already serving in the unit were most tolerant and helpful in teaching me the many appropriate methods of treating patients. As time passed I became more confident and so began to enjoy life in Singapore.

'The next significant event was when I was informed that I was to deploy with B Troop, on an operation in Malaya. This involved being transported by train, fixed-wing aircraft and finally helicopter, into the Malayan jungle.

'At the end of an exciting but otherwise uneventful journey, I arrived at base camp to be met by an array of injured personnel. Most of them had sustained cuts and lacerations while cutting bamboo to build their bashas; these injuries required suturing/bandaging, so I set about treating the casualties. By the time I had finished it was almost sunset. Almost everyone, with the exception of the sentries, had eaten and was bedded down. I had not eaten, washed or made any preparations for sleeping or stowing my kit. After shouting several expletives, loudly, one of the Troop Officers came to my aid and organised assistance. The lesson I learned from this experience was to ensure that on future deployments, I was in the advance party group and so organised before the main body arrived.

'The first of my visits into the 'ulu' proved an invaluable part of gaining knowledge, experience and confidence in carrying out my duties as an SBA. Often the only medic present, the fear of letting the side down was quite a responsibility and one of which I was very much aware.

'Of particular significance was the occasion of an accidental discharge, which resulted in a gunshot wound to the jaw and the evacuation of a casualty by helicopter. This was my first serious case and most importantly, I was able to perform the treatment necessary to the complete satisfaction of the incoming doctor. His comment, that his services had not been essential as the appropriate treatment had been administered, was a memory I treasured and remembered for the remainder of my service and a tremendous boost to my confidence.

'Apart from accumulating knowledge of building a basha, rigging a parachute hammock, snakes, fishing by detonator, leeches, jungle fever and jungle sores, the only other notable medical event was that concerning a PTI Corporal. I believe the story was that, whilst he was leading a patrol, his group came across a herd of wild elephants. In an attempt to draw the herd away from the patrol, he shouted and ran in the opposite direction. Unfortunately, the bull chased and caught him with its tusks and threw him to the ground. The injuries he sustained were a fracture/dislocation and wound to the shoulder. As he was being evacuated, he asked for a pencil and paper and wrote, *'Dear Mum, have been hit by an elephant, but not seriously injured. Your loving son'*!

'On return to Singapore it was back to normal Sick Bay routines, until the unit embarked in HMS *Bulwark* for an exercise in the New Territories, followed by some shore leave in Hong Kong. This proved most enjoyable and also afforded me my first opportunity to go to sea.

'We had not long been back in Sembawang before the unit was on the move yet again. This time it was to Borneo, to complete the reorganisation from Troops to Companies. The only medical incident of note was when a young local boy started to bang some rocks, one on top of another. Suddenly there was an explosion, and unfortunately the boy lost several of his fingers and had to be evacuated to the nearest local hospital. The report which followed suggested that the cause of the explosion was probably a detonator.

'On completion of the training exercises, we were given three weeks pay and allowed shore leave in the local township. The ensuing melée was best described by a visiting RSM, as similar to the scenes on 'V' Day in Belgium!

'Back in Singapore in early December, the main topics of discussion were of approaching Christmas and anticipated celebrations. I had gone to Johore Bahru for a weekend and on returning over the causeway into Singapore, noticed a heavy military presence. I was stopped by Military Police, asked for my unit and told to report back to barracks immediately. On arrival at the Sick Bay I was informed that L Company was on stand-by and preparing to move at a moment's notice. If I could pack my kit in time, I would deploy with them, otherwise, another SBA would go. In record time I had packed, reported to the Company lines and moved out with them.'

Brunei and Limbang

'Arriving in Brunei, we were billeted in a hotel and the first task I was given was to go with a party to commandeer some vehicles. During the course of this task, the vehicle I was travelling in came under fire and as the driver braked sharply I fell backwards inside the vehicle. It was first thought that I had been shot; however, I quickly jumped up, demonstrating that I had not been injured.

'I next remember the Company being fallen in and informed by the Company Commander of the situation in Limbang and of the action planned. His words, 'Gentlemen, this is war', will remain etched in my memory.

'The assault force boarded the Z-Lighters and left Brunei shortly before midnight, in order to be off Limbang by dawn the following day. It was pitch black and so I found myself a space and tried to get to sleep. It's an interesting thought that often in times of need, fear or panic people turn to religion for support – not necessarily for one's own safety, but for the strength and courage to carry out the task ahead. Usually there is a strong link forged between the medical staff and the Padre in a unit, for fairly obvious reasons. On this occasion, there was no Padre present and in these circumstances, personnel may turn to the 'medic', if only for a chat. I found it very difficult to sleep thinking of the day ahead and was more than happy to chat to anyone who thought likewise. I have to admit to saying a prayer or two!

SBA Terry Clarke, who was L Company medic and awarded a Commander-in-Chief's Commendation, laying a wreath at the Limbang Memorial unveiling. He has contributed to this Special Publication.

'Apart from the chugging of the Z-Lighters, there was no sign or sound of life in the area of the riverside kampongs. The jungle was ominously silent, as is always the case when dawn begins to break. As the craft rounded a bend in the river the bazaar area of Limbang suddenly sprang into life, firing commenced and all hell was let loose! I was told to position myself and prepare to open fire when directed and, be ready to deal with any casualties that might arise.

'The next event I recall was a shout for me to report to the bridge, as someone had been wounded. I grabbed my medical pack in one hand and my weapon (SMG) in the other and set off to get to the bridge. As I ran toward the stern of the boat, which I was told was the route, I saw an open door and threw myself through. In an instant I realised that I was in the 'heads,' with no access to the upper deck. I poked my head cautiously out of the heads and spotted a ladder on the open deck, which was totally exposed, but appeared to lead to the upper deck. Taking a huge breath I shot out of the compartment, onto the ladder and up onto the bridge where my casualty was lying – I don't think I have ever moved so quickly up a ladder in my life!

'The treatment for gunshot wounds was generally to clean the area and remove any loose materials and, having dressed the wound, to administer penicillin and streptomycin injections. This I duly did, before being called to deal with other casualties. Having dealt with the patients on board I was then told by the Sergeant Major that I was to proceed ashore to deal with further casualties.

'As I stepped on to the jetty alone, a Marine came running towards me and asked me where I was going. I replied by saying I was off to deal with shore side casualties. I clearly remember his words: "Don't go any further Doc, or you'll get shot to pieces"! I immediately stepped back onto the boat.

'The Sergeant Major then appeared and asked why I was back on the boat. I gave him the information passed by the Marine, upon which he said that I had to go ashore and there was nothing further to discuss. Plucking up courage – one rarely argued with a Sergeant Major and especially not when on 'active service' – I asked him bluntly what was the purpose of going ashore, if I would be seriously wounded within a very short period of time. He then paused, considered my comments and told me he would provide me with an escort and so off we went. Within a short distance I came across my second casualty, who had sustained a gunshot wound to his shoulder. I quickly set about treating him, but before I had finished, my escort had disappeared. Fortunately, further troops soon arrived, organised the evacuation of the casualty and directed me to the hospital. Here, I set up the Company Aid Post, where the dead and wounded were brought to me. I was ably assisted by the hostages, some of whom were already in the hospital, where they had been held captive.

'Later, a party arrived to collect the dead and wounded and return them to Brunei; in the group was an SBA who stayed overnight. During the late evening he became morose and started shouting about the dead and wounded. Outside the hospital the situation was extremely tense and sporadic firing could be heard. Suddenly he attacked me and in desperation I hit him over the head with an SMG magazine; then to be certain he would quieten down, I gave him an injection of pheno-barbitone, which did the trick and he soon fell asleep. This was the first case I had dealt with of what I suppose was Post Traumatic Stress Disorder. Other cases were to follow, but not until the Company returned to Borneo at a later date.'

Chapter 2

The Clean-up

Comings and Goings

December ’62 to March ’63

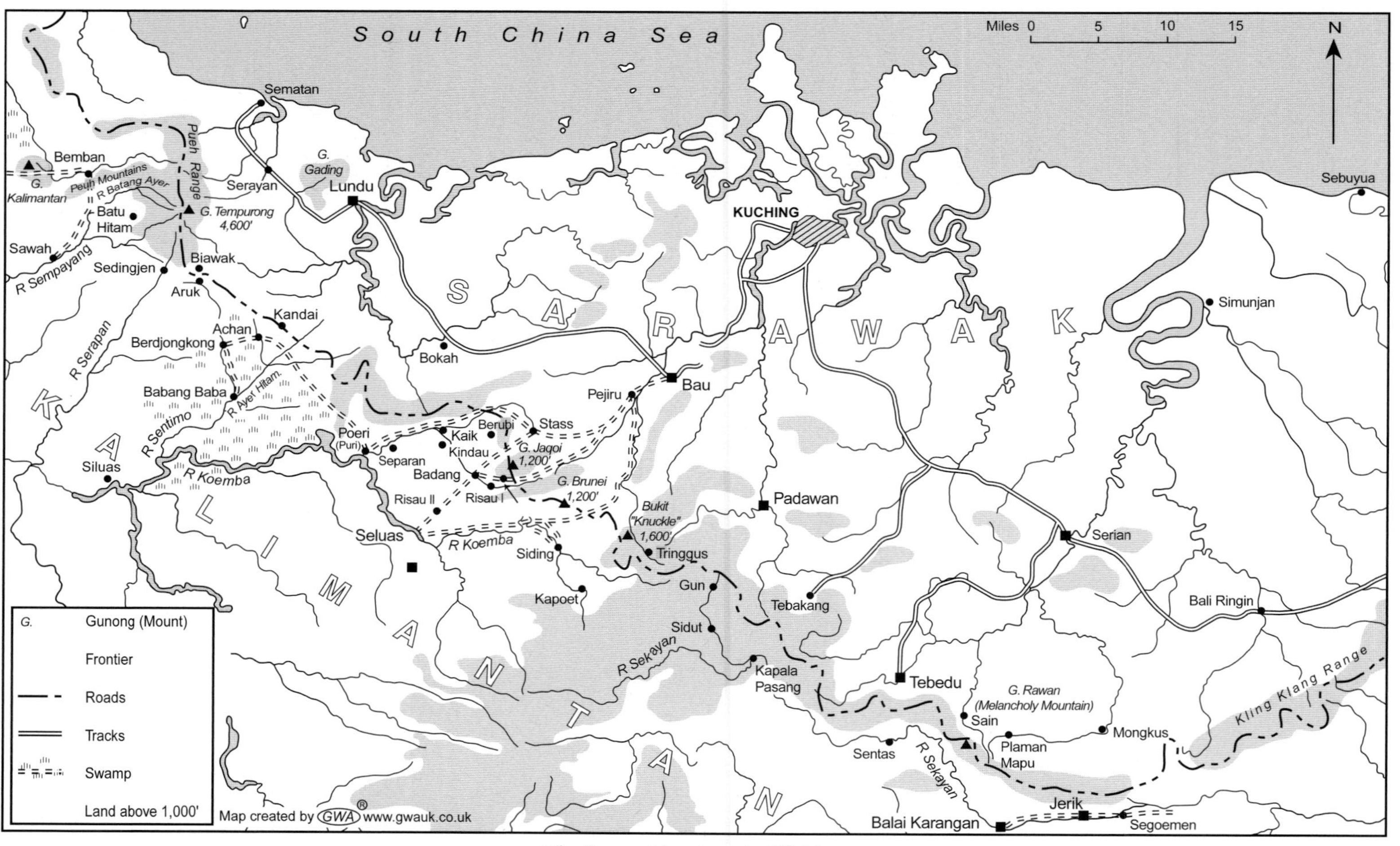

The Borneo Frontier – 1st Division

The Clean-up

Waiting on the Jetty

Derek Oakley – G3 Int

'As will have been seen, my part in the Limbang affair was comparatively small, just the finding and collection of the Z craft which took part in the assault. I spent a lot of 11 December driving from the temporary Brigade HQ in the town down to the jetty with messages to be transmitted to Singapore. It seemed extraordinary to me that the army had not provided themselves with the right (or sufficient) communications equipment to be in constant contact with Far East Land Forces in Singapore. The two RN minesweepers certainly had adequate signalling equipment though, in those days, there was no voice messaging.

'I found somewhere to park my soul in the Brunei Hotel – a very unremarkable establishment – with 42 Commando and I watched as L Company prepared for the assault ahead. Around about midnight I went down to the jetty and witnessed the two fully laden Z craft move out into the river at a very slow speed; as we saw them disappear round the first bend in the river, we said a silent prayer for their safety and success in their mission.

'I remember slumbering quietly but restlessly for a few hours – the previous forty-eight hours had held precious little sleep for any of us. It is astonishing how the adrenalin flows and how wide awake one stays when danger is round the corner. I had experienced that both in Malaya and at Port Said. I went back to the jetty and joined a group from the minesweepers, who provided us with some shelter and plenty of coffee or tea. They were just as alert and tensioned as we were. Occasionally the wireless crackled, but strict radio silence was being observed by the attacking L Company…'

Ray Frost – OC Signals Troop

L Company was due to land at dawn. At 0600 hrs the control signaller had an expectant audience willing him on as he tapped away monotonously at his morse key. Suddenly his head turned away slightly as he muttered "There they are". Faces peered over his shoulder to read what he was writing – '*Heavy fighting on landing. Some casualties…*'

"The interference is very heavy" said the signaller, "they are only about strength one." "Keep trying" I replied but I was thinking *they must still be on the lighter – get ashore, get ashore for God's sake and shove a decent aerial up.*

'Then in came the next message that Support Company had landed at Lawas unopposed. There were sighs of relief around the control set. Gradually L Company signals increased in strength – "Strength five – loud and clear, now, Sir!". "Well get them on voice and fetch Sunray". The Colonel had gone to Brigade Headquarters to report progress, so I spoke to L Company Commander. I must have sounded very agitated because he spent a lot of time assuring me that everything was under control. I did not tell him that we had no spare batteries nor any charging engines and he was probably going to run out of communications very soon.

'However, this difficulty was overcome by requisitioning the stock of car batteries in a nearby garage and sending them up by boat to Limbang…'

Derek Oakley – G3 Int

'Dawn breaks about 0600 hrs every morning of the year near the equator and even more vehicles and people arrived on the jetty. News was that both Z craft were returning to Brunei town with the dead and the wounded. At least two ambulances had appeared along with medical staff, mostly service, but with some civilians. We still had little idea of the actual casualties until, at about 0645 hrs, the two Z craft, with their white ensigns proudly flying rounded the last bend in the river and turned towards the jetty. There was a sense of cautious anticipation.

'As was usual I had my camera slung round my neck and was one of the few people to take any pictures of the wounded returning to Brunei. Later in that day I gave them to the naval press officer along with some quickly written captions, some of which were slightly wrong. These were flown out that evening to Singapore and it was my photographs that hit the front pages of several national Daily papers, including the Telegraph and Express at least. I also had one photograph published in the Illustrated London News of 29 December 1962. There was no acknowledgement and I did not know anything about these until several months later when I got a copy whilst in Kuching. Eventually I got the negatives back, and though lost for several years they are now in the RM Museum.

'We could see a number of stretchers strewn across the decks, several bandaged Marines, obviously wounded, standing up and a number of civilians. As they drew alongside, a civilian lady was almost the first ashore and, seeing me, she thrust two envelopes into my hands with the words "Can you please get these to my children in Australia as soon as you can?" It was my first, brief meeting with Dorothy Morris, one of the hostages and wife of the British Resident. Her first thought after battle had cooled down was to inform their children, Geraldine and Adrian, both at school in Sydney, that their parents were safe. She stood there chatting as cool and unflustered as anyone could be after her five-day incarceration. It was bravery and fortitude of a high measure.

'There was plenty to do that morning what with helping 42 Commando, reporting to the ad hoc Brigade Headquarters and signalling my own Commando Brigade HQ. About noon, I accompanied Brigadier Pat Patterson, commanding 99 Gurkha Brigade, who had taken over the operational role, and went down river to Limbang in the small motor craft, which was coxwained by a RM Sergeant. It was quite eerie trying to relive what it must have been like to go down the narrow winding river – lined with nipa palm and mangrove swamps – by night to confront an enemy.

'All looked remarkably peaceful as we approached Limbang Town, a smallish outpost of the British Empire. I met Dick Morris, the Resident for the first time, not realising how we should become such close friends for nearly forty years and how often we should later meet. There was ample evidence of a severe fire fight and bullet holes scarred some of the brick buildings. The Marines of 42 Commando were still engaged in the active pursuit of rebels and one could imagine a sniper hiding in every tree, waiting to take a pot shot.

There were no heroics here, just a lot of tired Marines and civilians contemplating a job well done but ruing the fact that they had lost five men killed that day.'

As the first Z Lighter returns to Brunei Town from Limbang, casualties can be seen on deck. Standing on the far side is one of the freed hostages, Fritz Klattenhoff, a United States Peace Corps officer.

42 Commando – The Clean Up

Major Peter Darling was then OC K Company but had become 42 Commando's Staff Officer Operations (SOO) when he wrote of the sequel to Limbang:

> "At dawn on the 13th 'M' Company moved to mount a similar attack on Bangar and K Company proceeded by river to relieve L Company at Limbang. The river trip was uneventful except that the boats grounded for over an hour on a sandbank whilst the CO put off in a small dinghy in his impatience to get on.
>
> "On arrival at Limbang, K Company took over the perimeter of the town, allowing L Company to have a well earned night's rest. Intermittent firing throughout the night made sleep impossible, as sentries engaged shadowy targets, many of which must have been imaginary.
>
> "On the 13th M Company arrived at Bangar to find no opposition as the rebels, hearing of the Limbang defeat, had taken to their heels up the Temburong River. K Company cleared the road from Limbang to Bangar without aid and so by the 14th elements of Commando HQ with 'K' and 'M' Companies were in Bangar, with L Company still in Limbang.
>
> "But what of 'S' Company..."

Keith Wilkins, Lieutenant – OC Recce Troop

'On Sunday 9 December 1962, my wife and I were sitting over breakfast in our flat in Singapore. In front of me lay a copy of the *Straits Times* carrying the banner headline 'Revolt in Brunei'. This meant nothing to me at the time because, apart from anything else, I had no idea where Brunei was. I soon found out, because, moments later, I was racing back to 42 Commando's barracks at Sembawang in response to the unit's recall. The following evening I was on my way in an RAF Hastings with the remainder of Recce Troop to Labuan Island, which lies just off the coast of Brunei. Shortly after take-off, the load master informed us that this same aircraft had just returned to Singapore carrying the bodies of three dead Gurkhas, who had been gunned down by rebels whilst trying to recapture Brunei Town. A sobering reminder, as if we needed one, of the situation that we were heading into.

'We landed at about 0200 hrs on 11 December, and spent the rest of the night stretched out on the edge of the airfield trying to get some sleep. Next morning, we were ordered to move to the nearby jetty and board a RN minesweeper which took us across to Brunei Town. I remember that on our arrival we were met by members of L Company, who had flown in earlier, and who told us to make our way to the Brunei Hotel which had been allocated as the unit's base. By this time, the town had been more or less secured by a company of 1st/2nd Gurkhas who had been the first British troops to arrive, but there was an eerie silence about the place, punctuated by the occasional shots that rang out from time to time. We therefore had to be careful as we moved forward.

'Shortly after arriving at the hotel, I was ordered to attend an O Group. I remember that the only other people who were present were the CO (Robin Bridges), OC L Company (Jeremy Moore) and the IO (Benjy Walden). The CO told us that, whilst Brunei Town and nearby Tutong had been retaken, the remainder of Brunei and parts of the neighbouring Division of Sarawak were thought to be still in rebel hands. The unit's immediate task was to recapture Limbang in Sarawak, release the British hostages who were being held there and retake Lawas, which was thought to be occupied by rebels. L Company was to deal with Limbang and Recce Troop, with elements of the Anti-Tank Troop – who by that time had arrived – was to go to Lawas.'

Lawas and Labu

'Shortly after first light the following morning, we flew from Brunei airport in six RAF Twin Pioneers to Lawas, a journey which took about thirty minutes. Shortly before touch down a party of armed men were spotted on the edge of the tiny airstrip, which caused the pilots to abort their first attempt at landing. However, it soon transpired that this was a group of friendly policemen, who were very pleased to see us because

An RAF Twin Pioneer of 209 Squadron embarking men later in the campaign, watched by VIPs. They could land on comparatively small jungle air strips and carry thirteen troops or 2,000 pounds of stores. Some civilian Twin Pioneers were also used.

they had been dangerously isolated for the last few days. They led us back to the town where we took up positions in and around the police station and, later that morning, we sent out patrols to visit the neighbouring kampongs to find out what was going on. All were found to be peaceful and untouched by the revolt. By that time, news of the Limbang action had reached us and I remember that all of us were saddened to hear that five members of our unit had been killed and others wounded but, at the same time, relieved that all the hostages had been released without harm.

'That night, the Recce Troop received orders to move next morning to Labu, a small town at the centre of a rubber plantation some seventeen miles to the west of Lawas. The first part of this journey could be travelled by road but the remaining fourteen miles had to be covered on foot through dense jungle.

'For most of us, this was our first experience of 'jungle bashing' and we were not particularly well equipped for it, given that we were still wearing SV boots and puttees, rather than the, still to be issued, jungle boots. We were, however, provided with two local guides and the whole journey, which took about seven hours, was completed without mishap. Once again the local inhabitants were pleased to see us. They were Brunei Malays who had remained loyal to the Sultan throughout the revolt, but felt very threatened by their neighbours from the Dusan tribe, who were sympathetic to the rebels. What made things worse was that they had run out of food and were getting close to starvation. In order to remedy this, I gave permission for one of the estate's cows to be slaughtered and this was done in the customary way by the headman, who slit the animal's throat with a large ceremonial parang. It all seemed a bit bizarre to us at the time, but I have to admit that the animal appeared to die very peacefully. Later that evening, an RAF Twin Pioneer appeared overhead to airdrop our rations for the next few days. The only trouble with this delivery was that the third package 'candled' and crashed straight through the roof of the mosque, which took a bit of laughing off.

'First thing on the following morning, patrols were sent out to check the local area. Most of the kampongs visited were empty or inhabited only by the elderly, plus women and children. There was a sense of hostility and sullenness in the air. However, by this time news of Limbang had filtered through to the local Dusan people and this had weakened their resolve to continue supporting the revolt. A few days later we were not surprised, therefore, to hear that those who had actively participated in the revolt were ready to give up and to be told that they would be waiting for us at a prearranged RV early on the next morning. A strong fighting patrol was mounted and, sure enough, we found a body of thirty-four frightened and dispirited Dusans at the appointed hour, squatting with their shotguns at the RV. It did not take long to disarm them and escort them back to Labu where they were sent by long boat to Brunei Town for interrogation. Two days later, they were back, looking happier and greatly relieved to be returning to their families, having been severely ticked off for their misdemeanours.'

Bahru Bahru

'By this time the revolt was virtually over with only a band of hard core leaders still at large and known to be hiding somewhere in the surrounds of Brunei Bay. Some weeks later, we left Labu to join up with the remainder of Support Company on an island called Bahru Bahru which was situated in the middle of this bay. The Company's task was to keep the whole of the eastern section of this huge area under surveillance, and to be ready to follow up any leads which resulted from information gathered. This turned out to be a somewhat frustrating role, because it was like looking for a needle in a haystack. What made things worse was that the entire surrounds of the bay were covered in mangrove swamp, which was almost impossible to penetrate. Two separate targets were identified, but both were found to be abandoned sites.

'As the weeks passed, the law of diminishing returns had meant that each Company was committed to days of arduous patrolling without tangible results. An epic long range patrol from M Company (Captain Tim Priest) was no exception. Notwithstanding, it was a demonstration of the tenacity of purpose and physical endurance shown by comparatively junior ranks and ratings in this campaign and arguably remains relevant as an example to sceptics of the value of this aspect of Commando training. The Patrol Commander wrote of his patrol in the Corps Journal…'

Rupert Van der Horst, Lieutenant

Bukit Pagon

'Company location Kampong Amoh, Temburong District, Brunei – frustrated, weary and bored after a day of fruitless patrolling and searching; wondering how much longer, what new jobs, if any, there would be for us…

"The Company Commander wants you!" He handed me a signal from the Commando Headquarters:

> WARNING ORDER – LONG RANGE PATROL – DURATION SEVEN DAYS – TEN FIT AND EXPERIENCED MEN REQUIRED FROM YOUR COMPANY. OFFICER WILL BE LIEUTENANT [VAN DER HORST] – FULL HELI SUPPORT – SIGNALS AND MEDICAL PROVIDED FROM THIS LOCATION – BRIEFING AT THIS LOCATION 0930 HRS, 28 DECEMBER – LEAVE PM 29TH OR AM 30TH – ACK.

'My heart and stomach leapt back about six feet. Something to do at last – may be interesting! That bit about fit and experienced men looks a bit sinister. I spent the rest of the night wondering what on earth was in store for me. Next morning after a short helicopter flight to Commando Headquarters, I learnt. Information had come in to Brigade that there was suspected rebel movement in the area of Bukit Pagon (6,070 feet) and it was thought that the rebels might be making a last ditch stronghold on top of the mountain. Brigade wanted someone to investigate. I had been given the job.

'I learnt at my briefing that Bukit Pagon was a mountain some forty miles south of Bangar and quite a long way from any form of human dwelling. It was on the southern most tip of the eastern part of Brunei – actually on the Sarawak border. The nearest LS was twenty-five miles by the easiest route from the top of Pagon, on a bend in the river, on some shingle.

'At 1600 hrs that afternoon my patrol flew into the LS in three Wessex aircraft, equipped with seven days rations and the usual jungle stores. My patrol consisted of myself and nine from my Troop, an SBA, two signallers and two Sarawak Rangers, Adjt and Bahru, who later proved themselves very useful at route finding and food finding. We were all reasonably fit but only half the patrol had experience in jungle marching and patrolling. They did not know that by the end of the patrol they would all be heartily sick of it.

'Well, after a short delay to start off with, due to the fact that we had no sort of accurate map, we set off up river heading roughly north. This we followed for two days. The going, despite the fact that we were continuously crossing the fast flowing river in water up to our waists, was fairly fast. As we got higher up the river the terrain changed. The ground, which was fairly flat and muddy to begin with, became hilly and marshy. The sides of the river valley started to get steep and to rise up to about 200 feet or more. With five days rations or so on our backs, it required considerable effort to climb these little hills, especially as the surface was slippery and we often had to haul ourselves up from vine to root to tree. Many a curse was heard as the poor signallers or the 'Doc' went sliding down the hill only to have to start climbing again…'

On day three the patrol was behind schedule but was instructed to continue, with the qualified promise of a supply drop on day six. By that time they were on the ridge at over 4,000 feet after a particularly arduous ascent through the jungle; continually soaked to the skin, feet had swelled so that boots removed could not be put on; food was getting short and the nights were bitterly cold. The supply drop came from an RAF Belvedere twin rotor helicopter – known to the locals as the 'silver longhouse' – with its wheels almost brushing the tree tops; sitting in the doorway was the SOO [Major Richard (Bull) Bavin] throwing out boxes of rations, cigarettes and spare clothing, including jerseys, allegedly pulled from the backs of the owners to provide the patrol with some protection against the nights' chill. Less welcome was the follow up radio message that told them that ridge that they were on was 'false' and that the main ridge of Bukit Pagon had yet to be reached…

Rupert Van der Horst, Patrol Commander

'…So next day we started out again. Here we found our worst going of the patrol. We had to cross an area of rocks covered in roots and moss. Half the time we had to crawl down mossy tunnels which with several days' rations on our backs was not easy. Eventually we got out, only to be confronted with a cliff face. This we had to climb with the aid of vines and stunted trees. As we were climbing this, our signals sergeant kicked a rock down on the Doc's head. The Doc was heard to mutter "I'll remember you at treatment time, Sergeant"!

'There was surprisingly little muttering, apparently, when shortly after reaching the main ridge and beginning the estimated two day ascent along it to the summit, the patrol was aborted – a recce by Auster light aircraft had declared the summit clear. On the conclusions of this air recce so late in his patrol, the Patrol Commander was relatively constrained in his comment… "I could have made a pretty good guess and told them so". The patrol struggled back to the LS, much of the time sliding on their backsides in the slippery mud. Once there, the clouds closed down, the rains came and the site flooded. It was a further week before they could be lifted out by Wessex and in the meantime they ran out of food. Starvation was avoided by a pig and small deer hunted down by the two Rangers, followed later by an air drop from a RAF Valetta fixed wing transport, flying at about 150 feet…'

Terry Clarke, SBA – 'Doc'

'After Limbang, I was transferred to M Company for a period, as their SBA had completed his tour and was leaving for home without relief. L Company had moved close to the Unit Headquarters, where the unit doctor and other medical staff were based and therefore had medical cover. I initially went to what had been the Brunei Governor's summer residence, where certain of the political prisoners were held. A very quiet period then ensued until I was informed that I would be going with a long range patrol of approximately seven days, to an area known as Bukit Pagon.

'Soon after arrival at the departure LS, the Sergeant told me that he was feeling a bit unwell and thought he was running a slight temperature. His signs and symptoms were similar to those of the 'jungle fever' which was fairly common in this environment and so I decided to treat him conservatively with aspirin and fluids. However, within a short time his condition became worse. I was taken aside by the Patrol Commander and told that I had to make a decision as regards to his fitness, as once the patrol left the LS there would be no further helicopter support for a while. Despite the Sergeant stating that he felt well enough to continue, I decided to evacuate him. It transpired that he later became quite ill and so, (thanks goodness) the right decision had been made.

'Rupertforce', as the patrol led by Lieutenant Rupert Van der Horst was named, turned out to be one of the most physically demanding treks I was ever to undertake. There were times when I really believed I was not going to make it. I did hear that some of the group were hoping I might 'conk out', as without an SBA the patrol would not continue. So just to be awkward, I kept going! Another fact which I can substantiate, is that the anticipation and drinking of a brew of tea worked miracles.

'Fortunately during this patrol, no major illnesses or injuries occurred. However, when we returned to our LS to await helicopter evacuation, I was quite concerned when the weather worsened. We had not received an airdrop due to the cloud level being too low. The river level began to rise and the ground became a muddy stinking swamp. Food was running out, (we in fact dug up the food we had dumped and buried previously) and the batteries for the radios began to malfunction. Personnel began to have headaches, feel dizzy and listless and generally unwell.

'Imagine the sheer joy when eventually a Valetta flew over our position and dropped supplies. Having gorged ourselves over the next two days, we were finally lifted out and returned to Brunei. On arrival, we were met by a welcoming committee and it appeared that we were somewhat celebrities.

'After an overnight stay, we flew to Bangar to change our clothing and equipment and were sent on two days leave to a Shell Hotel in Labuan. Once there, we ate ourselves silly, drank ourselves even sillier and were thoroughly spoiled. We also met up with the crew of the Valetta and had the opportunity to thank them personally for 'saving our lives'. This ended my deployment with M Company and I rejoined L Company.

'Shortly afterwards, I bruised the soft under-pad of my foot, which caused me to hobble. I reported the fact to the Company Sergeant Major, as I felt that if the Company had to deploy, I might not be fit to accompany them. Following the evening 'O' Group, he came to see me. He said, rather tongue in cheek, that considering my past history with the Company, the general consensus at the meeting was that if I was unfit to deploy, at least there would not be bullets flying about!…'

Major Peter Darling summed up 42 Commando's activities between mid-December '62 and early February '63…

> "The … two months were spent rounding up the rebels in the Temburong district – except for S Company who remained on the River Tusan. It was largely a game of hide-and-seek and as far as I know no shots were fired at our forces during this period. Over 500 prisoners, including the leaders, and over 250 weapons, mostly shotguns, were recovered. The back of rebel resistance in this area had been broken by the Limbang attack and by the rapidity of the Commando's deployment by helicopter

> and by boats along the main rivers. The timely arrival of Naval Helicopter Squadrons only two days after our arrival in Bangar was undoubtedly a major reason for our success…
>
> "This was the heyday of the junior leaders, the Troop Commanders and their Section Commanders. A great deal of very valuable experience in patrolling and ambushing was gained which was to stand us in good stead in Sarawak three months later."

In February the Commando was deployed back to Brunei; of this last six weeks Peter wrote…

> "It was hard work and much of the élan had gone out of the campaign. S Company in particular had a gruelling time hunting in the swamps bordering Brunei Bay. However, our efforts met with little success except for K Company's capture of two leaders in the Senkurong area. On 1 April, with a feeling of a job well done the unit embarked in our 'alma mater' HMS *Albion* for the trip back to Singapore."

Coming and Going

Derek Oakley – G3 Int

'For my part, after Limbang things began to move very quickly. The lack of communications became even more apparent when I was sent for on 13 December by Brigadier Glennie, the overall commander, and asked why HMS *Albion* was disgorging 40 Commando at Kuching, the capital of the First Division of Sarawak, as he urgently required the Commando for active operations in the Sarawak areas surrounding Brunei state. He said there was no signals link, either air or land, between Brunei and Kuching and I was to proceed there and inform Brigadier Billy Barton that 40 Commando was to re-embark immediately and *Albion* was to steam north.

'How was I to get across 300 miles of impenetrable jungle? I used my initiative and went to Labuan civilian airport to try to find some means of transport. I, along with my signaller, luckily found a small civilian airliner, commandeered a seat by turfing off a couple of erstwhile refugees fleeing from the battle zone. It's not easy to fit into a small passenger aircraft with signal set, full pack, weapon and kit, but we managed the turbulent journey fairly quickly.

'When I reached Kuching I found that the majority of 40 Commando had landed by helicopter; I located Brigadier Barton in the Police HQ and explained to him the problem. He immediately ordered A Company of 40 Commando to re-embark, contacted Singapore with whom he had plenty of communications, and *Albion* proceeded north east with all due speed. It transpired at the wash-up which I attended some months later in Singapore that the C-in-C Far East Fleet had ordered *Albion* to drop 40 Commando off in Kuching and then go back to Singapore for more reinforcements – but they had not told the Army GHQ. Many lessons were learnt from the early days of this campaign about inter-Services cooperation.

'I spent a very pleasant evening in the luxurious Aurora Hotel, a hostelry I was to get to know well in the coming year. Good food, plenty to drink and a warm bed. I went back to the rather less comfortable Brunei but, as 99 Brigade HQ gradually arrived, there was little for me to do, so I returned to Kuching well in time for Christmas; so ended my first phase of 'Confrontation' in Borneo. I did not realise the second phase would follow quite so quickly.'

An oblique air photo of Kuching pinpointing the police station (arrowed half left centre), where HQ 3 Commando Brigade (and subsequently West Brigade) shared the Police Station and operations rooms

Kuching

'My job as Brigade Intelligence Officer also included being the Public Relations Officer. I had been to Kuching a year earlier when Brigadier Billy Barton and I had been over to make initial arrangements for 42 Commando to carry out jungle training. Indeed I have a photograph of us sitting beside the pool at the Sarawak Club with the Deputy Commissioner of Police. I had not expected to meet him and the Head of Special Branch, Roy Henry, again quite so soon.

'We now shared the Police Headquarters with the Police, setting up a combined operations room and sharing duties with the Sarawak Constabulary. It was the typical arrangement that had always been made when we were supporting the civil power. Our accommodation was in a large bungalow (a house really) called 'Angby' where we enjoyed an almost peacetime Officers' Mess life. I slept on the upper floor in a large bedroom, which held five of us on camp beds. It was about half a mile to the Police Headquarters with the Sarawak Club about half way. I suppose there were about twelve of us living in the Mess but with operational duties and watches, we more often than not just 'passed in the night'.'

40 Commando – East and West

At the time of the Brunei outbreak, 40 Commando had been on return passage from Aden, where the two Commando ships had completed their turnover. Among the newly joined Troop Commanders was Ian Uzzell…

Ian Uzzell, Second Lieutenant – OC 7 Troop

'On completion of the first part of my Young Officer training in October 1962, I was posted to 40 Commando who were at that time stationed in South Malaya. So I was very surprised when my flight took me to Aden, the home of 45 Commando. All soon became clear as Aden was to be the location for the change over of the two Commando Ships HMS *Bulwark* and HMS *Albion*. On board *Albion* was a squadron of the then new Wessex Mk 1 helicopters. I was put into Charlie Company (Captain Frank Reynolds) in command of 7 Troop with Sergeant Jan Exelby as my Troop Sergeant. I was surprised to realise that at the age of nineteen I was the youngest person in my Troop.

'As we were leaving Aden on board *Albion*, one of the tugs helping her to manoeuvre was accidentally capsized killing two crew members. We were held back for the Board of Inquiry and during that time I was given my first flight in the cockpit of a Whirlwind 7 helicopter and that is when my interest in becoming a pilot first started – not something that I would have thought of doing when I joined the Royal Marines as I do not have a good head for heights. The experience was not without its problems: I was filming our flight at low level with my brand new cine camera when I became aware that the pilot was shouting at me. It seemed that as I was changing my film around I was clutching the control column between my legs and he could not properly control the aircraft.

'We left Aden for Mombassa to exercise with the new Wessex aircraft and were delighted to find that an entire section could be embarked in each aircraft as opposed to using two Whirlwinds to lift the same section. However, we did not travel with full equipment as the exercise was only short in duration. This was to prove a problem the next time I was to use the Wessex helicopter.

'On 5 December we finally set sail for Singapore and the return of 40 Commando to Burma Camp in Johore, Southern Malaya. Halfway across the Indian Ocean, one of our officers, Lieutenant Vic Courtice, was listening to his radio on the flight deck when he heard that there were problems in Brunei, and suddenly we noticed by the widening of the wake that the speed of *Albion* had increased considerably. We were told that we were to 'make all speed' to collect stores in Singapore and go from there direct to Borneo. We started to train for jungle warfare, mostly on the flight deck, and we were introduced to the 'JEWT' – Jungle Exercises Without Trees!

'On arrival in Singapore married families were given a couple of hours together on the dockside whilst we took on stores, before again setting sail. We heard of the five deaths of members of 42 Commando during the assault at Limbang, and assumed that we were going to assist them. But after we had left Singapore we were told our destination was Kuching in the First Division of Sarawak. We were to fly ashore in the Wessex helicopters and land at Kuching Racecourse on 13 December. On this occasion, as our time ashore was indeterminate, we each took much more kit. I had misunderstood the briefing we had been given about the aircraft loading and instructed those in my Troop to put their heavy packs in the small room to the rear of the aircraft, so when we took off the nose of our aircraft rose alarmingly and we were very quickly deposited back on the flight deck, where ground handlers redistributed our load to give a safe centre of gravity and we were off. My learning curve about helicopters went up another notch.

'We did not know what sort of reception we would be getting on our arrival and so I had put my Troop into all round defence ready for anything – or so I thought! What I had *not* expected was an ice cream man circulating our landing area on his tricycle with the cry "Ice creams! Lollipops!" I accepted the cone offered by one of my Section Commanders.'

Serian and Tebedu

'C' Company was deployed to Serian which we were to use as a patrol base, whence we would go to visit the local villages to check on shotguns and licences. My first task was to go by road to a police station at Tebedu and patrol from there to the border with Indonesia. It took the most part of a day on a very poor jungle road. We were based in the police station for a couple of days whilst we patrolled towards the border and carried out the required checks. There was a large trade in raw rubber being brought across the border and we had also to search the packs of rubber for weapons.

'Within a few days we were told that we were being redeployed north and we moved to Kuching Airport, embarked in Beverley aircraft and headed – as we thought

– for Jesselton. On our arrival our company second in command disembarked from the aircraft, looked around and said "So this is Jesselton!", only to be told that it was Tawau which is on the east side of North Borneo. From here 7 Troop was tasked to do river patrols and to observe Indonesian Gunboats based at Nunuken.

Tawau – River Patrol

'My first patrol was to Kampong Serudong, close to the Indonesian Border. The boat broke down en route and I took Sergeant Exelby with me to walk to the village in order to get a tow for the boat and to arrange repairs. I noticed that he was not wearing jungle boots, but standard UK boots, so I asked why. "Because of the snakes, sir" was his reply. I pointed out that snakes were very sensitive to vibrations, would sense our movement and would move out of our way. "I know that, sir, I just want to make bloody sure they hear me coming!"

'On arrival at Serudong the boat was recovered and whilst we were waiting for the repairs I let the members of the Troop go swimming in the local river. The current was a bit fast but not excessively so. As they swam I spoke to the headman of the village and during the conversation he mentioned that they never swam in the river as there were too many crocodiles. I advised the swimmers that it was time to finish, but did not disclose the reason.

'Christmas day was spent patrolling Wallace Bay and checking boats in the area. We were working from the destroyer HMS *Barossa* in a requisitioned boat. Whilst moored alongside we were visited on several occasions by a white dolphin. On one patrol I had the ship's Navigation Officer with me as we were to moor our boat close to the border and observe the port at Nunuken. We had a disagreement over which headland was closest to the border. I felt that we should be closer but as he had seniority we anchored overnight where he decided. That night as I walked around the boat I was aware of something glowing on the deck. As I approached it, it moved away. I followed it for a short time before I discovered one of my Marines with a fishing rod reeling in a luminous prawn. "Got you sir!", was his triumphant shout.

'The next morning we observed the area and the Indonesian gunboats for several hours before our task was completed. I had a further disagreement with the Navigation Officer on returning to our base as to whether what was marked on his chart was a sandbank or an island that we could see nearby. I insisted that it was a sandbank and that if we proceeded on that course we would probably run aground. Again I was outranked, but it was difficult to hide my satisfied grin as we waited for two hours for the tide to get us off the sandbank.

'Our stay in the Tawau area was not long and we were relieved, returning to Singapore on 10 January 1963, where we settled down to the usual round of range work and training and I completed a Jungle Warfare Instructor's course.'

Meanwhile the rest of 40 Commando had been similarly active, first in Sarawak and later in Brunei. For much of the initial time off Sarawak, 'A' Company Group (Major Peter (Pug) Davis) had operated from HMS *Albion*, acting as Brigade Reserve and being committed ashore as required in Wessex or Whirlwind helicopters of 845 or 846 Naval Air Squadrons respectively. Over the period they netted sixty-nine wanted men and some 300 weapons. By Christmas Day it was B Company that was aboard *Albion* en route to Brunei, where they were flown ashore on Boxing Day and where they quickly noticed a much more charged atmosphere among the people – more frightened than hostile, but nonetheless demanding caution. Here 40 Commando was to be reunited before returning to Johore a fortnight later.

846 Naval Air Squadron

The two squadrons of helicopters from *Albion* had played a vital part in the mopping-up operations after the insurrection. Shortage of Wessex helicopters had meant that, unlike her sister 845 Squadron, 846 Squadron was equipped with the ageing Whirlwind Mark 7 with its limited payload. Writing in the Corps Journal one of the pilots testified to their contribution and concluded:

> "The most intense period of flying the Squadron has carried out during the stay in Borneo has been in support of 42 Commando, when 193 hours were flown between 15 December '62 and the 5th January '63. This covered the campaign from the arrival of the Commando at Bangar and its subsequent very successful mopping up in the Temburong District.
>
> "Despite its limitations the Whirwind has been getting through a great deal of work whilst ashore. The number of troops moved now runs into thousands in over 4,000 sorties and the amount of 'brass' and senior civilians runs into tons. Our loads have varied from dead rebels to expectant mothers, although none of the crewmen qualify for midwifery badges, but so far their luck has held. There have been two incidents of broken aircraft but no broken bodies. In both incidents – one an engine failure which resulted in the aircraft collapsing on its side after landing in a paddy field, the other where the tail rotor flew off after striking a tree stump – the aircraft have been successfully recovered by courtesy of the other 'firm' (the RAF had lifted them out) and are flying once more.
>
> "Possibly the greatest contribution the Squadron can make in this type of operation is its ability to lift out casualties without tying up one of the large load helicopters for one or two people. Another advantage – or disadvantage, depending on the viewpoint – of the Whirlwind is its use for carrying Commanding Officers around all the outposts in hours as against days of walking…"

The article also drew attention to the rocket firing capability that had not yet been called upon and cast a wistful eye at the Commando Carrier concept that seemed to be in abeyance in a period during which 'out of 2,500 hours flown only 430 hours were flown with the Squadron embarked.

A Whirlwind Mk 7 of 846 Naval Air Squadron

More Coming and Going

Derek Oakley – G3 Int

'The situation in Sarawak quietened down and it was decided that a full Brigade Headquarters was not necessary and the military presence was reduced to a small Headquarters, British Forces West Sarawak, and one army regiment. We were relieved on 16 January 1963 by 'C' Squadron of the Queen's Royal Irish Hussars; their CO was Lieutenant Colonel John Strawson, a serious looking soldier with a deep voice and even deeper military convictions. They were an armoured car squadron to give mobility around the enormous area for which they were responsible – the 1st, 2nd and 3rd Divisions of Sarawak and a border of 750 miles with Kalimantan (Indonesian Borneo).'

Brief Interlude

'Whilst 42 Commando remained in Brunei, Brigade HQ and 40 Commando were now in Singapore and Johore at immediate notice to return to Borneo if a crisis arose, so it was decided that there should be a Brigade liaison officer over there. Two weeks after getting back to Singapore, I drew the short straw and was the one who returned, leaving a wife and five children in Singapore; the youngest, Philip, was barely six months old. It seemed unfair to me at the time, especially as the other officer from the Headquarters who might have gone was our Sapper, Captain Bill Marks who was unmarried – at least he was then. I think I managed a spot of swimming and a couple of games of cricket before I left.

'So in February I was back in 'Angby'. There was little to do, so I spent some time exploring and learning about the wonderful colony of Sarawak. There was an excellent Museum and wonderful flowery gardens where young ladies, dressed in their Sunday best, paraded through the orchid filled grounds every weekend, in their very colourful costumes. I learnt about the many tribes who lived deeper in the jungle, the Kayans, the Kelabits, the Ibans (or Sea Dyaks), the Penans the Muruts and the Land Dyaks, along with the Malays, the Chinese and the Indian communities. So many different cultures and tribes, most of whom lived in longhouses deep in the vast jungles of northern Borneo and many of whom had never set eyes on a white man.

'Dick Morris had returned from leave to become Resident of 1st Division and was joined shortly afterwards by his wife, Dorothy; they were the most hospitable hosts. I also met Hedda Morrison, a pictorial historian, who had lived in Sarawak for a dozen or so years. Her husband was in Government service. I became fascinated by the Land of the Rajahs, the Brooke family who had ruled Sarawak for over 100 years. I also met the legendary Tom Harrison, the curator of the Sarawak Museum, who had fought with the tribesmen during the Japanese occupation of World War Two and was probably the most knowledgeable man about the country. He was a fascinating, if at times mildly truculent, man, who was held in awe by the tribesmen of the country. I learnt about the wildlife, championed by the orang-utan and hornbill, papaya and pepper, blowpipes and headhunters.

'I had a Land Rover to myself and was able to drive down to Bau, across the rope ferry, or to Simanggang, the capital of the 2nd Division, some 100 miles eastwards. 'A' Company of 40 Commando in Semengo Camp, near Kuching, became my particular responsibility as far as liaison duties were concerned. I ensured they got all the best supplies, but being Royal Marines, part of the Royal Navy who also had a helicopter squadron nearby, they were never short of the essentials. From the outset there was always a Gurkha presence in West Sarawak and I met a large number of excellent officers, mainly British, but as I did not speak Gurkhali I did not really get involved with the NCOs and riflemen. What amused me was that, whilst a helicopter might carry twelve Royal Marines, you could easily pack twice that number of Gurkhas into one – very good for logistics.

Arrival of the SAS and Setting up of the Border Scouts

'It was during this period that a clandestine group arrived, in fact a Squadron of 22 SAS Regiment, who hardly ever seemed to wear a recognisable uniform, nor badges of rank, and were not amenable to any advice or direction. In fact their commander,

Lieutenant Colonel John Woodhouse had been on an initial recce early in January and the squadron arrived in plain clothes a few at a time. Their task was 'Hearts and Minds' deep in jungle kampongs and along the border and in due course, together with the Gurkha Parachute Company, they set up a sort of Home Guard organisation called the 'Border Scouts'. This was an esoteric organisation and frightened the local police as well as many of the British troops. They seemed to live a life of their own, seldom brought in any intelligence that was shared with us, but obviously relieved British troops of unenviable tasks deep in the jungle.'

Life in Kuching

'There was a very reasonable social life in those days in Kuching; the Club, the Aurora Hotel and hospitality amongst British colonial residents, the Shell Oil Company, and so on. There were a number of eligible young ladies in the Secretariat and amongst the teachers, so there were plenty of mixed company parties and banyans down the Sarawak River to some excellent beaches. It was colonial life par excellence.

'One remarkable day I actually commanded the whole of the British Troops in West Sarawak, in fact if not in name. It was St Patrick's Day, 17th March and I was serving with the Queen's Royal Irish Hussars, whose CO, Lieutenant Colonel John Strawson, was then designated as Commander British Forces, Kuching. Naturally I volunteered to be duty officer in the operations room – or perhaps I had no choice. I had no idea what the celebrations were going to be like. They seemed to start well before dawn; the whiskey, Guinness or whatever flowed freely from breakfast onwards. By morning stand-easy, I reckon, I was the only sober person in the force. There were games, sports, pipes, drums and lots of noise. I am sure if the terrorists had realised what happens on Paddy's day, they might well have created military mayhem in Kuching. It was a long day, and whilst I was invited to join in several times, I did feel, for once, a sense of responsibility. The day, and night, passed off peacefully – the Squadron slept well.

'A couple of weeks later Bill Marks [SORE] did indeed relieve me – this time as a married man. That was why he didn't come in the first place! I was delighted to be home again in Singapore with the family. I thought life would settle down to a more routine pattern, particularly as it was just coming up to Easter – how wrong I was!'

Chapter 3

Sarawak Alert

First Division; Incursion and Counter Measures

March to July ’63

Sarawak Alert

Intermission

By the end of the first week in April '63, 3 Commando Brigade Headquarters, 40 Commando and 42 Commando had each returned to Singapore or Johore. It had been a busy four months but the respite was to be short lived. Indeed, in March 40 Commando had already deployed B Company (Captain Pat Gardner) to relieve an Artillery battery in providing a military presence in Sarawak's First Division.

Pat Gardner, Captain – OC B Company

'We were relieving a gunner battery, which had detachments scattered over a wide area so it was important that we arrived at Kuching on time. After a fiendishly early start we got to Changi (apart from Peter Cameron who couldn't be woken – it was later discovered he was ill). It became apparent that, for social reasons, the RAF had no intention of flying that day although pressure was brought on them to do so. They went through the motions of taking us and as the ancient Hastings took off a fire alarm sounded; we flew round jettisoning fuel and finally came down with a hefty bump. We got off the following day.

'We were spread thinly over a huge area of the First Division of Sarawak that was basically peaceful. After about a month the Indonesians came over the border and attacked a police post. The senior officer in the area was Colonel John Strawson, a cavalryman, and we went to see the Governor; John told him, in his deep 'whiskey' voice, that if he wanted a Brigade, he could have a Brigade and the following day 3 Commando Brigade flew in.'

Meanwhile, in April, Derek Oakley had returned to Singapore in early April; a keen sportsman and notable cricketer, he had soon been on his own travels..."

Derek Oakley – G3 Int

'I played a couple of games of cricket and was delighted to be picked for the State of Singapore against Selangor in the annual two day match in Kuala Lumpur over the Easter weekend. I was one of only two servicemen to be picked, but was surprised to find, for the first time in my life, that I was down to bat at No 11. I had been picked as the wicket keeper though the selectors must have known that I normally opened the batting for Singapore Cricket Club. In some ways this was a sporting double as I had played for Singapore at hockey in 1954 when I was serving in HMS *Newcastle*.

'We travelled up to Kuala Lumpur on Good Friday, 12 April, for the match over the weekend. The two-day game was played on the beautiful Selangor Club padang, one of the most luxurious clubs in the Orient and known colloquially as 'The Dog' – though I'm not sure why. The first day was played, extremely slowly as it was always a 'we mustn't lose encounter'. I remember keeping wicket reasonably well in the heat and being not out for 0 at No 11.'

Attack on Tebedu

'As we came off the field I was handed a note which said that I was to ring Brigade HQ in Singapore urgently. I did so, whilst sipping a 'Tiger' and was told that I was to get back to Singapore immediately as the balloon had gone up in Sarawak with a guerrilla attack on the village of Tebedu in the First Division and several policemen had been killed. Brigade HQ was moving across at speed to Kuching and I was to get to Singapore by the fastest possible means. Bill Beckett, our Camp Commandant, told me that they would get my wife, Pam, to sort out my uniform and accoutrements ready for my arrival. I quickly explained that the fastest means was the midnight train from Kuala Lumpur to Singapore.

'This meant that I was able to enjoy the social evening with dinner and a reasonable amount of alcoholic refreshment before I caught the train. I had a sleeper booked and was met at the station by a Land Rover and driven home to 6 King's Road to drop my dirty cricket gear off and collect my belongings. I was then driven straight to Changi to catch some RAF transport, probably a Hastings, for Kuching. I arrived in Sarawak before the players in Kuala Lumpur went on the field for the second day's play. It was some four months later before I discovered the result of the match – as expected, a draw.

'The balloon had indeed gone up and troops were being flown and shipped into Sarawak at a rate of knots. 40 Commando and L Company of 42 Commando were among them. We took up residence once more in 'Angby', where Lieutenant Colonel John Strawson QRIH handed over to Brigadier Billy Barton and there we remained for nearly a year. It was much tougher work this time and we were fully occupied. As the G3 (Int) I worked in a roster of three duty officers in the Ops Room, along with Bill Marks, SORE and the G3 (Ops), at that time another army officer. The Brigade had the same responsibility, covering an area of about 30,000 square miles where some of the outposts that were set up were 175 miles apart.'

First Division – Deployment

'On arrival with the rest of the unit, HQ 40 Commando and S Company moved into Semengo Camp, where Tac HQ opened on 17 April. The Camp was close to Kuching Airport and took its name from the neighbouring river, itself named after a young man who – by local legend – was eaten by a white crocodile. The unit correspondent wrote of the arrival...'

> "Semengo is a recently constructed atap camp built for about 200. As, together with the QRIH and 846 Squadron, we currently number something like 400, this appeared to present a problem, but the PWD workmen soon proved the value of atap huts when they were extended without even disturbing the occupants..."

The Officers' Mess at Semengo Camp, near Kuching airport, where HQ 40 Commando and subsequently HQ 42 Commando were based.

'A' Company once again remained initially aboard *Albion*, but subsequently took over Lundu District from a detachment of B Company, which at that stage held Bau District. C Company returned to their previous District at Serian, in which also stood the police post of Tebedu.

'In addition to the establishment of border outposts, the first task to be undertaken with the aid of the police was to collect in shotguns and other firearms from non-natives, in particular the Chinese, fruitful material for recruitment to the internal Clandestine Communist Organisation (CCO). The Chinese population was grouped significantly in townships, including the District of Kuching itself; it was for operations in this area that Lieutenant Colonel Parsons requested an additional Company from 42 Commando and for which L Company was nominated. 42 Commando's correspondent wrote of the deployment...

'They had scarcely collected their jungle greens from the laundry than they were packing them again. The language was unprintable but they had a very real task to perform in Sarawak...'

Above: A Whirlwind of 846 NAS. Below: A Wessex of 845 NAS.
Two typical landing sites cut from the jungle specially for helicopter landing pads.
These illustrate the skill required by pilots, not only to locate them, but also to land on them.

Operation 'Parrot'

In compiling this publication my prime concern has been to link the experiences of others. However, on this deployment and on the next three deployments of 42 Commando my own involvement is sometimes relevant. In February, two months earlier, I had been on Salisbury Plain at Warminster, undergoing a Company Commanders' course during the worst winter in a decade. The experience had been interesting but the course was directed towards mobile operations in a potentially nuclear war in North Europe, not perhaps ideal preparation for the tactics and climate to which I was committed.

I had reached Singapore at the end of March, just before 42 Commando arrived back from Brunei, my wife had followed a week later and we had been given temporary refuge with Captain Robin Patteson-Knight, OC Rear Party. I had since taken over command of L Company from Captain Jeremy Moore – a difficult act to follow. The command team had also changed and Lieutenant Ricky Targett-Adams of 6 Troop was then the only officer remaining who had been with the Company during the previous deployment. He, like others among Brunei campaigners, had yet to recover fully from the injuries, sores or fungal infections acquired after four months of operations.

On 18 April we flew to Kuching in a RAF Beverley, a double-decker transport aircraft with rear doors and a ramp, rather like a flying elephant but ideal for ferrying a Company with the minimum vehicles of a couple of Land Rovers and trailers. Ian Moore, who had left the post of Assistant Adjutant, was one of the Troop Commanders…

Ian Moore, Lieutenant – OC 5 Troop, L Company

'Harking back to the spring of 1963, I become conscious of just to what extent L Company were required to 'lift and shift' at that time. After 42 Commando's return from the eventful four months in Brunei, during the two week's well deserved and much relished post deployment leave, the Company changed its command team.

'Now under Captain Brian Edwards, with Lieutenant David Morris as Second-in-Command and QMS Peter Gibbons as Sergeant Major, we were crash-moved to Sarawak First Division in mid-April, to support 40 Commando in confronting a new and apparently growing threat, following the raid by the TNKU on Tebedu Police Station on Good Friday.

'I had taken over 5 Troop, after many months as Assistant Adjutant, and it is likely that I did not fully appreciate the mental disruption this sudden deployment imposed on our people. Four months earlier 5 Troop had borne the brunt of casualties in the Limbang assault, and earned two MMs in the process – Corporals Lester and Rawlinson. I took over from Colour Sergeant Len Poole, who was well respected by the Troop, and who had, some four years before, been the Platoon Weapons Instructor (PWI) of my YO batch. I remember that his hand over was both sympathetic and concerned – probably concerned whether an officer whom he had trained would measure up and not mess up the Troop with too much 'pusser's' protocol!

'On 18 April the Company flew to Kuching and was allotted as Company base a wooden school building, equipped with 'kindergarten' furniture and one tap, at the seventh milestone out of Kuching. From here we were to help with the enforcement of the recent amnesty to surrender shotguns (Op Parrot). Our tasks were also to involve cordon and search operations following any 'tip off', as well as standing patrols at police stations that might be vulnerable.

'The task at police stations included filling sandbags, laying dannert wire, and waiting through the night in case of a TNKU attack. On 22 April guerillas attacked the Kampong at Gumbang on the border; they were fought off by a section from B Company, 40 Commando, and five days later a repeated attack on Tebedu was similarly repulsed. The threat seemed real enough and some Limbang veterans found it hard not to be edgy…'

Operation Parrot had begun on the 19 April, the day after arrival, L Company HQ was at the 18th Mile Police Station with patrols on the Serian Road between the tenth and twenty-fourth milestone, where there was another police station and at Siniawan on the Bau road, where there too was a police station. By 2000 hrs on 22 April, when that phase of the operation ended, 462 shotguns, 126 air rifles, two pistols and one .303 rifle had been collected in the Company area. The total for 40 Commando Group had been around 2,800 weapons.

Full Circle to Brigade Reserve

On the same day there had been warning of a pending attack in the Second Division on Semanggang, garrisoned by a company of the King's Own Yorkshire Light Infantry (KOYLI), which L Company was sent to reinforce. The town was linked to Kuching by a rough road that ran for much of its length close to the border with Indonesia; the move was made by three ton truck and was escorted by Ferret scout cars and Saladin armoured cars of the Queen's Royal Irish Hussars (QRIH). Ian Moore wrote…

> "Recently the Company has completed an interesting encircling movement. Alerted at midnight we moved east to Simanggang at 0200 hrs, a distance of 120 miles. Here we sat at border police stations, subjects of likely attack from Indonesia, which is only twelve miles away; a mysterious line of grey green jungle hills, reached by straggling paths. Wire, trip flares and sandbags were erected and troops stood by in trenches for the arrival of TNKU that never came. The following morning we moved by air to the organized and air conditioned hospitality of HMS *Albion* with a task of operational reserve. This however was not to be; at 1500 hrs on the following day we moved by Wessex round full circle back to 7th Mile school…"

As the time away from 42 Commando and Singapore progressed, a reserve role with the school as a base was not ideal…

Terry Clarke, SBA – L Company Medic

'…The Company was initially billeted at a school close to Commando Headquarters. The conditions were cramped and there was only a very limited water supply for washing and cooking. Tempers became a little frayed at times and morale lowered. Thankfully, the Company was later moved to empty flats in Sekarma Road, Kuching, which proved much more habitable and morale improved considerably. I had little work to do medically during this period, apart from the morning sick parade, so I spent most of my time trying to cheer others up. I have always believed that part of a medic's duty is to keep a close contact with all ranks and contribute to improving morale whenever possible…'

The move to Serkama Road in Kuching eventually took place on 5 May, meanwhile the importance of an active involvement was obvious…

Ian Moore – OC 5 Troop

'We practiced helicopter drills from Whirlwinds of 846 Naval Air Squadron – payload five men – prior to being 'choppered' out to stop points in cordons, reacting to hot tips. Establishing a routine was difficult, but it was important to keep busy with training and sport. We were working around the edge of Kuching, the bright lights never far away. It seemed a different scene from Brunei. These were suburban jungle villages. I recall dawn patrols and cordons, lamps being lit in village homes coming to life, smoke from morning fires glimmering out from under the atap.

'The article that I penned for *The Globe & Laurel* on behalf of L Company included the following…

> "The latter days in Sarawak were spent in two locations of widely different character. Bau, situated in the West, about two hours away from Kuching, is a beauty spot for all of Sarawak … One Troop was deployed here at a time, with a roving commission of exploring possible enemy approaches, preparing defence positions, 'against the day', and generally making ourselves felt to counteract communist influence in all the distant and obscure suburbs … Each kampong was a separate revelation as one came upon it in the jungle clearing. Insecure stilted bashas, tottering up the hillside, hazy in the early morning smoke and mist, guarded by smiling naked children, and girls in sarongs crouched by their laundry in the stream shingle. Mostly the men folk had been out working in the rubber plantations since the small hours, but in one corner of the longhouse the headman was normally to be found, with an entourage of breast feeding wives. At this stage thick gritty coffee was offered, and the headman produced from his biscuit tin his credentials and his headman's badge, and pointed proudly to three identical prints of Her Majesty, set on the atap wall, among the pagan fetishes…"

'This excerpt perhaps conveys some of the sense of wonderment and old style colonial paternalism with which a young Troop Commander saw life in the early sixties – before the world we lived in became much more weary and self effacing. Though we didn't know it then, L Company would in due course get to know the Bau area very much better.

'Meanwhile, two weeks crash-deployment extended to six and we finally returned to Singapore on 28 May on the open decks of a Chinese manned LST and over a glassy sea with only the occasional downpour.'

C Company – Serian District

It had been the attack on Tebedu Police Station in the Serian District that had sparked the arrival of HQ 3 Commando Brigade and 40 Commando Group. Close to the border, the Station was normally occupied by three policemen and their families and was to remain vulnerable to attack. It had therefore become a Troop patrol base. On 27 April there was a second attack…

> "This raid was made by a small party of two or three men at 2150 hrs. The enemy crawled to within fifteen to twenty yards of the position cutting alarm systems, laying them aside and removing panjis. They opened fire with a shotgun followed by LMG fire over a period of five minutes. The ranks in the police station defensive positions, a Troop of C Company, were in the process of changing sentries. They returned the fire and the attackers made off. A follow up revealed nothing, tracker dogs failing to follow the scent on the main track, as it was impossible for them to reach the location for some hours."

Ian Uzzell – OC 7 Troop

'On the Saturday of that Easter weekend 7 Troop was having a night out in the Golden Venus bar in Singapore when word reached us that 40 Commando was being recalled. Tebedu police station had been attacked and two police corporals had been killed. Within twenty-four hours we were back in Borneo and we found ourselves returning to our original base at Serian, our Company Commander now being Captain David Shallow. This time we were to be there on a more permanent basis.'

Kampong Muara Mongkos

'7 Troop was sent to patrol from a base at Kampong Muara Mongkos, near the Indonesian border. As there were no roads leading to this village we travelled by native boats on a river journey, along the Sungei Kedup, which lasted most of the day. The boats carried a large supply of shear pins for the propeller. Frequently as we were travelling through shallow waters the propeller would hit the bottom, and as a safety measure the pins shear thus reducing damage to the propeller itself.

The type of river boat that was used to transport the Marines to Muara Mongkos

A typical Dayak longhouse in the First Division.

'On arrival at Muara Mongkos we set about building the defences around the village area before starting patrols to the Indonesian Border and the three border villages of Kampongs Mongkos, Mujat and Bunan Gega. Patrols were usually of half Troop strength with the other half responsible for the running and defence of the camp area. We had an emergency 'Stand To' one night shortly after we arrived when a trip flare had been activated. Investigation showed it to be one of the domestic animals from the village that had been the culprit.

'On return from one patrol I was informed that the remaining part of the Troop had been treated to a magnificent pork meal. Sergeant Mitchell had informed the headman of Muara Mongkos that it was Royal Marine Remembrance Day and on this day it is the custom to eat pork. A pig was duly slaughtered and feasted upon. The fact that it was actually some weeks after the event seemed immaterial. It also transpired that the meal coincided with a visit by the Commanding Officer, Lieutenant Colonel John Parsons – who was most impressed. There was no pork left for my patrol.

'We had a naval medic attached to us for the duration of our stay as we were so far from any medical assistance. He was equipped for most things up to a minor operation. His work was taken up mainly with helping the local villagers with their medical problems. Daily sick parade consisted of one or two Marines and many more locals, some of whom had travelled for some hours to get there. The main medication needed seemed to be 'Golden Eye Ointment' as eye problems were the most common ailment. Word soon spread and we actually had some blind villagers appearing after several hours walk through the jungle. We did what we could for them but had to tell them that we could not cure their blindness. Several locals arrived with letters, written probably by a local schoolteacher, asking for medical assistance. Again, where we could help we did.

'We were re-supplied by airdrops from Hastings aircraft. The drop zones were several hundred yards from our camp and the local villagers willingly helped to bring the stores into the camp and were paid for their efforts with such things as ration pack biscuits – or pieces of damaged parachute – sometimes the 'damage' happened after the drop had been collected. Other items were frequently damaged, which we reported by signal, and were replaced at a later airdrop. We could not understand why potatoes were loaded on top of such things as bread and eggs. We might not have been too truthful about the amount of beer and cigarettes that were also damaged…

'This type of soldiering was a Troop Commander's joy. We were almost entirely separated from the main unit with poor radio communications which was reduced to Morse code at night. Visits by the Company Commander and the Commanding Officer were few and far between and were by helicopter. So as a Troop Commander I was in charge of a very large area of jungle with a number of villages which we

St. Michael School
Kampong Tapu.
18/8/63.

Dear Sir.

Thank, you, very much for you.
I am very sorry to write this few lines of
words to you, I tell you about this.
Excause Sir. I want you to come to Tapu.
And see my mother, she was very ill.
Last night she counld slept, because
she was very painful.
I hope you will be coming at this afernoon.
and see her here.

Sir if you have anytime
~~please~~ please came here as quick as
possible. I want her go down to Serian
but I am very porr.
I hope you will be coming Sir
Thanks very much.

From Tony Dawi.

A letter received by C Company asking for medical aid from Kampong Tapu

regularly visited in order to get information and also to boost their confidence. In effect these were 'Hearts and Minds' operations. The area was generally quiet apart from one incident in which I heard what appeared to be a burst of heavy machine gun fire on the Indonesian side of the border area. I took bearings as visibility was strictly limited by the trees, and reported it back to Company HQ. It was possibly an anti-aircraft gun but we never heard it again.

'Between two of the villages there was a small clearing in which was located a school. On my first patrol through the area I was delighted to hear singing coming from the single school building and as we got closer I could hear the words: "This old man, he played one"… etc. The children were being taught English. On several occasions, as we visited various villages the children acted as interpreters for us. Their games were also influenced by our presence. As I entered one village a young boy raced past wielding a wooden airplane his father had made complete with a side opening and as he passed us he threw something up into the air. It was a stone with a parachute attached to it to represent an air drop. The parachute was made from an air drop parachute. I was also impressed by the numbers of photographs of the Queen that were in the longhouses that we visited.

'On one occasion as we were sitting in a longhouse being treated to the local rice wine – tuak – the skulls hanging from the roof were pointed out by my host who informed me that 'Dayaks eat people'. Fortunately we were not on the menu. The tuak was to be a problem, as it seemed to be expected that we would drink some on each visit to a village. If we visited several villages on a patrol it could result in us getting a little merry. At one time I tried to circumnavigate the village by following the river but the undergrowth became too dense to penetrate and as I had to divert inland I suddenly came across our own footprints; so we went through the village and I sent word that I would prefer them on future patrols to offer us coconut milk instead.'

Terbat Bazaar

'7 Troop returned to Serian and was later helicoptered to Terbat Bazaar where we were based across the river from the local village. The helicopters were Whirlwind 10 helicopters flown by the RAF. They were powered by jet engines so were able to carry more than the Naval Whirlwind 2s. Our routine was similar to that of our previous location but in addition to assistance in recovering air drop supplies some of the village ladies would wash our clothes. My particular wash lady was named Mandin; her payment was a new sarong and as much soap as she needed.

'For those who were not on patrol there was a morning briefing at 0900 hrs each day. For some unknown reason at this location there was a tame white rabbit which wandered freely – sometimes giving the night-time sentries a start when it moved across the front of their position. If not on duty members of the Troop could wear flip flops to enable their feet to get some air. I must admit to having some difficulty in keeping a straight face one particular morning as the rabbit was licking between my toes whilst I gave my briefing.

'After leaving Terbat Bazaar I was tasked with patrolling an area to the South East of Serian with 7 Troop. We were based at a school next to a river, and patrolled for several days. Most of our patrols started and ended with fording the river which was just over waist deep. I noticed that subsequently, as we approached puddles on the tracks, even though they were still very wet from the river, every single Marine went out of his way to go round them.

'Returning on foot to the main road we had to stop and bivvy overnight and as I was setting up my shelter I heard a shout from lower down the hill. Lance Corporal Fagan had been bitten by a large spider. I looked at the bite on his arm and in the absence of anything else put on some antiseptic cream. The offending spider was produced for me in two pieces. I told Lance Corporal Fagan that the best thing he could do was to lie down and get some rest. "I dassen't go to sleep, sir" he said "I mightn't wake up". So I pointed out to him that this particular spider was not too dangerous and that he would not die from the bite. The following morning his arm had swollen considerably and we arranged for a vehicle to collect him and take him to hospital when we arrived at the road. When he recovered he came to ask me what kind of spider it was – I told him that I had no idea whatsoever.

'In July we returned to Burma camp and in October I returned to UK to complete my training. I applied to return to the Far East for my next posting, requesting that I go to 42 Commando, and this was granted. I also applied to specialise as a helicopter pilot. At that time the only choice was for the Troop lift Wessex helicopters.'

B Company – Bau and Lundu Districts

During the first week a patrol from B Company was attacked at Kampong Gumbang. In the Bau District. Lying only a few hundred yards from the border, the Kampong was to become a frequent target for the TNKU…

> "On 23 April there was a raid on one of our patrols at Gumbang. The attacking force was thought to be a patrol of eight men led by a Second Lieutenant Gusti Noya, who kindly left a card to say he was leading a TNKU raiding party. The Marines quickly returned the fire, severely wounding one of the enemy in the knee – as reported by the locals. The patrol, a section of B Company, sustained one casualty, who was the signaller, with slight wounds in the elbow. A follow up revealed nothing, a blood trail ending about seventy yards from the position…"

The process took time but towards the end of the year Lance Corporal Radford was awarded the Military Medal and Sergeant Locke received a Mention in Despatches for their part in repelling this raid. Defences were strengthened, border patrols continued and things appeared to quieten down. Towards the end of May, A Company took over Bau District, while B Company found themselves in Lundu District during the run up to 'Malaysia'…

Pat Gardner – OC B Company

'When B Company took over from the gunner battery in March they were very thinly stretched over a huge area. Our initial forward bases were fixed as we took them over from the gunners. I was not convinced that these sites were in the right position. In several instances the kampongs seemed to be protecting the bases rather than vice versa. However, they were so established that they could not be moved immediately. Then we were overtaken by events.

'Our tasks – so far as I remember and I am not sure that we were given any! – were to protect the border crossing points by having defendable bases from which to patrol and ambush. From my experience in Malaya in the 1950s my main priority was to promote 'Hearts and Minds' to ensure we had the locals behind us, so we had the intelligence and early warning, Co-operation of the locals was vital and basically we got on well with them.

Captain Pat Gardner, commanding B Company, 40 Commando (left, rear standing in the doorway), with locals at Stass in the First Division

'This was a Troop Commander's war and Company HQ was there to provide the sinews of war – which had yet to break out. Wireless (or had it become radio?) communication was very poor during this first period. It improved vastly with the advent of the 'Yagi' aerial and the support of helicopters.

'The skills of District Officers, Police Officers, Headmen, Public Works Department, foresters, traders and later Border Scouts were all used and proved invaluable.

'After about a month there was the incursion and B Company were in due course sent to Lundu – a remote area without any roads where we patrolled, tried to sell Malaysia as a viable project and generally guarded the border.

'Towards the end of our first tour there was a border incident. One night a party of people attacked the house of a police sergeant in a border kampong. Shots were fired and a grenade was thrown, which apparently landed on the police sergeant's lap.

'Sergeant Callow, whose patrol base was within earshot, went to assist, secured the kampong boundary but sensibly did not try to follow up in the dark, especially as it was so close to the border. He tried to render medical aid to the police sergeant whose abdomen was terribly injured. The man was in agony and asked Sergeant Callow to put him out of his misery, which he could not bring himself to do. Sadly he died, still in agony, just before dawn. Sergeant Callow, a natural sea Marine, did really well.

'I got to the Kampong late in the morning. It was eerie as the inhabitants had set up a constant wailing. We searched for evidence, picked up a few used cartridges and discovered an unexploded hand grenade on the main path through the Kampong. The pin was out, the handle missing but the striker was still in place. We hadn't the wherewithal for a controlled explosion. Something had to be done and someone had to do it. I had that awkward feeling that this could only be me. I had the area cleared and asked for a container of water. I then undid the base of the grenade under water, hoping that if the striker was dislodged I should have four seconds before it went off. Having seen what a grenade could do to the poor police sergeant, there was a distinct incentive to make a fast move if anything went wrong. All went well but if I ever had a Walter Mitty dream of becoming a heroic bomb disposal expert, this quickly evaporated.

'I was never fully convinced that this attack was necessarily a policy incursion by Indonesia but might have been a settling of border scores.

'I believe this was the occasion when the Colonel later joined us by helicopter and appeared less than 'gruntled'. Apparently the helicopter pilot saw a military camp and landed, only to be surprised when everyone ran away – presumably they expected that this was the lead helicopter of a commando attack. It was quite a diplomatic embarrassment and the Colonel confessed later that his reasons in writing for an invasion of Indonesia reached the Prime Minister's desk in No 10 Downing Street! You can't win them all.'

A final fanfare came from B Company's correspondent...

> "We were kept busy to the end, as 5 Troop under Sergeant Fink was clearing up the mess after a nasty border raid on an undefended kampong; then on our last day a combined patrol of 6 Troop and K Company, led by Sergeant Callow, killed one Indonesian and think they wounded another in an ambush. Who could ask for a better leaving present? During the Commando's time in Sarawak, B Company could claim all the units kills – not a bad record!"

42 Commando's K Company (Major Alex Higson), which was relieving B Company, was also quite pleased with itself, having just excelled in a unit Sports meeting; however, in the tile competition at the rifle meeting they had been outshot by the MT 'B' Team – a result that might have encouraged a little humility. Just as B Company sounded its own farewell fanfare, so K Company heralded its arrival with its own emphasis on the same event...

> "If we expected to find ourselves in Lundu, with time to settle in before going out on location, we were to be disappointed; in fact, at short notice three patrols were to leave straight from *Albion* on 2 July to relieve 40 Commando in their border locations. This

was duly done and, to the excitement of all those waiting for the second lift, a signal was received from Sergeant Goodwin's section at Kandai – 'AMBUSH SUCCESSFUL. COLLECT BODY MY LOCATION..' K Company had arrived."

Pat Gardner, the outgoing Company Commander, has a copy of the Patrol Commander's report, signed by Sergeant Callow, who was the only NCO in the party; with him were two Marines from his company and six from the incoming company...

> "Having left Kampong Kandai at 1900 hrs, we set out for the ambush area; this being twelve minutes away on the Kandai – Panchon border track. All went well as we quickly and silently settled in for the night. At 2003 hrs voices were heard. Section stood to waiting; three figures appeared. I waited until distance closed to twenty-five yards and shouted: "Berenti"! Immediately a torch flashed, a sub-machine gun fired; fire was returned to the maximum and ceased at 2005 hrs. Loud moaning was heard from track.
>
> "No move was made to search the track until daylight. 3 July at 0615 hrs track searched; found one body with sten-gun and three magazines. Body and weapon brought to Kandai. Border Scouts have now set out to search area completely for any further evidence – Callow, Sergeant RM"

Amoebic Dysentery

Shortly after return to Johore, Pat Gardner recalls that he went down with amoebic dysentery. Water borne diseases and parasites are always a problem in jungle operations; each man was equipped to boil and sterilise water, but the amoeba are removed only by filtering. The filtering arrangements at patrol bases became quite sophisticated, though often – perhaps usually – they were outside the perimeter. There was also the Millbank bag for filtering and I note that an award – albeit a paltry sum of £8 each – was paid at about this time to a RM officer (Captain Sears) and a RM SNCO (Colour Sergeant Slater) for developing a filtering kit for use with water bottles and canvas 'chagils'; filtering, however, took time that was not always available on patrol. Commanders at any level were in any case at risk from the coffee that they could hardly refuse to share with the Headman or 'Kapitan China' on a visit to a Kampong or village as part of the campaign for 'Hearts and Minds'.

Chapter 4

Company Group

Bau District; 'Hearts and Minds' and Brief Encounters

July to October '63

Company Group

West Brigade

Derek Oakley – G3 Int

'Life was always busy, not only was the Brigade now responsible for some five scattered battalions or Commandos, but we had more visitors than we could reasonably expect to cope with.

'One particularly important event happened during this period, Malaysia. Malaya and Singapore was seeking independence and the territories of Sarawak and Sabah (North Borneo) were to be integrated as East Malaysia. We had a group of United Nations observers visiting when a 5,000 strong anti-Malaysian demonstration gathered in Kuching, leading to minor riots. With the Sarawak Constabulary we stood by to 'keep the peace'.

'On Independence Day, 16 September 1963, a large parade was held on the Kuching Padang at which the Governor handed over to the Malaysian authorities. On parade were contingents from both the British and local armed services and organisations. It was good to see Paddy Davis acting as ADC to the Governor that day, having made a remarkable recovery from his wounds received at Limbang nine months earlier.

'One pleasant and relaxing duty I had was to accompany the Commando Brigade band on their week's visit to the country. Apart from playing in Kuching itself, we all embarked in one of the RN Minesweepers for a trip to Sibu, the capital of the 3rd Division, situated some 100 miles up the huge Rajang River. The band would play at Kampongs along the river, where crowds of locals gathered, and entertain in schools. It was the perfect 'Hearts and Minds' public relations exercise. I also met many of the troops in the field.'

As 42 Commando – now under the command of Lieutenant Colonel Ian Gourlay – relieved 40 Commando on what was to become a system of 'Roulement', K Company deployed to Lundu District and M Company to Serian, while L Company Group went to Bau.

Bau District

Situated at a road-head on the most direct route from Indonesia and the focal point for a number of tracks from the border, Bau was an important location in which A

The Headquarters hut of L Company, 42 Commando at Bau, flying the Company flag

A Ferret scout car of the Queen's Royal Irish Hussars at Bau.

and B Companies of 40 Commando had already served. In support was a Troop of the Queen's Royal Irish Hussars (QRIH), while under operational control were fifty Border Scouts, initially led by Gurkha riflemen, and sixteen Field Force Police of the Sarawak Constabulary.

There was also the Mortar Troop...

Keith Wilkins, Lieutenant – OC Mortar Troop

'On arrival, the Mortar Troop was placed under command of L Company which had responsibility for the Bau District. Company Headquarters was based in Bau, a small town of about 2,000 mainly Chinese inhabitants, situated some thirty miles from the border. The Mortar Troop was also based in Bau to help defend the town, carry out disruptive patrolling in the rear areas and also to act as the Company's reserve. Bau was linked to Kuching by some twenty miles of metalled road and to the patrol bases by jungle track.

'Supplies to these bases were normally delivered by helicopter or air drop, with the occasional loads carried in by porters, usually escorted by members of the Mortar Troop. Communication with the patrol bases was, at first, difficult, particularly at night, because of the inadequacies of the radios that were in use at that time.

'Throughout most of July and early August, things remained pretty quiet in the Bau area. 30 July saw a visit from the Brigade Band, while the small scale riot staged by protesters during a visit by the UN Investigating Team was dispersed by the Sarawak Police, using tear smoke grenades and without our assistance. There were plenty of rumours of enemy activity circulating around the border, spread by the local Dyaks, but most of these were either false or greatly exaggerated, and all had to be treated with considerable caution. However, by late August things started to hot up. The section base at Gumbang, a few hundred yards from the border was attacked on several occasions but each time the rebels were driven off and casualties were inflicted. There were also a number of minor incidents at the other patrol bases. Meanwhile, the Mortar Troop had been kept busy patrolling the rear areas, and carrying out a number of cordon and search operations in order to disrupt the activities of the Clandestine Communist Organisation (CCO). One search at the village of Musi, a known 'hot spot', revealed a large quantity of communist documents but no weapons.'

Curfew Breaking and the Cost

'From the outset, a nightly curfew had been imposed throughout the forward areas from 1700 to 0600 hrs, so that ambushes could be set up to cover tracks and other areas known to be used by Indonesian Border Terrorists (IBT).

'At the end of August, the Company Commander decided to extend the pattern of these ambushes by using elements of the Mortar Troop and a section of 145 Battery,

Royal Artillery, which had been allocated to help with the task. I was ordered to set up a forward command post in the kampong of Opar in order to coordinate the activities of these ambush patrols and act as a radio link to the headquarters at Bau. Just after 1700 hrs on 24 August, we heard a ripple of shots from the direction of the gunner ambush position, but no radio contact could be made, and we had to sit out the remainder of the night wondering what had happened. Early the following morning, the gunner patrol appeared at the edge of Opar carrying two dead bodies.

'They reported that shortly after their ambush had been set at 1700 hrs the previous night, three men had entered the killing zone and fire had been opened. Two had been killed and the third wounded. It transpired that they were young Dyaks from the neighbouring kampong of Serasot who were trying to get home 'before' the curfew started. The arrival of the bodies at Opar had caused near pandemonium in the kampong. The women, in particular, were the most disturbed, rushing forward to try and cradle and caress the bodies. There was mounting anger amongst the men and I realised that our presence and that of the gunner patrol was only exacerbating the situation. I therefore ordered an immediate withdrawal to allow the kampong people to get on and deal with the problem. I remember, however, that the incident caused us considerable concern, not that the gunner patrol could be blamed in any way for what had happened. Nonetheless, it had damaged our good relationship with the local Dyaks, which was important to the overall success of our campaign. 'Bridges' needed to be rebuilt and more emphasis was placed on 'hearts and minds' in that area during the next few weeks, which resulted in most of the damage being repaired. There was one positive result from this incident in that it brought home to the local Dyaks the importance of strictly observing the curfew hours; as far as I know, no similar incidents occurred thereafter.'

The three principal forward locations in the Company area were east Pang Tebang, west Stass and in the centre Serikin; the grain of the country ran across the border, so that on the flanks of each location were jungle covered ridges of varying heights, making lateral movement between them more difficult. The natural traffic routes were across the border, which was unmarked, while family relationships, day-to-day occupations and trade were similarly cross-border.

Ian Moore – OC 5 Troop

Serikin

'We had five weeks to shake down, before the next major deployment, when 42 Commando relieved 40 Commando 'in situ' in Sarawak. We trained in jungle ambush and anti-ambush drills. A unit rifle meeting was held and also a unit athletics meeting in which Paddy Ashdown seems to have won most of the cups for Support Company where he was then OC… Troop. I remember how he relished the prospect of the coming deployment. He used to sport a Meerschaum pipe, and both he and Sergeant French (his Troop Sergeant) required regular supplies of Erinmore Flake in their supply drops.

'On 9 July, 5 Troop was 'choppered' out in Wessex helicopters from the deck of HMS *Albion* to Kampong Serikin in Bau district. On my right at Stass was deposited 6 Troop, and on the left 4 Troop at Pang Tebang.

'Serikin and nearby Serabak were in the middle and just an hour's march from the Indonesian border; hence 5 Troop were in a direct line between the Indonesian enemy – with their base not far over the border at Babang – and Bau, with Kuching beyond. Kampong Serikin lay in a valley between wooded hills of secondary jungle, where loggers were at work and the whooping of monkeys could be heard morning and evening. The Wessex placed us in a field next to a fast river, before returning to *Albion*, presumably taking with them the outgoing Troop from C Company – a company I was to command ten years later.

'I cannot remember a hand over, but I shall always be grateful to Lieutenant 'Spud' Murphy and his Troop for the outstanding job he and his men had done over the past weeks, creating a well sand bagged fortified longhouse, with sentry bays and good fields of fire extending to a wire perimeter fence two hundred yards out. There was a wild west sign 'Fort Murphy', which remained. This was to be 5 Troop's home for the subsequent months.

'Just four hundred yards down the track was Serikin, a cluster of land Dyak houses, mainly on stilts, with pigs underneath. There was a small coffee shop in the centre. From the start the locals appeared well disposed. We had inherited good will from our predecessors and were to generate more.

'The Company Commander had made it clear that we were to become acquainted with our territory as a matter of urgency and this 5 Troop proceeded to do from morning one, deploying a spread of half section patrols to locate and visit all dwelling places, particularly those towards the border. The patrols of the Troop relished this fresh challenge to get out into the ulu on a roster, and get to know the locals in their atap and tin houses in the jungle clearings. These were simple dwellings, without electricity or running water, the jungle dense and encroaching all around.

'Back at the fort was usually a section on stand-by as a reaction force. In the dawn and at last light we stood to, and through the days and nights our SLR's were always with us. Those stand-to moments in the dawn remain etched in the memory, with the smell of the jungle, fire smoke rising from the kampong, the rush of the river, gazing out from our block house, the morning fog heavy on the hills, the heat and humidity yet to brew, and the monkeys whooping. What would the next twenty-four hours bring?

'Stand-down was swiftly followed by the noise and smell of the hydro-burner starting up in the cook house and by those other distinct smells of compo beans and sausage on the brew. The first cup of char in the bamboo mug, with whole meal block, the contemplation of life from the thunder box – sited for its fields of fire – SLR at hand. Patrols had been warned off and given orders the night before, so it was not long before we hit the track on our patrol, be it six hours or forty eight.

'From the outset there existed a dilemma in command and control arrangements. As Troop Commander I wanted to be out on my patch, seeing and hearing for myself, and understanding my area. On the other hand our only link was the heavy company net set (WS 510) which had to remain central at Troop HQ; it was not mobile, there was no wheeled transport and even had there been it would have been impossible on jungle tracks. The Company needed to know that the Troop Commander was able to receive and react to developments. It was the age old question that John Keegan poses in his books on command – *'how often at the front/on the ground?'* I imagine we reached a balance.

Lieutenant Ian Moore presents an arm band to a member of the Serikin 'Home Guard'

'After some three weeks the operational tension tightened. I will never forget 2 August and the voice of our Company Commander on the set telling us that 'last night Sunray Call sign 2/1 was shot and killed by own troops. Thus we received the tragic news of the death of Graham Rolls at Pang Tebang, out on the wire. I had only worked with Graham for a couple of months, since he had just come out from UK as a Young Officer on his twelve month appointment to a Commando; nonetheless his was a firm and mature personality that immediately impressed and that one doesn't forget.

'At about this time more information started to come in about a massing of TNKU and Indonesian guerillas on their side of the border. No doubt Babang was reported as a central gathering point, although at this stage there was no question of 'going across' the border. Kampong Serikin was definitely positioned 'in harm's way', so I decided to institute a more active defence of the village under our care. Operation Parrot had not applied to the native locals, and there were many local farmers and householders with their own shotguns. Moreover my request to Company HQ for a supply of cartridges was agreed and acted on. I enrolled some forty to fifty stalwarts into the Serikin Home Guard; their badge was a strip of parachute silk, titled in marker pen, worn on the right upper arm. We agreed to fight shoulder to shoulder against incursions.'

Fortress Village

'We proceeded to turn Serikin into a fortified village. Each house had its walls thickened with mud and wattle, to a height of two feet from the ground. A bullet penetration demonstration was carried out – in retrospect, a somewhat two edged impact on civilian morale! Inside these shelters women and children would go to ground during an attack. Outside the dwellings we dug trenches and parapets covering the main axes of approach from the border. These were to be manned, principally through the nights, by a roster comprising a mix of Royal Marines, members of our Border Scout Detachment, and members of the Serikin Home Guard.

'The border districts of Sarawak were subject to a night curfew. This enabled us to booby trap approaches to this defended area with electrically detonated grenades and to supplement them with panji plantations in the ditches beside the tracks. Further down the track, some 600 yards towards the border, we deployed from dusk to dawn a two man listening patrol. Lance Corporal Manning from Recce Troop was a key operator, in a hide beside the main likely enemy axis of advance. This post was equipped with that rare commodity, an infrared night sight; it emitted a faint buzz, luckily masked by the incessant nocturnal noise of jungle toads etc. Clearly a voice warning of hostile presence was impossible, with the enemy moving along just yards away; our solution was that the listening post would apply depressions on the pressel switch of their A 40 set – one depression for each ten enemy; this would interrupt the mush on the A 40 set 600 yards away in the HQ of the defended position. Looking back fifty years to this idea, it seems ingenious, but pretty ad hoc.

'After an initial burst of excitement, this defended village stratagem settled into some sort of nocturnal routine, and then, after three weeks or so, was phased down, when the threat appeared to reduce – though, as we shall see, in reality it didn't. The main value of this exercise was that it was an excellent way for us to get to know the locals we were there to defend, and vice versa. It generated a good spirit of unity against a common foe, whose aim was to claim Sarawak for Dr Soekarno.

'This winning of the 'Hearts and Minds' was augmented in many other ways, such as the implementation of a mass inoculation programme for families, administered by our company Medic, SBA Clarke.

'It was a tense time, punctuated by pin prick incursions. I find from the War Diary that on 10 August thirty-seven unarmed suspects were detained just this side of the border by 5 Troop; twenty-five were later released, but those further detained included 4 TNKU, 1 TNI (Indonesian Army), and four Chinese illegal immigrants; clearly fire power had not been required on this occasion. Three days later Gumbang, in 4 Troop's bailiwick, was again attacked by a raiding party. The following day near Serabak we discovered a TNKU Flag, and a five man ambush position, just our side of the border crossing.

'Tense and expectant though we were, I remember morale throughout the Troop was generally buoyant. One was encouraged by visitations. One gala day we paraded the Serikin Home Guard, forty strong, with their armbands, shotguns, bandoliers and parangs, for an inspection by Lieutenant Colonel Gourlay. The finale was an unexpected and triumphant fanfare, blown down the barrels of many raised shotguns.

'The Company Commander came to see us regularly, as did the Second-in-Command, David Morris, who sent this signal from our base:

> 'SUNRAY MINOR ARRIVED THIS LOCATION STOP REQUEST PERMISSION TO REMAIN OVERNIGHT STOP AM SHATTERED.'

He was in the midst of visiting the round of Company location on shanks' pony to pay the men. A stalwart and encouraging presence was our CSM, WO Peter Gibbons, with whom I had enjoyed serving two years before, when he had been TQMS of an old style Troop in 41 Commando.

'We were engaged in an unremitting round of patrols, night ambushes, and sentry duties. With this demanding physical programme, food was a preoccupation. At this stage patrols used the standard European twenty-four hour ration pack. In ambush all had to be eaten cold, and very quietly in the harbour area. We all knew how far the scent of hexamine travelled. The arrival of new self heating soups was a bonus, but the aroma of hot oxtail also travels on the air. Those on rotation at Troop base subsisted on compo, cooked by the GD Cook. Hence the arrival of fresh rations, by Wessex or by para-drop from a Beverley or Hastings aircraft produced an invigorating surge of optimism. Never has roast chicken tasted better. I had arranged with a book shop to mail out the occasional book, though clearly time for reading was at a premium. But I remember dipping into something by Robert Graves and something else by Dylan Thomas. We managed a game or two of scrabble by the 'tilly' lamp at the end of the long house – Sergeant Friel, Corporal Derbyshire and myself. My transistor radio was picking up songs from a new group called the Beatles, performing somewhere on an entirely different planet.

'In these weeks there were moments of farce as well as of crisis. One dark night, at about 0300 hrs, the sentry in the bay at the end of the long house challenged an approaching body of men twice. They kept coming, so he fired long bursts of tracer into them. My Verys light showed this unstoppable foe to be the clothes on the Troop dhoby line, rhythmically moving in the breeze. By contrast grim disaster struck when Corporal Murphy, a stalwart and ingenious Section Commander and a qualified Assault Engineer, detonated a grenade on our perimeter wire while disarming it, the standard procedure on stand-down after the curfew. He sustained severe stomach wounds. On that occasion, communications back to company worked and the casevac helicopter arrived after an agonising two hours. To the immense relief of us all Corporal Murphy survived, but was invalided. This event overshadowed my last days with 5 Troop. I believe I left on schedule in early September on draft to CTCRM, Lympstone.

'Those few short months in Sarawak, at the outset of the Confrontation, stay firmly in the mind. For me expectation was everything; I was essentially unblooded. Some three weeks after I left, the village of Serikin was subjected to five rounds of two inch mortar fire in the middle of the night – happily inaccurate. About a week after that, the Troop under Sergeant Friel arrested two Chinese terrorists, trying to get back over the border, who confessed to being in that raid, which would have been followed by an attack had there been any coordination. So one's plans and fears were clearly not based upon chimera. I was touched to see later in *The Globe & Laurel* that the Serikin irregulars continued to be known as 'Lieutenant Moore's Own.' Sergeant Mackie, veteran of the Gumbang raids, had returned to 5 Troop, and had taken them over.'

Lieutenant Alan Hooper had served in the unit before, during his training attachment, and had rejoined 42 Commando in June '63, with a newly acquired specialization in mortars and anti-tank weapons and an anticipation of related employment. On arrival in Singapore he had been surprised to be met at the airport by Peter Waters, the Assistant Adjutant, who had taken over the job from Ian Moore. Peter had been L Company Second-in-Command at Limbang, only to be shot in the leg and to become a casualty, albeit protesting, before he could get ashore. His purpose now was to inform Alan that he was to deputise for the unit Intelligence Officer (IO), Lieutenant Benjy Walden, while that officer was recovering from an appendix operation. On deployment to Sarawak Alan, therefore, had been fulfilling the role…

Alan Hooper, Lieutenant – Acting IO

'On arrival in Semengo Camp, adjacent to Kuching Airport, where Commando HQ was based, I soon settled into the routine of being the Intelligence Officer under the watchful eye of the Staff Officer Operations (Major Peter Darling). Apart from the fascinating work of Intelligence – which I was also to put to good use several years later during an operational tour in Northern Ireland – I also learnt a great deal about how a Commando Headquarters becomes effective on operations. Under the guidance of individuals such as the Second-in-Command (Major Bob Loudon) and the Signals Officer (Captain Ray Frost), there was a methodical approach, involving a great deal of 'unsung' hard work, which encouraged people to deal with crises and emergencies with calmness and logic.

'A few weeks after our deployment, Benjy Walden rejoined HQ having now recovered from his operation and, naturally, wanted his job back! So what should we do with Hooper? Anticipating that I was about to become a 'spare' officer (and alert to what this might mean!) I seized the initiative and suggested that I become the Assistant IO and, in particular, spent time gaining more intelligence in the field. A bit to my surprise, Peter Darling agreed to my suggestion and, even more to my surprise, so did the CO! As a result I spent the next few weeks gleaning intelligence across the Commando's area of operations, sometimes in the company of the G3 (Int) from Brigade. By now I had settled into the routine of Commando HQ – but that routine was about to be interrupted.'

42 Commando Intelligence Office at Semengo Camp, with the acting IO, Lieutenant Alan Hooper (standing left with pipe)

Alan Hooper – OC 4 Troop

Pang Tebang

'Late in the evening of 1 August, Peter Darling [the SOO] called me into his office and informed me that 4 Troop Commander (Second Lieutenant Graham Rolls) had tragically been shot dead by his Troop Sergeant, whilst investigating a suspect intrusion on the perimeter wire of the Troop base that night. I was called in to see the CO and told that I was to take over as the Troop Commander in the next twenty-four hours. He stressed that I would be taking over in very difficult circumstances as Graham Rolls had been a popular young officer and this had been a tragic accident. To make things more difficult, there would not be time for me to see the Company Commander personally before deploying, as he was flying out the following morning to spend twenty-four hours in the post, and the helicopter that would take me in would take him out. However, we did – I believe – manage to talk briefly over the phone.

'4 Troop was located at Pang Tebang which was an isolated small kampong about one and a half hour's walk from the border with Indonesia. There was a reinforced section forward at Gumbang which was just two minutes from the border. The Troop base was established just outside the kampong beside a river, and above it was the helicopter LS, the only means of swift communication with the outside world. During the helicopter trip from Kuching I reflected on my situation. I was twenty-two years old, had commanded a half Troop as a YO having just caught up the old Second World War Commando organisation that comprised five Rifle Troops, each of some sixty men. I was trained in heavy weapons and had 'stood in' as the unit's IO; I was now going back to 'the day job' as a Troop Commander. It would be good to be in command of Royal Marines again but I had some apprehension about what the atmosphere would be when I arrived. How would they react to a new boss who had been imposed on them after losing a popular officer in very difficult circumstances?

'The helicopter hovered over the LS; I jumped down and then helped with the off loading of rations. We crouched down breathing in the avgas fumes until the helicopter lifted off and wheeled away. Silence at last! I was alert to signs of apprehension as I was introduced to the Troop by the senior Corporal, the Troop Sergeant having been flown out earlier to take an essential week's break. I was met by the usual 'dead pan Marine' 'look.' It was a few days later, before the Troop Sergeant rejoined, that people started to open up; they had to be comfortable with me first and they took a few days to weigh me up before they could confide in me. With typical Marine pragmatism, they had decided on the night of the accident that it was just that – a very unfortunate accident. The situation had been particularly difficult for them because the shooting occurred just after last light and the body could not be removed until a helicopter was able to fly in the following morning. They attributed no blame to the Troop Sergeant and were happy to see him back a few days later. So they decided that nothing could be gained by wishing things could have been different, and just got on with life. As they shared this information with me I realised that I was privileged to command such men, and learnt from them the benefit of rationalising difficult situations – and then moving on.

'I knew the Troop Sergeant well as he had been a PT Instructor when I was undergoing YO training. Having checked that he was OK, we soon established a good rapport and it was reassuring to have his support for the rest of the deployment. I soon settled into the Troop routine which involved constant patrolling of the area, I was keen to get up to Gumbang as soon as possible as I wanted to size up the situation of this vulnerable location so close to the border. Given the fact that day to day movement off jungle tracks was impracticable due to the thick jungle, and that Gumbang sat astride a main track from the Indonesian border, it only seemed a matter of time before our defences there were tested. The problem was that we were forbidden to cross the border, so the only early indication we would get would be from the local tribesmen who went freely to and fro; this situation provided little comfort since rumours abounded, and emphasised the importance a very alert sentry.

'Apart from patrolling, much of the time was taken up engaging with the local tribes in a 'hearts and minds' campaign. As our predecessors had learnt during the Malayan Emergency, the best means of gaining the confidence of the locals in counter-terrorism operations is to live amongst them. Whether the locals really understood why we were there is a matter of debate. Their life was one of simple subsistence and, provided they could tend their crops and live in peace, they were content. As for the villagers of Pang Tebang, they still remembered the previous Indonesian incursion and believed that so long as we kept our patrol base there, they were safe.

'Given the focus on 'hearts and minds' one of the trickier dilemmas was what to do with villagers who were sick or had an accident such as the one of ours with a bad gash in the foot from stepping on slit bamboo. They would often walk for days to our base realising that we could provide medical assistance. However, much of this was limited to the knowledge of the Marine who had undergone a rudimentary course before deployment. For anything more complicated the only solution was to get then back to the nearest civilisation – and in their case that was a three day canoe journey. The alternative was to use a helicopter, but we were discouraged from using them because of limited availability and it was also reckoned that the locals would become too dependent on air evacuation, which would not be a good idea once we had left. A reasonable idea in theory, but not helpful when you are the commander on the ground apparently refusing to provide the transport that could perhaps save the life of a villager whom you have got to know well.

'Another factor of operating in the jungle in the 1960s was that it was not possible to communicate via VHF after dark. At least this meant that the Troop Commander could not be badgered by his Company Commander at night – which just meant that we had the conversation before last light!

'As my Company Commander frequently needed to talk to all three of his Troop Commanders at the end of the day, there was many a time that I was summoned to the radio whilst I was having my last cup of tea before darkness. As we could not use lights after dark this meant, inevitably, that I drank my tea cold and in the dark – a habit that stayed with me for a while.'

Incursions at Gumbang

'One of the characteristics of jungle warfare is that the opposing sides manoeuvre around each other trying to find their opponent in very difficult terrain, with visibility often restricted to a few metres, so that endless hours are spent in unrewarding and apparently fruitless patrolling. The ratio quoted was ninety hours patrolling for an hour's contact. Well, 4 Troop had its ninety hours and the monotony was about to be rudely interrupted.

'It was just before first light when, from our patrol base at Pang Tebang, we heard the sound of small arms fire coming from Gumbang, down on the border. There was nothing I could do immediately to help as it was an hour and a half's walk away. I was conscious not to disturb Sergeant Mackie (the Senior NCO in command there) in the middle of a fire fight, so I waited a very long four minutes before I called him on the field telephone:

"Sergeant – Sitrep please."

"Bit difficult at the moment – I'm trying to win this bloody battle!"

'I got the message, curbed my frustration and kept off the line. Sometimes commanders have to learn not to interfere! The fighting did not last too long and, once it had died down, Sergeant Mackie was on the phone to inform me that there had been an incursion just before first light but, although Gumbang was only two minutes from the border, the enemy had been spotted by the sentry positioned for just that eventuality. He opened fire at a man on the track leading from the border. Fire was returned immediately by at least three enemy but Mackie's men won the fire fight and forced the enemy to withdraw.

'At about the same time, two more enemy worked their way round to a flank but were heavily engaged and were forced to withdraw. Sergeant Mackie waited another ten minutes until it was light and manoeuvred part of his force forward to an old slit trench where it was again engaged by the enemy. Firing continued for a few minutes but ended when Sergeant Mackie threw a 36 grenade. The enemy gave up at this point and withdrew back to the border, using fire and manoeuvre.

'I was soon on my way to Gumbang by foot with a section and met Brian Edwards there, who had flown in by helicopter. We debriefed Sergeant Mackie and it was apparent that he and his section had done a really good job in holding their prepared positions

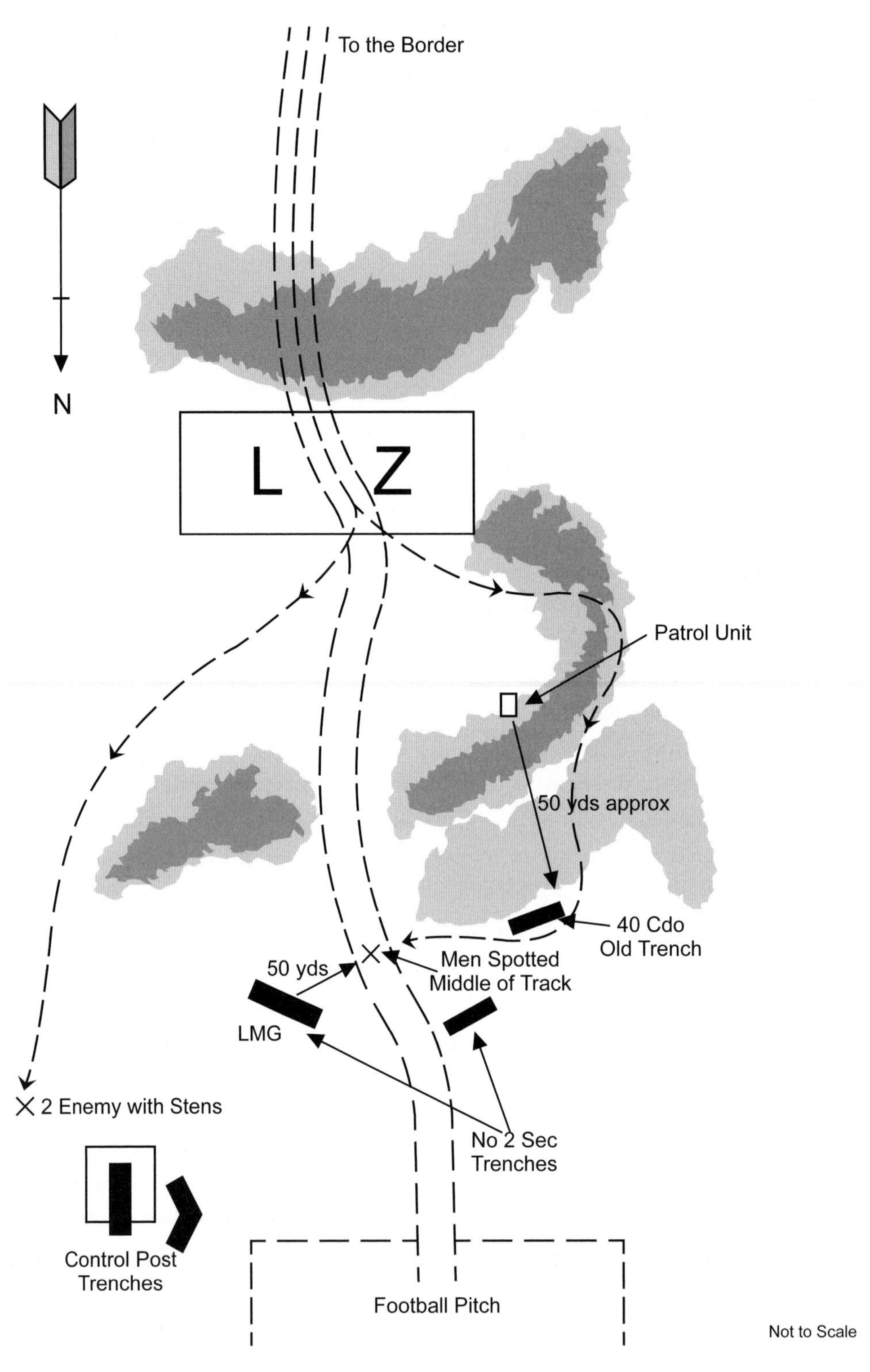

The enemy attack on Gumbang on the night of 19 August 1963, from a sketch map

and forcing the enemy into killing areas. By the time we got there Sergeant Mackie had thoroughly searched the area and discovered two ambush positions covering likely follow-up routes. There was also a blood trail back to the border so we knew that we had hit someone. Perhaps the most encouraging thing was that the villagers who formed the 'Home Guard', some armed just with rudimentary rifles, had held their positions alongside the Marines and had given a good account of themselves.

'I discussed options with Brian and said that I would stay in Gumbang for the next night. He allocated Colour Sergeant 'Gilly' Howe to stay with us and also lent us one night sight which was one of very few in theatre. We gave this sight to Marine Downey – a forthright Geordie and a very good shot. I was delighted to have the experienced Gilly Howe with us. He had already won a DSM and an MM and was a legend in the SBS. I had no doubt that his steadiness would prove invaluable when the Indonesians returned as I was sure that they would – and I hoped it would be that night.

'As we took up our 'stand-to' positions at last light I looked around the alert faces of the villagers and recognised what a good job Sergeant Mackie had done in developing this discipline in them. We were only going to win this counter insurgency war by having the locals working with us and being prepared to protect their kampongs. And so we waited… and waited… and… nothing! Once the dark had become pitch black we stood down realising that there would be no attack that night.

'I returned to Pang Tebang the following morning, content that Mackie and Howe could handle the situation well between them and that I would only get in the way of what was a section operation. Nothing happened for the next few days, and then on the 21st the enemy had another go – this time shortly after dark.

'At about 1945 a torch was seen flashing on the track at the North end of the kampong. Mackie waited for about fifteen minutes and then fired a para-illuminant which revealed some eight men, armed with an LMG, SMGs and rifles, moving up the track. Fire was opened up immediately and the man with the LMG was hit. The enemy took cover, taking their casualties with them. Brief exchanges of fire continued until about 2130 when three 36 grenades were thrown by the Security Forces and one of the enemy was heard to cry out.

'We had just stood down at Pang Tebang when the firing commenced and this time Sergeant Mackie rang me, and then kept the line open so that at least I could hear the battle and the orders being given. Brian Edwards and I met up at Gumbang the following morning and, by then, the dawn search revealed marks, where wounded and dead had been dragged from the track and there were bloodstains in the bushes. In the subsequent debrief Sergeant Mackie's force reckoned that they had hit at least four during the engagement. An elated Marine Downey greeted me: 'I got one, Sir!'

"How do you know?"

"Cos I saw him fall, through my night sight!"

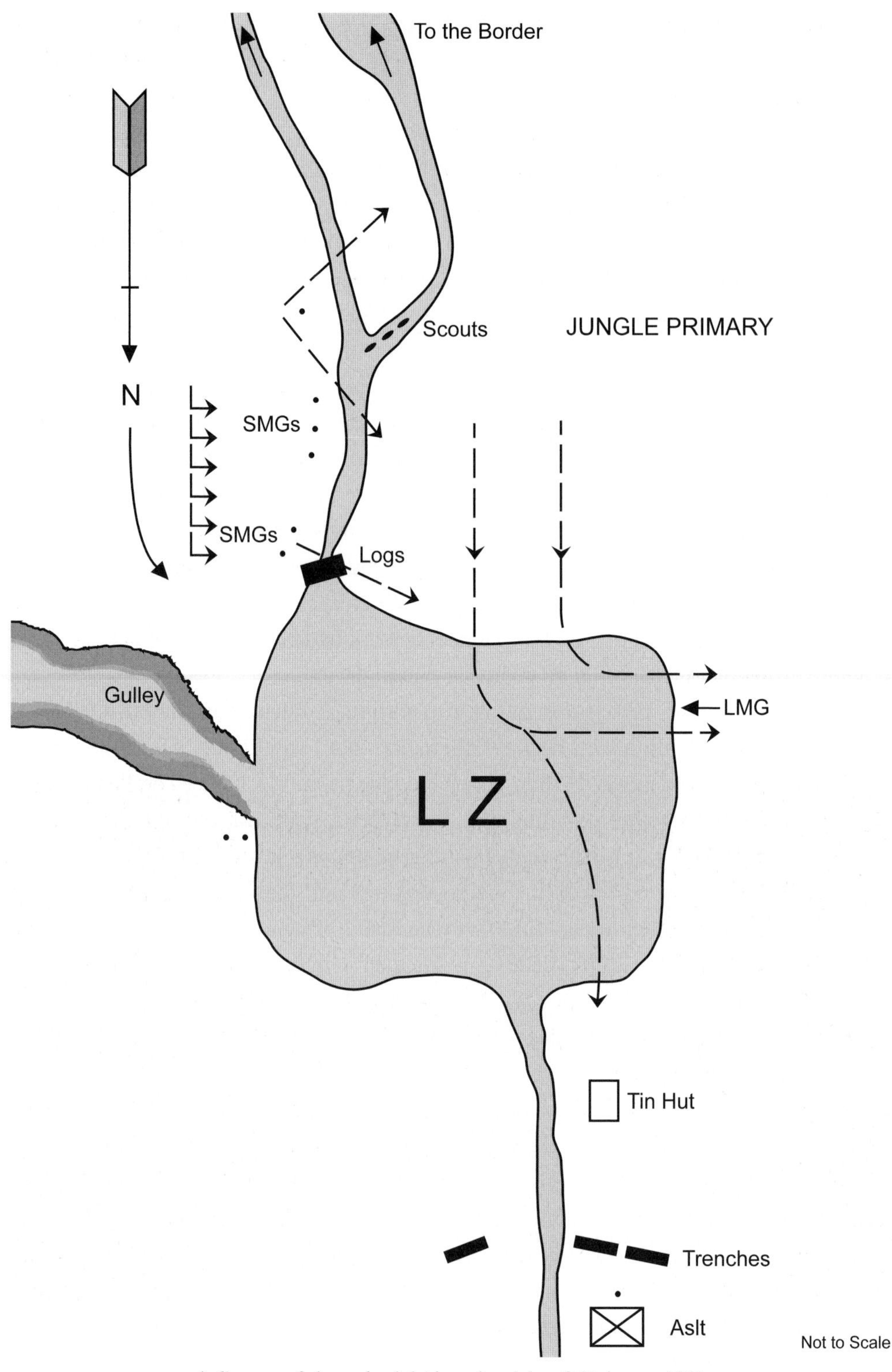

A diagram of the ambush laid on the night of 21 August 1963

'This was a revelation to us because this first generation infrared equipment enabled us, for the first time, to see what we were shooting at in the dark without the aid of illuminations. Subsequent intelligence reports revealed that five bodies were buried across the border and that Dagang, a prominent bandit leader and Guntor, another leader, had both been wounded in the raid, the former seriously.

'I had assumed that this 'bloody nose' would convince the enemy that it was not worth having a go at Gumbang – but I was wrong. At 2200 hrs the following night a shot was fired by Marine Downey using the night sight. Another figure was fired at near the track but he moved into dead ground. Two more figures were engaged near an unoccupied house.

'The dawn search proved inconclusive but we were not taking any chances and set an ambush the following night overlooking a log crossing and track junction nearby the Landing Site. At about 1915 hrs noises of movement were heard in the jungle parallel to the track, and behind it. Shortly afterwards two men appeared at the second track junction. The ambush party reckoned that they might be scouts for a larger party.

'The two 'scouts' turned back on their tracks. The noises behind the ambush position seemed to indicate that the enemy was closing in. The ambush party opened fire in the direction of the sounds, by now at very close range. It was then about 2020 hrs. Several shots were returned and the ambush party then used fire and movement to withdraw back to the main position in the kampong, having first made voice contact to avoid confusion.

Captain Brian Edwards (L Company Commander) and C/Sgt Gilly Howe briefing Major General Walter Walker, the Director of Operations and Brig 'Billy' Barton, (Commanding 3rd Commando Brigade) on the landing site at Gumbang

'Meanwhile both north and south defence positions in the kampong engaged small enemy parties. The Northern position believed that they hit one using the infrared equipment. The enemy withdrew eventually at about 2200 hrs. Subsequent intelligence revealed that this had indeed been a much larger enemy raid, involving between thirty and sixty men. It also appeared that they had employed the military tactic of moving parallel to a known track but in the jungle. This indicated that they were probably TNI or trained TNKU.

'This last engagement seemed to convince the enemy that there was no advantage in continuing to press in 4 Troop's area and there were no further incursions before we handed over to 40 Commando on 15 October. We had more than our share of our 'exciting hour' and resorted back to the relative tedium of the '90!'

Sgt Mackie was later awarded the Military Medal and Marine Downey was mentioned in Despatches for their part in the defence of Gumbang. In due course Second Lieutenant Cameron Mackie took over 4 Troop and Alan Hooper the Anti-Tank Troop.

Stass

Each Troop Commander carried out similar tasks in his own way, imposing his personality and ideas on the area in which he operated. Lieutenant Paddy Ashdown with 6 Troop at Stass was, as anticipated, 'relishing' the opportunity and was an experienced Troop Commander. A Malay speaker with a tendency to go native when in base – flip flops and sarong, with or without a shirt – he was in his element squatting in a kampong chatting with the headman while organising cross-border intrigue, or simply campaigning for 'hearts and minds'.

Marine Patterson, a signaller 'mastering' a blowpipe in the Signals Office at Stass

His enthusiasm for things native communicated itself to his signaller who was mastering the blowpipe. The Company correspondent wrote…

> "6 Troop had as a primary task the defence of Stass the largest Kampong in the area. Most of the inhabitants had farms in Indonesia, only thirty-five minutes march away, and as a result were a fund of information and of undigested rumour. To discern the one from the other provided Lieutenant Ashdown and headquarters at all levels with a fascinating task. Rumour became reality, however, towards the end of August when the rebels commenced a scorched earth policy towards the farms on the Indonesian sides. This led to an influx of refugees. The subsequent wanton killing of one of their number, as an act of terrorism, had the reverse effect on the villagers.
>
> "A party of Stass Dyaks in a series of ambushes claimed to have killed up to ten TNKU with their shotguns and on one occasion brought back an ear to prove it. In order to lure 6 Troop patrols into an ambush the rebels fired some shots into the air from a position near the border on Thursday 12 September. The spent rounds fell into Kampong Stass. On Friday 13 September a patrol led by Corporal Reece turned the tables by reaching an ambush position in rear of the enemy. Neither party was in fact aware of the presence of the other. There was some surprise therefore, when the rebels selected Corporal Reece's killing ground as a rest area. The first member who chose to use it was allowed to enjoy his meal and a last cigarette before being mortally wounded by Marine Herwin, who considered the rebels' conduct provocative. Following up they were greeted by a burst of fire from the enemy ambush party which briefly revealed itself, only to depart with haste through the jungle to the border. So ended 6 Troop's first and only contact with the rebels, though they too had a spate of leaflet dumping, some of a pornographic nature, designed apparently to lower morale but which finished up as indifferent 'pin ups' in Company HQ"

In these operations, working from patrol bases in comparatively remote jungle locations, Company Headquarters had a primary role of supply, the province of the Second-in-Command and the CQMS, who coordinated the air drops and the helicopter lifts. Of almost equal importance was the role of the Company SBA…

Terry Clarke – L Company Medic

'After a five week period in Singapore, L Company returned to Sarawak. As the Company SBA I was at Bau, but at each of the Troop locations there were two medical orderlies. These were Marines of the Troop whom I had trained in advanced first aid and were able to suture, give injections and, if necessary and with my permission, prescribe antibiotics and other forms of treatment.

'When possible, I would visit these locations, either by patrol or helicopter, to ensure there were sufficient medical supplies and discuss any medical/hygiene issues. There was also radio coverage although at night this was difficult. There were a number of incidents during this period, of which the following were of particular note:

'On a patrol from Bau to one of the Troop locations, I was point man. As I turned a corner and looked down the track, I could see a small smouldering fire in the distance. There was no one in sight, so I halted the patrol and called the officer forward and we discussed the situation. It appeared as though a person or persons had made the fire, but on hearing our approach had made off in a hurry. The officer then suggested that I should make my way down the track, slowly and cautiously and he would give me cover from behind. My reply was that seeing as I was the medic and he the Marine, perhaps it would make more sense for him to lead and me to follow. Furthermore, if he got shot at least I could treat him, whereas if I got shot would his medical expertise be sufficient to treat me? Also, one had to consider the Geneva Convention! After a short hesitation he agreed with this solution, provided I give him my solemn promise to follow closely behind and give him cover. As luck would have it, there was no one in the vicinity and the patrol carried on its way.

'This brings to mind the time when I visited the Regimental Medical Officer (RMO) at Headquarters in Kuching. He took me to one side and asked me the reason why I was not wearing a red cross armband on my jungle greens. I explained that wearing a red cross would distinguish me from other personnel and might make me a particular target. He then gave me a lecture on the Geneva Convention, to which I replied by asking him if he thought or knew that the enemy was aware of said Convention. In a desperate attempt to end the discussion, he stated that the Commanding Officer felt it was appropriate that medical personnel should wear a red cross. My parting response was to ask the RMO to give my compliments to the Commanding Officer and, remind him it was *me* and not him who was at the sharp end! Interestingly, this subject was never raised again.

'On another occasion, I was called to the radio set to talk to one of the medical orderlies, to advise him on the treatment for a Marine who had developed the signs and symptoms of 'jungle fever'. He had shivers, was running a slight temperature and felt weak. I suggested that he be given aspirin and lots of fluids and I asked to be kept informed as to his progress. I mentioned the incident to the Company Commander, who asked if I wished to go and visit the location in question. It was past midday, the climate was warming up and no helicopters were in the vicinity. This would therefore require a patrol of several hours duration, to escort me to the location. Call it intuition, but after a short deliberation I decided that I should visit the sick man. Thank goodness I did. When I arrived on scene, I found that his temperature had risen and he did not look too well. During the evening and early morning his temperature rose further and he became delirious, unconscious and incontinent. I discussed the case with the RMO and at first light requested a priority 1 casevac. The RMO was at first reluctant to approve this priority category, but following a heated exchange, eventually acceded to my request.

'The patient became critically ill and was subsequently diagnosed as having encephalomyelitis and was urgently evacuated to Singapore, where he eventually make a full recovery from his illness.

'I thoroughly enjoyed this, my final tour with L Company, in the Bau district and was kept quite busy at times. Even the Company Commander was not immune from the hazards of Far East scourge, as was shown when he acquired a parasitic infection. This was successfully treated by the administration of an 'elephant'-sized tablet! I learned much about radio procedure and visiting the forward locations kept me in touch with most of the Company personnel. In addition to treating our own people, I was able to play my part in the 'hearts and minds' campaign, visiting Kampongs and treating local Dyaks, both adults and children. It proved difficult to refuse a gift – sometimes a few eggs – for treatment dispensed, the locals were not particularly wealthy but one was also wary of causing insult by not acceding to local custom.

'I played soccer for the Company and the games against the Malaysian troops were often fiercely competitive! At Bau there was also a lake, which proved popular and where either swimming or fishing was possible. One evening, a Marine returning to camp decided to go for a swim. Unfortunately, he mistook a small pond for the lake and in diving into it, sustained a rather large laceration to his forehead. As I recall, at the time, there had been a small celebration taking place in the Longhouse which housed the Sick Bay. However, with the help of several signallers and a storeman, I managed to suture the wound. When I cautiously checked the wound next morning, it was one of the best suture jobs I had ever performed!

'As 40 Commando arrived at Bau to relieve L Company, amongst the advance party was an SBA who was a colleague and friend from my Haslar days. This was his first draft and – similar to my previous situation – he only had nursing experience from the hospital wards. He admitted to feeling quite apprehensive and asked my advice. Fortunately, I had kept records of all the patients, both Service and civilian, I had dealt with, including diagnosis and treatment. This included a log of radio calls I had made or received, which referred to medical matters. As I was shaking his hand and wishing him well, a call came from the longhouse,

"Doc required on the radio set".

"There you go", said I, as I jumped on board the transport, "Nothing like starting off at the deep end. "Don't worry – you will be fine"; and I disappeared around the corner in a flurry of dust.

'On the voyage back to Singapore, I thought about the past eighteen months I had spent in the Far East. My first Commando unit, my first time at sea on Commando Carriers and all the other events I had experienced. I felt quietly confident that I had carried out my duties as an SBA – and on occasions, non medical duties such as sentry – in a professional and competent manner and I felt ready to face future challenges.

There had been some fantastic moments, runs ashore and the travel by air, sea and land. I thought of the friends I had made in the unit and felt I had been a part of an elite group of men, whose esprit de Corps and comradeship I would treasure and would further experience during the years that followed. I felt sadness too at the loss of comrades who had died at Limbang and in Bau district. Death is always tragic, but none more so than when it occurs as a result of an accident.

'Before departing from Singapore to return to the UK at the end of my eighteen-month tour, I was invited into the Sergeants' Mess for a drink with L Company SNCOs – a special moment that I thoroughly enjoyed.'

Chapter 5

The Yagi Saga

Sarawak; Solving Problems in Communications

1963

The Yagi Saga

Problem Solving

Experience tells me that the Corps is fortunate in its communicators and Captain Ray Frost's Signal Troop in 42 Commando was certainly no exception. His article in the Corps Journal, quoted earlier and written under the pseudonym of 'Pronto', describes some of the difficulties of those early days after Limbang...

Ray Frost – Signals Officer, 42 Commando

'Things were never quite so exciting again but even so, crisis followed on crisis. We almost ran out of A41 batteries before a resupply system started to work. When we were down to one battery, a box arrived from *Albion* in response to a frantic note I had sent by hand of the RC Padre. A long range patrol of M Company ran out of food and was fast running out of its last A510 battery before the supply dropping plane managed to reach them. The signal stores at Bangar were snatched away from the rising flood in the nick of time and telephone lines had to be re-laid from a boat.

'Everything that could go wrong went wrong but somehow the communications went on working. It was a far cry from the faint messages from L Company to the complicated combination of nets that were operated in the later stages in Brunei and even further to the sophisticated arrangements in Sarawak.

'But through it all the signallers were never allowed to forget what a vital part they had to play in the operations and, whatever the difficulties they encountered, they remembered their unofficial motto... *Get the message through!*'

Reference has been made to the difficulty of communication in Sarawak and the limitation of VHF radios after dark. For me, the long drawn out attempt to receive a message from 4 Troop, on the night when Graham Rolls died, had emphasised the restriction that this problem could impose at Troop and Company level in any emergency. Things were about to change.

Ray smoked a pipe, which at times lent him an unflurried, contemplative and almost philosophical air, all of which was entirely appropriate to his calling; he also had a dry sense of humour. He died in 1996 but has left an account in his own name, first published in the Corps Journal, of the development that he and his Troop pioneered in mid-1963 and that was to improve the communication scenario throughout Borneo.

'The Yagi Saga'

'I suppose it first started when one of the Company Commanders turned up in the Commando Headquarters in Semengo Camp and quite ruined my lunchtime beer by buttonholing me and talking about communications.

'At that time the Commando communications in Borneo followed the well tried pattern of using high frequency (HF). The 62 set was used from Commando to Company Headquarters and the small Australian A510 set from Company Headquarters to Troop bases and patrols. In 'conventional' training we used very high frequency (VHF) radios such as the A41, since VHF gives a very clear signal in daytime or night-time. It is for this reason that VHF is used for television broadcasting which will not work unless the signal is particularly clear and free from interference. But VHF signals are very easily blocked by obstructions such as hills and trees. Whatever else is lacking in Borneo there are plenty of hills and trees, so it had been assumed that VHF would not work there and so we used the HF sets, whose signals could and did bend and twist around the obstacles and reach the other end.

Note: somewhere round here put in a full page with four Yagi aerials and their captions

'HF signals work better at night but an awful lot of stations, service and commercial, work in the HF band. Their signals are often much stronger than those put out by our small sets, so our own HF transmissions get swamped and unreadable during the hours of darkness.

'Between Company and Commando Headquarters we could use the civilian telephone or send a truck in an emergency but from Company Headquarters forward to Troops and patrols there was very little in the way of communication between 1800 and 0700 hrs each day.

'It was just this fact that the Company Commander was complaining about. He wanted communications all day and he particularly wanted them at night. I explained the difficulties; I expanded on the problem; I drew little pictures of radio waves. The Staff Officer Operations joined in the fight and my back was to the wall. The real nub of the argument was that I was the Signals Officer and my job was not to make excuses but to 'bloody well get on and provide communications'. I did not sleep very well that afternoon. Could they perhaps be right?

'The next morning I attended the usual daily signals 'O' Group in the Signal Centre. We disposed of the standard problems – the battery charging storeman had made too much noise with his engines after 'pipe down' – the Adjutant refused to make out seven copies of every signal – the MT Troop had been using our telephone cables as dhobey lines again – and so on. With the third cup of coffee I slipped in my bombshell.

"L' Company Commander wants communications".

"He's got some" says the Radio Sergeant."

"I know, but he wants them at night".

'There was a ghastly pause – then they all spoke at once, the Colour Sergeant, the Radio Sergeant, the Control Corporal, my MOA, the duty intelligence clerk (he had only come in to get a cup of decent signals coffee). "Can't be done"; "He would"; "In the jungle?"; "He's crazy".

'Then we settled down to consider the problem. For night communications we must have VHF. We had plenty of A41 VHF sets and had used them in Brunei in the previous year.

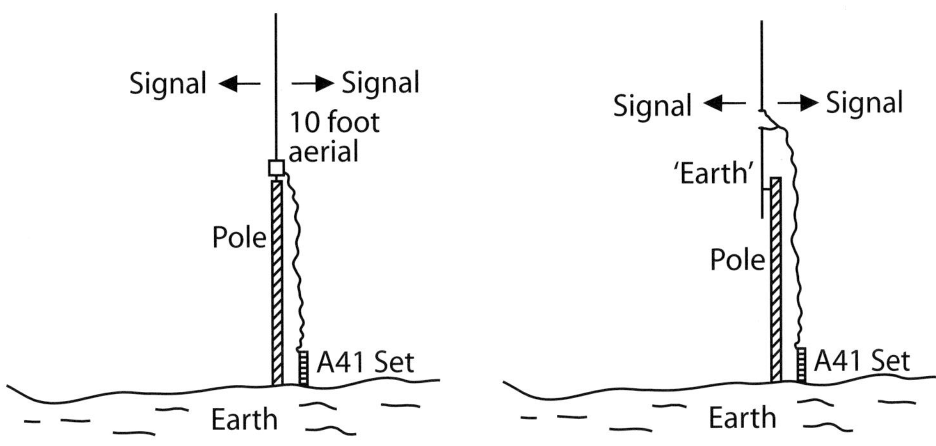

Fig 1. With the aerial on a bamboo pole we could send six miles.

Fig 2. The aerial is both 'aerial' and 'earth'.

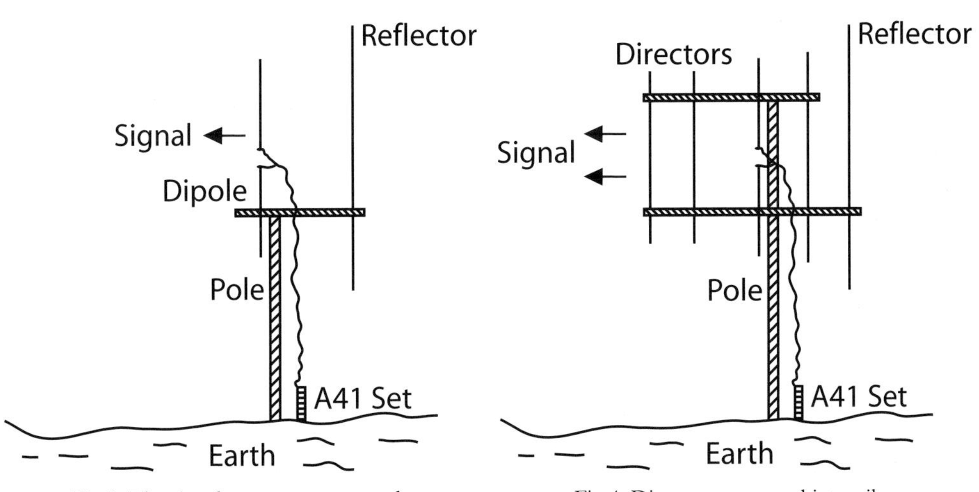

Fig 3. The signals were concentrated.

Fig 4. Directors gave us thirty miles.

The Yagi Aerial, from an article in *The Globe and Laurel*

'By raising the aerials on bamboo poles we had been able to communicate over distances of about six miles but if the aerials were raised too high the communications got worse instead of better. Now we were being asked to communicate over distances of at least twelve miles (Fig 1, previous page).

'The first question therefore was *why could we not just put up an enormous pole and push the signal as far as we wanted to?* The Troop Colour Sergeant (who was technically minded) applied himself to this and came up with what appeared to be a reasonable answer.

'Any radio aerial is really in two parts. One of the parts is the metal rod or wire which we can see and move; the other part is called the 'earth'. With most service aerials the 'earth' part is the real earth on which we stand. So, the higher the visible aerial is raised above the earth, the less the two interact until above a certain height the combined aerial/earth becomes less efficient and the signal does not go any further.

'It is a fairly easy exercise to construct an aerial which is both aerial and earth. The 'earth' in this case is either a metal wire or rod the same size as the 'aerial' and pointing in the opposite direction. This type of aerial is called a 'dipole' (Fig 2). So we did this. Then we stuck the dipole on top of the longest piece of bamboo we could find and set off in a truck to see how far this would work. We got results up to about eight miles but this was not good enough.

'The next question was *why did the signal peter out at all?* I knew the answer to this one. A rod aerial, dipole or otherwise, sends out the radio signal equally in all directions (omnidirectional is the OK word). Therefore the signal gets weaker and weaker as the receiver gets further and further from the transmitter; but, and here's the rub, if the signal is being transmitted to a receiver four miles away and to another eight miles away, the strength of the signal received at the distant receiver is not half that received by the nearer but only a quarter (mathematically minded readers may care to work this out). The effect of this is that after a certain distance the signal fades and becomes undetectable very quickly.

'It so happened that the Rifle Troops of the Company we were fussing about were all sited in a fairly narrow arc; Company Headquarters, the Indonesian border and most of the patrols were within the same narrow arc. The next step, therefore, appeared to be to so arrange the signal that it was only transmitted in one direction. Then of course it would travel very much further before it became too weak to detect.

'It was at this stage that the Troop Colour Sergeant said the magic words – "What we want is Yagi aerials." He was prevailed upon to explain this cryptic remark and the explanation went something like this.

'Radio waves work in some ways like rays of light and can be reflected from metallic surfaces. If we took our dipole aerial and fixed it on a frame and then fixed another metal rod, rather longer than the dipole, parallel to it and the correct distance behind it, the radio waves would be concentrated in one direction (Fig 3).

'It sounded hopeful so two of these Yagi aerials were made with a wooden frame on which were fixed the dipole and the reflector. When they were completed I realised that they were exactly the same sort of aerial arrays [as those] which are fixed on the roofs of houses to receive television signals. Again one was erected on our trusty bamboo pole and the other was precariously balanced on top of a Land Rover and I set out to test them for distance working. We set up at eight miles and then at nine miles and so on. At last we were over twelve miles from Commando HQ and still getting through.

'Now came the final test. The next day I went to L Company HQ with one Yagi, whilst the Radio Sergeant thumbed a lift in a passing helicopter and went to one of the Troop bases with the other Yagi. Ignoring cries of: "Are we going to get television, then?" I erected my Yagi and tuned in the A41 five minutes before the agreed time of opening up. Dead on time I sent a couple of plaintive calls over the air. No reply! Fifteen minutes later I was still calling, then, suddenly I heard the unmistakeable voice of the Radio Sergeant answering me explaining that he had some difficulty in finding a suitable bamboo pole in his Troop location.

'It only remained then to keep the link open well into the night and to invite the hitherto sceptical Company Commander to have a conversation with his Troop Commander before going to bed. This communication barrier had been well and truly broken.

'Thereafter the Troop Colour Sergeant and Radio Sergeant worked like beavers making more Yagis, taking them out to Company and Troop locations, erecting them and indoctrinating people in their use. Improved Yagis were also made with 'directors' in front of the dipole and the signals were then covering distances of over thirty miles (Fig 4).

'Shortly after this we were relieved by 40 Commando and then relieved them again in due course. By this time Yagi aerials were sprouting all over the First Division of Sarawak. They provided good VHF communication between all the static bases and headquarters; it also meant that patrols could communicate with their own headquarters at any time of day or night using their A41 sets…'

To the Company Commander, the Yagi was a breakthrough that restored his ability to respond to an emergency as quickly as possible and/or to make appropriate plans, regardless of the time of day. To the Troop Commander, wanting to talk to mobile patrols on a wide arc and not equipped with a Yagi aerial, the boon may not have been so obvious. Though I never heard anything but praise for the concept, Ray Frost's postscript may not have been entirely apocryphal…

‘I was sitting in the Mess at Semengo Camp one lunchtime, quietly drinking my beer, when two Rifle Troop Commanders walked in looking rugged and operational. They glared at me with such concentrated venom that I choked on my beer.

“You and your damned ‘Yagis’!”

“Oh?”’

“What did you want to make those bloody things for?”

“Well…”

“There used to be a time when we were on our own for twelve hours a day.”

“…Running our own thing, making our own decisions”

“Well, I only…”

“Now we have the Company Commander breathing down our necks all the time…”

“Yes, but…”

“…Giving us orders, demanding SITREPs!”

“You ought to be court-martialled! Ought to be shot!”

“…Ought to be sent to a rifle company!”

‘After this last sadistic suggestion I crept sadly away to my bunk. You can’t win, can you? I mean to say, you can’t actually win…’

Chapter 6

Roulement

Bau District: Soldiering On

October ’63 to May ’64

Roulement

Bau District

Malaysian Independence had seen the arrival of 'C' Squadron of the 1st Malaysian Reconnaissance Regiment and had altered the operational structure within Bau District. As Keith Wilkins recorded, the Squadron had relieved a Troop of the QRIH and had spare capacity, taking responsibility for the security of Bau itself and freeing his Mortar Troop from that commitment. The Squadron continued to support the resident Commando Company, providing patrols on the limited stretches of road. Coordination was achieved through an evening O Group at the resident Company HQ.

The Squadron Commander, Major Baljit Singh, describing himself as a mechanised Sikh – that is he wore neither turban nor beard – was an urbane and sociable character; friendly and easy to get on with, he would from time to time reveal a 'chip on his shoulder'; perhaps understandably, he felt that he should have the command of the whole military operation in the District. As was to be demonstrated both here and in Sabah, Malaysian units were not yet ready for the responsibility, nor had they the numbers. British and Gurkha troops would soldier on in the forefront of operations for some three years after Malaysian Independence.

Tringgus

It had also been decided to man a Field Force post at Tringgus, a Kampong in the remote south east corner of the District. The Kampong was close to the border but not on the direct route to Bau or Kuching, being separated from the rest of the District by miles of jungle and a high ridge. A section of 42 Commando's Assault Engineer Troop (Lieutenant St John Grey) had been flown in to help with construction of the landing site.

The arrival was timely; the area had become something of a 'no man's land' and there were persistent rumours of visits by parties of TNKU. On their first day the Assault Engineers had helped to repel a party of invaders and, for the rest of the time that they were there, they remained alert to attack by day and shared the watches by night.

Towards the end of October, B Company, 40 Commando arrived to take over Bau District. Before 4 Troop left Pang Tebang, a unit plaque was presented to the 'Kapitan China', head of the local Chinese community, from whom they received the following letter:

To: The General, 42 Commando.

My Dear Sir,

With many thanks for presented a gift. I shall keep it as a remembrance. And I shall never forget the kindness that you gave me.

Sir, I have the honour to inform you that all 42 Commando are very good and kind here, especially the officer and sergeant.

Well I have nothing more to write about, I only hope that "God Bless you always".

I remain, yours faithfully, Chung Siong
The Kapitan, Pangalan Tebang.

Pat Gardner – OC B Company

'When we returned to Sarawak things had hotted up. My three Troops were located on border villages astride the main route to the capital, Kuching, and my Company Headquarters was by the lake near the road-head. I also had a squadron of the Malaysian Army under command. They were a multi-racial force commanded by an amusing Sikh, Baljit Singh; their second in command was Chinese and the Troop Commanders were Malay. As a fighting force they were useless but, for political reasons, I was ordered to put one of their Troops on the border. I chose to send them to Stass, where the villagers were a pugnacious lot, well capable of defending themselves and the Malay Troops.'

Not yet ready

'I was not happy about this Malaysian Troop and the Colonel came out to visit them. They were living well but not doing anything. I demanded that they put out two ambushes that night. I said that I would go with one and the Colonel then volunteered to go with the other... 'as we wanted to see how ambushes were really organised by experts...'! The little Malay subaltern seemed a little put out and asked if he should come as well and we indicated that it would be a nice gesture. He drew himself up to his full height – which wasn't very much – and told us he was used to guards of honour and that sort of thing but ambushes were not his scene! He gave out some fairly inadequate orders and I sited the ambush positions for the patrol I was with and insisted that a guard rota should be instigated.

'I was due to be woken at 0100 hrs to do a watch. I woke only to discover that the rest of the ambush party was fast asleep. Shortly afterwards firing broke out not far away; it sounded like a major battle and went on for quite a while. When we met up in the morning, I rather naughtily asked the Colonel whether he had got anything. He was white-lipped with rage but, after a cup of tea, was almost prepared to see the funny side of things. His ambush party started firing, no one ever discovered who started it or why, and the rest just joined in and blazed away. The Colonel asked a machine-gunner what he was firing at but got no reply; the man just went on firing until his ammunition ran out. Then, in the darkness, the barrel of his weapon glowed white hot! At least the Colonel began to have more sympathy with my problem.'

Around the Patch

'I spent much of my time walking out to visit the forward Troops, spending a night with them, before going on to the next. The nearest was about four hours walk away so one got quite fit! These forward Troops were supplied by airdrop. Once I was up in an Auster spotter aircraft, piloted by Ian Munro who was clocking up hours to become an airline pilot, when we noticed the airdrop aircraft cut a corner and fly over Indonesia. Over the air we heard them complaining that they had been shot at. Then something went wrong with the Auster's engine and we were covered with warm oil but fortunately we just made the airport. As soon as we landed I was handed an urgent message from my Sergeant Major to say that the locals had seen an Indonesian fire at the plane and had immediately beheaded him – *"Please, what did I want done with the head?"*!

'The locals used to burn the jungle on the side of a hill and then plant their hill paddy. Then the hillside was allowed to grow until the next time it was needed. However a Peace Corps girl – in amply filled Bermuda shorts – got some locals together and explained that a bit of fertiliser would increase the crop, obviate the need to burn the hillsides and provide the village with a surplus to sell. The locals were, as ever, very polite but didn't take easily to advice from women. *"Why should they want to grow more? What should we do with it? For more money? What do we want money for?"* I think she gave up and realised that there would have to be cultural change before any other changes took place.

'The climax to my year as a Company Commander was when the Indonesians made an incursion through our area towards Kuching. We made contact and inflicted some casualties but sadly Corporal Marriot was killed in one of the skirmishes. The operation lasted about ten days; I should have been relieved in the middle of it to go to my new job but my relief went down with a temperature. I had over 600 men under command and for those ten days, I was very stretched. However, we cleared the area and honour was satisfied…'

> "On New Year's eve a band of about 100 Indonesians crossed the frontier in the Bau area. During the subsequent operations Corporal Marriot was killed when the patrol he was leading came across a large party of enemy resting in thick jungle. After a fierce fire fight lasting about half an hour, the remainder of Corporal Marriot's patrol withdrew. A number of enemy weapons, including American Armalite rifles, were recovered during

> the follow up operations and two enemy dead were also recovered. Unfortunately the bulk of the enemy party escaped across the border…"

On leaving the Company to take up a job as a GSO2 with the Headquarters 17 Infantry Division, Pat Gardner concluded…

> "B' Company had done well; it had earned more honours and awards than any other company of the Brigade; it was a going concern which people wanted to join and it was a happy group to be with."

On Line

During this tour there had been improvement in the radio coverage through the use of Yagi aerials but OC B Company had also been doing his own research. Norman Parker was Signals Corporal with the Company…

> "The episode I remember best was in 1964. B Company was at Bau, with sub-units at Gumbang, Stass, Serikin and Bukit Knuckle. Captain Gardner was the Company Commander and he had been reading about the Japanese positions during the Second World War. They had telephone communications between Bau and what were now our outstations.
>
> "He asked "Could we do it?"
>
> "I said that with enough D10 cable I would give it a go. He organised the cable, I organised the Dyaks to carry it and we successfully laid cable for about twelve to fifteen miles – I forget the exact distance but a map will help.
>
> "I laid the lines – hard work – and the telephone communication worked; it was not easy but it was successful; only the repairs later gave me nightmares."

*

Back in Singapore, Keith Wilkins, having commanded 42 Commando's Recce Troop and currently still commanding the Mortar Troop, had been demonstrating the versatility of the 'Heavy Weapons' specialisation by turning his hand to the potential of the anti-tank weapon in the campaign…

Singapore Interlude – The SS 11

'Some time earlier, the Royal Navy had purchased a quantity of French SS11 wire guided anti tank missiles for use by the Brigade, and the Naval Air Squadrons in the ground and air roles. In April '62 I had been one of seven Royal Marines to attend an aimer's course run by Nord Aviation. In 1963, it was thought that the missile could be usefully employed in the surface role at sea to intercept Indonesian craft trying to infiltrate IBT into the First Division of Sarawak. I was therefore ordered to run a course for SS11 aimers.

'Volunteers were sought and eight students were assembled at Sembawang for training. The first ten days were spent learning about the missile and its firing circuits, and also developing aiming skills with the use of a simulator. The remaining three days of the course were spent at Asahan Range in Malaya carrying out live firing at the end of which six of the students were considered to be qualified and were passed for duty.

'In the event, the missile was never used in this role, largely I believe, because it had no night firing capability. However, I later discovered that in March 1965 Wessex helicopters of 845 Naval Air Squadron fired five missiles to very good effect at a hillside occupied by the Indonesian Army in the Second Division of Sarawak, whilst supporting an attack carried out by a company from 2nd/10th Gurkhas.

'In November 1963, I relinquished command of the Mortar Troop on being promoted to Captain, and was appointed as Second-in-Command of K Company...'

Keith Wilkins – Second-in-Command K Company

Back to Bau

'42 Commando returned to the First Division of Sarawak in mid-January 1964, and I found myself back on my old stamping ground at Bau, but this time with K Company. By then the intensity of operations had increased and the unit's TAOR had been correspondingly reduced. At Bau, the Federal Recce Squadron had taken over entire responsibility for IS in the rear areas which enabled K Company to concentrate fully on the protection of the border in its shortened sector. Two Rifle Troops were deployed forward to patrol bases at Pang Tebang (Serikin?) and at Bukit Knuckle, with a Police Field Force Detachment at Tringgus under command; the third Rifle Troop and Company Headquarters were based in the camp at Bau alongside the fresh water lake.

'Shortly before our arrival in Bau, there had been a major incursion into the area by some eighty IBT, stiffened by elements of the Indonesian Army, which had resulted in a Corporal from 40 Commando being killed and others injured. This had made the civilian population apprehensive and, by the time we arrived, local morale was low. Our Company Commander (Major Alex Higson) was determined to tackle this matter without delay; he therefore asked me to organise a demonstration of fire power to show the local people just what means we had available to deal with any future incursions. The nearby lake lent itself perfectly for this purpose and, on the chosen day, a large number of locals turned up to watch.

'The demonstration started with the firing of the full range of company weapons into the large hill on the opposite side of the lake; no sooner had this finished than a Saladin Armoured Car from the QRIH rolled up and let fly with its Browning machine gun, followed by a round from its eight-pounder gun. Finally, to finish things off, a

RAF Javelin came out of the sky and swooped low over the lake showering everyone with its vapour trail. In reality, it was all a bit of theatre, but it had the required effect, confidence was restored and spirits rose amongst the civilian population.

'On 21 February, the police post at Tringgus was attacked and two policemen were killed and six wounded. The raiding party had withdrawn back over the border, but there was clear evidence that it had suffered some casualties. A tracker team from the Recce Troop (Lieutenant Peter Montgomery) had been sent in immediately with a section of 2 Troop, reinforced later by police Field Force…'

> "Out in the Tringgus area everybody settled down in their ambush positions. It proved to be a quiet night but early next morning shots were heard and shortly after the police confirmed that they had killed four enemy; just retribution! About an hour later, two exhausted and bedraggled enemy surrendered to K Company and were quickly whisked back to Bau by 'chopper' for interrogation. It was then believed that the remainder of the enemy party, about ten men, had retreated back across the border…"

'It soon became apparent that the enemy had also become very active in the nearby Pang Tebang area. 3 Troop mounted a series of operations, supported by the tracker team and after nine days it was clear that the enemy had been driven out, but not before seven had been killed and a further six captured…

> "The interrogation and inspection of captured documents showed that a second party of about fourteen enemy had infiltrated into 3 Troop's area around Pang Tebang. Accordingly this morning patrols from 3 Troop supported by another tracking team and a section of drivers from Semengo moved in. Our suspicions were confirmed by the locals who reported that a party of enemy had visited the local shop last night and taken away food. One section of 3 Troop then had a contact and killed one enemy in a small camp; and so the chase is on. The enemy have split up and are trying to make their getaway but in considerable confusion. A great deal of equipment, ammunition and documents have been captured and these – at this very moment – are proving most illuminating … our patrols will be on the move again tomorrow…
>
> "Shortly afterwards Corporal Watson and his section from 3 Troop found and attacked an enemy camp. The main body of enemy split up and made tracks for the border. Corroborative reports state that they carried with them four dead bodies and others were wounded. We then embarked on a series of mopping up operations. The IBT left behind were widely scattered and out of food, and slowly but surely they surrendered. Most of them were very demoralised and two, in particular, were so emaciated and weak that they required immediate hospital treatment. The Grand Finale was provided by the Headman of Pang Tebang who shot and killed two IBT who had come in search of food. This typified the tremendous support we received from the local people…"

'Hearts and Minds' – Major Alex Higson, commanding K Company, 42 Commando, with the District Officer emerging from Bau Lake at the 'baptism' ceremony of the newly constructed lido.

'This response seemed to have had a salutary effect on the Indonesians and for the next few weeks the border area remained quite quiet. In the meantime the rains came and before long Bau found itself cut off by floods. It was a case of all hands to the pump and those of us at Bau were kept busy rescuing locals and their animals and ensuring that essential supplies reached the town; it was a job well done that clearly enhanced our 'hearts and minds' campaign.

'At about this time the police received information that there had been some further CCO activity in that familiar old 'hot spot' at Musi. A cordon and search operation was mounted which involved those of us based in Bau, and I remember having to rope down from an RAF Belvedere helicopter into the cordon with other members of K Company. A hooded police informer was used to identify suspects and, as a result, nine arrests were made and a quantity of documents was seized. All of this helped to keep pressure on the CCO and to disrupt its activities.'

Border Activity Renewed

'In early April '64, information started coming across the border thick and fast and it was soon apparent that the Indonesians were back to their old tricks. On 7 April, a patrol from 3 Troop had a contact right on the border. The fire fight lasted about ten minutes before the enemy withdrew, having suffered some casualties. Unfortunately, a week later, at almost exactly the same spot, another patrol from 3 Troop was heavily ambushed and Corporal Hind, Marine McCrea and two Border Scouts were killed – a sad event that for a while stunned the whole Company.

'However, there was no let up in our operations and morale was quickly restored. Despite this success, the enemy remained quite subdued for the next two months, and I feel sure that this was because we continued to maintain a robust presence along the border. Shortly after this incident a top level political decision had been made to permit cross-border operations to be mounted to a depth of 2,000 yards. It was known that the Indonesians dropped their guard on their side of the border and it was considered essential to try and keep them off balance and gain some initiative.'

Cross-Border Plans

'Towards the end of this tour, K Company was among those chosen to mount one of the early cross-border offensive operations.

'The decision to cross the border was in itself considered to be politically sensitive in the extreme and the utmost secrecy was imposed. It was known that the Indonesians had set up an anti-aircraft gun on a hill just a few hundred yards on their side of the border, constituting a threat to airdrop and helicopter operations on our side. The plan was to take this out by a hit and run attack. 1 Troop was selected for this task, and for the next few days carried out intensive planning and preparation. For whatever reason the operation was cancelled at the last minute but nonetheless the episode marked the beginning of a cross-border offensive by British forces that was to have an immense impact on the final outcome of Confrontation...'

Certain units had been invited to submit plans for specific operations to be considered individually at the highest level; these operations went under the codename 'Claret'. The threat from anti-aircraft fire was real; two aircraft had been hit by fire from across the border in Lundu District. Nonetheless it is likely that the proposal to take out an Indonesian Army anti-aircraft gun – arguably legitimately defending its own airspace, however provocative the siting – was difficult to justify politically at such an early stage in cross-border response. It would certainly not have met one of the initial criteria for 'Claret' operations – that they should be deniable. Aircraft making supply drops near the border at this time were escorted by RAF Javelin fighter aircraft which might be expected to respond to hostile fire.

'...This important, albeit abortive event more or less brought to an end this deployment to Sarawak, but not before we had opened a brand new public lido by the Lake at Bau as part of our 'hearts and minds' campaign. We also succeeded in burning down much of the patrol base at Bukit Knuckle, when a hydro-cooker exploded and set fire to the central basha. This happened just three days before we were due to depart and demanded some very hasty repairs to be carried out before we handed over our area to a company from 1st/6th Gurkhas.'

Chapter 7

Escalation

Lundu District; 'Dragon's Teeth' and 'Indian Chief'

July '63 to April '64

Escalation

Lundu District

Lundu District forms the western tail of Sarawak's First Division, tapering to a tip in the Sematan peninsular. There was then no road link with Kuching and the rest of the Division. The main river is wide for much of its length is navigable initially by small coastal and thereafter by river craft. There were a few PWD trucks, a Citroen CV and one wide mud road running West from Lundu as far as Serayan and a creek, in turn crossed by boat to the Sematan peninsular – the tip of the tail. Sematan also had a landing strip for light aircraft.

Lundu itself and the whole of the north-central area of the District was dominated by the Gunong Gading, a high forested feature, round which there were intermittent patches of cultivation – 'gardens' – mainly worked by Chinese. Below the Western end of the Gunong was the village of Perigi.

Back in July '63, after the initial success during the takeover, in which Sergeant Callow's joint patrol from B and 'K' Companies had sprung a successful ambush, hostile activity had not been noticeable but time was not wasted…

> "Working on the old adage that 'any fool can be uncomfortable', we at Lundu have done a great deal to settle ourselves in properly… Patrols out were still doing fourteen day periods of night ambushes and day patrolling, but with some AE assistance and the help of the locals a complex water catchment appeared in one kampong, a water filtration device in another, yet another boasted a deep trench latrine and all of them had constructed galleys and dining halls. In a variety of ways ingenuity had helped to make life easier although signs of any enemy in our area remained dishearteningly few."

Independence Day and Malaysia Day had each been celebrated, boycotted by the Chinese but otherwise undisturbed. Things were indeed so quiet that towards the end of the deployment an ad hoc Troop had been withdrawn to Semengo to form a small Brigade Reserve.

In October '63 K Company was relieved by A Company of 40 Commando and was ferried by a combination of river craft, fast patrol boat and minesweeper to HMS *Albion* for the return trip to Singapore.

For the next two to three months, Troops of A Company continued to rotate between Lundu and the border patrol posts, where possible by boat. Christmas came and went, having been celebrated in various ways and on different days, depending on location and patrol programme. At Lundu there had been a party for local children, enjoyed reportedly as much by the Company as by the children. For the patrols there was little let up but still no contacts…

> "We have had a busy time during the first two and a half months, trying to watch eighty-eight miles of border and fifty-three miles of coast line for invading Indonesians. We haven't caught any – we have frightened a few and we have had our few moments of tense expectation and breathless suspense.
>
> "We have had two tragic occurrences when an RAF helicopter and an Auster had to make forced landings near one of our Border posts [Biawak]. In the latter the passenger, a RAF Chaplain, died of his wounds. Sergeant Foster and all men of Corporal Allsop's section, with Marine (S) Dougal their 'pronto', did a magnificent [rescue] job, and showed that the resourcefulness and personal bravery of the average Marine is of a very high order."

It was only in mid-January '64, at the very end of A Company's tour and following the incursions in Bau District, that the situation at Lundu escalated fairly rapidly…

> "Shortly before the unit left Sarawak at the end of January '64, more Indonesians were reported to have crossed the frontier, this time in the Lundu District. Operations by land and sea were directed against them involving Marines, SBS, and Gunners…"

According to 1 Troop (Second Lieutenant Simon Julian) the last fourteen days had been the most energetic of the tour and there had been unfulfilled hopes of 'bringing the enemy to battle'; a local who had been impressed as a guide or porter by the raiding party had escaped and reported that a helicopter had circled their position though apparently nothing had been spotted. The Company was now to be relieved by L Company of 42 Commando.

*

The use of Commando Carriers as troopships was an occasional necessity or convenience, but as an ongoing concept it was costly, if not wasteful. In any case the availability of a carrier at any given moment to support the 'Roulement' programme could not be guaranteed and, so, the Motor Vessel *Auby* was reborn. I wrote of her first voyage…

Maiden Voyage

'The MV *Auby*, owned by the Straits Steamship Company, had been a coastal and river vessel which conveyed cargo varying from deck passengers to cattle between Singapore and Borneo, and onwards up the wide jungle rivers. Now she was a troopship, after a hasty conversion, and it was thus that we found ourselves in the role of guinea pigs boarding her for her maiden trooping voyage, almost before the last dockyard 'matey' had removed his tools.

Marines on the mess deck of the MV *Auby,* which ferried troops from Singapore to Borneo

'Embarking on 27 January '64, we commenced the slow, plodding voyage lasting three days over 400 miles to Kuching. The Master, Captain Davis and his officers did all they could to make the voyage pleasant, but the ship had its drawbacks. The mess decks were hot and space was cramped; the food however was good but the crumbs from the mess deck tables, perched on the hatch combings, fell through onto the top bunks below, leaving the occupants with the itchy feeling that they might just as well have had breakfast in bed.'

'Berthing at the now familiar Biawak oil jetty, we deployed by road and helicopter. HQ and Support companies went to Semengo once again; L Company to Lundu, K Company to Bau and M Company to Padawan. By 31 January the relief of 40 Commando was complete and 42 Commando was back in business.'

40 Commando, the outgoing unit, had this to say…'

> "The change-over itself was complex, involving every available helicopter. At one time no less than four companies were passing through Krokong – a small landing site at the end of narrow road [south] west of Bau. Eventually the unit embarked in three ships, the MV *Auby*, the LST *Maxwell Brander* and HMS *Plymouth*."

Incursion

In the process of relief within Lundu District, the Sematan peninsular had now become the responsibility of a Gunner battery, with a number of coastal OPs established near the western tip. Within L Company area, 4 Troop (Second Lieutenant Cameron Mackie) was at Biawak, central-south and on the border; 6 Troop (Lieutenant Paddy Ashdown) was at Rasau, on the southern most bend in the principal river, covering the Sempadi Forest and connected to the border by several tributaries; at Lundu, with L Company HQ, was 5 Troop. On the evening of our arrival the reported IBT crossed into the Company area…

Duncan Christie-Miller, Second Lieutenant – OC 5 Troop

Jungle Paradox

'In 1964 I was a nineteen-year-old Second Lieutenant commanding 5 Troop of L Company, 42 Commando. We deployed to Borneo in January and my Troop was collocated at Lundu with Company HQ. I kept a journal and have used this to refresh my memory in order to write this contribution. What now strikes me as being a constant theme of this six month tour is the number of paradoxes and incongruities that were then a permanent part of my life.

Lieutenant Duncan Christie-Miller

'We went out and back using a converted Straits Line cattle steamer called the *Auby*. She was tiny, with a bridge set far forward to allow visibility when she entered the rivers of Borneo. The accommodation for the Marines was cramped [as the photo on the previous page shows]. There was no air conditioning. I slept with Paddy on the aft deck. The trip took three days and my journal tells me that I organised a series of aircraft recognition tests – there was certainly no chance of doing much else. As thereafter we rarely saw an aircraft – apart from Whirlwind and Belvedere helicopters – even that particular effort seems to have been somewhat useless, especially as once in the jungle you would in any case not see the sky.

Lundu Debut

'We moved to Lundu by twin rotor Belvedere helicopter staging through a temporary LS near to Bau where K Company was to operate. These ungainly large helicopters strained to take more than seven or eight passengers with their baggage at a time and the move must have taken ages. At Lundu we took over from A Company, 40 Commando. I managed to spend fifteen minutes with an outgoing batch mate of mine – Simon Julian – who assured me that nothing had *ever* happened in that area. There was no formal hand over, no briefing and certainly no intelligence.

An informer (with mask) trying to pick possible suspects at an identity parade following the incident in which Corporal Chappell was killed.

'At 2315 that night I was summoned to the Ops Room and told to take my Troop out to search an area about four miles away, up the western dirt track 'road' that bordered the large hill feature called Gunong Gading. There were rumours of an elusive group of fifty Indonesian infiltrators. I duly briefed the Troop – not that sure what to tell them, to be honest – and we duly left in a Public Works Department dipper truck; an interesting, incongruous and possibly unique way to go on one's first operational patrol.

'I decided arbitrarily where to leave the truck and we duly set off in to the darkness along a path. I had been told that the last thing you ever did was to use a track but here – as in a subsequent contact – we had no choice.

'After spending the night lying on the ground in a loose lying up position, we pressed on to a kampong called Keranji where we started to search for signs of the elusive group of Indonesian infiltrators and – did I mention – it was raining? We found an Indonesian camp, including a sentry roster and some pornography. I never knew what happened to the latter. We followed a good track towards the Gunong Gading. My journal records: *"Streams very swollen and up to fifteen feet in some places"* – so those toggle ropes had a use after all! And it still rained.

'We lost the trail after about a mile and then spent hours searching for it – needle and haystack stuff. This went on for three days before we walked back to Lundu.'

Patrolling

'It is the small things that still stick in my mind… at night I used a Zoot suit of black parachute silk, which a number of us had made up in Singapore. We slept under a poncho on the ground with our '44 Pattern packs for a pillow. I did require sentries to be posted at night and took my turn but with hindsight feel that they were quite useless in most situations and would only have been useful at first light. Putting on wet and cold OGs in the morning was uncomfortable. As some patrols took us up to about 4,000 feet it was often wet and very cold. Not what the jungle was meant to be.

'Obtaining water was no problem – you filled your water bottle from a stream coming off your poncho or dipped it into a stream as you crossed. But then you needed to purify it with two different tablets – white for purifying and blue for taking away the taste of the white one. Or was it the other way round?

'Map reading? Well, the maps showed rivers and contours but generally were white with no obvious features. I think I was technically lost for most of the time. I just aimed for a main feature like a river and then decided which way to go once we arrived.

'Patrolling itself was a strange business. I was always concerned that the Marines tended to bunch up and I seemed constantly to be nagging them to stretch out. This meant that you could see only the back of the man in front and, when turning around,

A patrol moving out from Lundu with tracker dog during Operation 'Dragon's Teeth'

the face of the man behind. I used to be the third in the line as this seemed a good position to be in if there was a contact.

'Then there was 'Wait a Minute'. Anyone who has been in the jungle will know how aggravating the barbed creeper can be. It seemed to reach out and grab you, pulling off your sodden jungle hat, snaring your clothing and requiring a careful backwards movement to disentangle yourself before moving forward again.

'My MOA – Marine Raine – carried the A41 radio set, a spare battery and his personal kit. At the start of a patrol he could be lugging around seventy pounds. On one occasion I swapped packs with him – as a result the patrol had never moved so slowly. The radio sets themselves were almost useless and getting through each evening to send a SITREP was nearly impossible, while the Section sets (A 40s) would not work at all in the jungle. My Company Commander must have thought that every time we went on patrol we disappeared into some silent pit!'

'Dragon's Teeth'

It had been almost a year since the deployment of B Company (Captain Pat Gardner) to the First Division of Sarawak. Since that date the territory to be protected by the Commando units and sub-units had been always too large to allow for any significant reserve. Capacity for reinforcement and follow up remained ad hoc. Headquarter Company had supplied a section of drivers to support K Company's operation in Bau District; elsewhere another section from MT had provided a patrol to guard a party of surveyors. Elements of Support Company usually provided some flexibility of response. The Recce Troop of 42 Commando (Lieutenant Peter Montgomery) had combined with the members of the Anti-Tank Troop to provide follow-up teams that included Iban trackers, as well as tracker or patrol dogs, the handlers of which included volunteers recruited from across the unit. On this occasion there was also Mortar Troop.

By January '64, HQ 99 Gurkha Brigade had taken responsibility for Western Sarawak (West Brigade) in succession to HQ 3 Commando Brigade; with them came the apparent call on a more substantial reserve.

The incursion on 31 January had consisted of a party that made its way into Gunong Gading. They had instructions to lie low and await further orders and clearly were being supplied with food and information by the Chinese farmers in the Perigi area. Food denial became the first priority to which 5 Troop patrols were already contributing. The operation, code named 'Dragon's Teeth', led to a buildup which eventually included 5 Troop, Mortar Troop, part of Recce Troop and a Company of the 2/10th Gurkhas; there was also a detachment of 225 Squadron, RAF, flying Whirlwind 10 helicopters, and an offshore Naval patrol. Early on in the operation Lieutenant Colonel Ian Gourlay established a Tac HQ at Lundu.

Operation 'Dragon's Teeth' – A RAF Whirlwind 10 hovering
with a winchman directing the pilot while sitting in the open door

A Whirlwind 10 disgorging troops during Operation 'Dragon's Teeth'

The arrival of the Gurkha Company heralded a deadly game of hide and seek in which the IBT rattled around inside the jungle, in small and large parties, moving camp frequently, with Gurkha patrols in hot pursuit and with Mortar Troop, Recce Troop and 5 Troop patrolling the fringes and rivers around the Gunong Gading…

Duncan Christie-Miller – OC 5 Troop

Gunong Gading

'After two or three weeks of routine patrolling – up to five days out followed by twenty-four hours or so back at Lundu – all changed. 5 Troop was to be used to dominate the East side of Gunong Gading, where a band of Indonesian infiltrators was still believed to be concentrating with support from the local Chinese.

'The area contained farmed plots and secondary jungle interspersed. There was a single but well used path from Lundu to a kampong called Siar. I gave each section a stretch of the track, where they had to mount intermittent blocks, stopping and searching locals for unusual amounts of food. When not on a track block they were silently observing the traffic. At night I gave them a requirement to mount ambushes on the approaches to selected houses. I based myself at a kampong called Sekambal with 6 Section under Corporal Chappell. We used a ruined mosque, made of atap, as our base and as far as possible I made friends with the villagers. I remember writing in a one headman's book that I would like to visit his village once the conflict was over.

'I patrolled with Corporal Chappell and a half section and on alternate days visited my other sections – Corporal Fulton to the South and Corporal Derbyshire to the North. On one such patrol with Corporal Chappell we searched a house on the jungle edge, about 2 miles North of Sekambal and found an outboard motor; the house was about half a mile from the main river exit to the sea. The engine was new, clean and stuck out like a sore thumb. It aroused my suspicions. The next day I visited Corporal Derbyshire by walking up the track – having first briefed Corporal Chappell that I would return in time to carry out an ambush that night on the house with the outboard motor.

'I had with me a Field Force policeman and one Marine. We visited Corporal Derbyshire, checked that all was going well and began the return journey of three miles. As I entered Sekambal I met Corporal Chappell leaving with a half section – he had decided that I would not make it back by nightfall and had decided, quite correctly, to take the initiative and to carry out my instructions without me. I decided to let him go on as I needed to send the evening SITREP.

'He was killed and four of his Marines were wounded in the approaches to the house where he was to place his ambush. Marine Howes was wounded in the chest but made his way to Sekambal to tell me what had happened while his wound was treated.

'Now was decision time. Having been taught not to use tracks and not to move at night, it was clear that both edicts would have to be ignored. Amazingly the radio to Company HQ worked. Captain Edwards asked me "What are your intentions?" There was only one option – to move up the track, relieve my patrol and then follow up as best I could. I told him so. He promised to send in a helicopter with Leading SBA Allwood.

'There was no Landing Site at Sekambal but we set to cutting an improvised LP as best we could in the dark. I placed a torch shining upwards in the middle of the so called LP and, when we heard the helicopter, I spoke on the radio to the pilots – Flight Lieutenants George Warren and Brian Danger – and told them to descend vertically on the light. I believe that when they took off they had about three foot clearance. Amazing flying, though so far as I know it was not recognised by any award.

'Then with the remainder of Corporal Chappell's section, my Troop HQ, and the Leading SBA we set off on a night move up the track. Marine Howes insisted on returning with us and was later awarded a well deserved Mention in Despatches (MID). It was so dark that I got them to use toggle ropes like umbilical cords to the next man in line. The move took three hours.

'The house was in a pepper garden. There was a light showing. I had not yet thought how I would actually get into the building without being shot. Eventually I crawled forward and decided to shout out the name "Balderstone!" and heard a somewhat strained voice reply – "We're here. Sir"!

'Once we had secured the house and made the wounded comfortable, I was completely overcome by exhaustion. I sat on the floor and crashed out for twenty minutes – so thank you 5 Troop for that brief respite; you were magnificent in all respects!

'There were to be many more patrols, many sodden nights, new locations and fresh incidents, stretching over a further two tours in Borneo but this period was the most stark and carries the greatest clarity over the years.'

Surgeon Lieutenant Evans and I flew in at first light and the casualties – Marines Findlay, Gardiner, Balderstone and Howes – were evacuated, after which the Doctor and I placed the body of Corporal Chappell in a body bag; rigor mortis had already set in and it was not an easy task, but, as I had already found at Pang Tebang, one with which Marines are particularly reluctant to become involved. For all the buildup it was still largely a Troop or Section Commander's war; Company Commanders disposed tasks and resources, after which they provided support, encouragement and, where necessary, helped to pick up the pieces.

A follow up by a Gurkha mortar platoon found blood trails but was abandoned by the Patrol Commander, who did not feel that his patrol was sufficiently strong to advance further into the Gunong.

Before deployment L Company had won the unit football league; Marine Balderstone, who had been shot in the leg, had been a key player; he was particularly incensed by the Chinese house-holder who had appeared briefly at the door with the IBT leader; he had been smiling, had somehow escaped the retaliatory fire and surprisingly was still around to be arrested and taken in for questioning at the police station.

Although K Company had ensured that the resident Company now had its own accommodation, it remained collocated at the police station. The Special Branch interrogator was a Chinese Inspector and a' reformed' leading Communist Terrorist from the earlier Malaya Emergency; he knew his business. The interrogation room was next to the room that I had occupied since the arrival of the CO and the unit's Tac HQ. He warned me that my night might be disturbed but there was nowhere else to doss down.

The Inspector was right; it was a comparatively sleepless night; the questioning was strong and the noise considerable, though there were no sounds of physical violence, nor indeed, on the following morning, were there any signs of injury; the process did, however, eliminate one or more links in the chain of IBT contacts.

The incident took place on 20 February, only two miles north of Lundu; the firing had been clearly audible at Company HQ. The move by IBT to the east of Gunong Gading came as a result of three weeks of sustained patrolling. Food denial had been the aim; in the end it succeeded and the system of communist contacts was broken. The IBT became fragmented and demoralised with survivors filtering back to the border. By the time Operation 'Dragons Teeth' had ended, Gurkha and Marine patrols with the aid of the local Dyaks had accounted for five killed, seven wounded and four captured. The captured included the platoon Commander, an Indonesian regular NCO named Kassan bin Somento. The remainder had been driven to the border.

As the pace slackened there had been lighter moments, for example the invitation of Colonel Ian and I to lunch with the Kapitan China of Serayan; a convivial occasion with the Kapitan beaming over his steam kettles and chatting amiably, while both parties wondered silently what the other really thought and how much the other knew. There was also the helicopter 'patrol' which Colonel Ian led to Turtle Island offshore; it was not the breeding season and there were no turtles but the beach and the sea air were a brief but welcome relief from the close atmosphere of Lundu; the visit also confirmed that the Island was not apparently being used by dissidents.

'Indian Chief'

Within a few days there were reports of lights at night and of tracks to the North of 6 Troop's post at Rasau (Lieutenant Paddy Ashdown) initiating a new operation codenamed 'Indian Chief'.

"The area consisted of much primary forest and was sparsely populated by Dyaks, the platoon of terrorists was therefore carrying its own army rations. Tracking was made easy by a veritable paper chase of discarded wrappings. After a report from a Border Scout patrol, a patrol led by Marine Vick followed the trail for twenty-four hours before being reinforced by tracker dog and the rest of the section under Corporal Bell. By nightfall on 5 March they were about two hours behind the enemy whose numbers were estimated at about forty. Reaching the main river [the Batan Kayang] next morning the patrol was welcomed by the debris of the enemy's breakfast floating downstream. They camped on the far bank. Patrols from the 1/6 Gurkhas, Mortar Troop and L Company were also moved into stop positions. Whilst Corporal Bell's patrol watched the crossing point a mixed Troop from 6 Troop and 1/6 Gurkhas crossed about a mile upstream and took up the chase. Corporal Fulton took the lead with his section for some hours, before being relieved by a Gurkha section…"

Paddy Ashdown – Lieutenant, OC 6 Troop

'…As dusk approached on the third day [6 March] our trackers told us that we were now very close to our enemy, who were within three hundred yards of our position. I discussed with the commander of the Gurkha contingent, Lieutenant Kakraprasad, whether we could risk a reconnaissance to locate exactly where the enemy were and what their dispositions were. We agreed that it was too big a risk to take. If we were discovered we would have to attack immediately and it would be too late in the day to do a proper follow-up.

'We agreed we would attack at dawn the following morning. All fires were forbidden as was any noise or talking, and we ordered the Marines and Gurkhas to eat cold rations and lie down were they were for the night. The following morning we were on the move as dawn broke. I was up near the front of the column, with a Gurkha section on point ahead of me, when a shot rang out. I discovered later that one of the enemy had come down to fill his water bottle at a stream which lay across our path and stumbled into our lead scout, who had no option but to shoot him. We would now have to go into a headlong attack in order to make good our surprise.

'I was just calling up my Marines when the Gurkhas, who weren't waiting for any one's orders, tore through in an uncoordinated attack on the enemy. Without waiting we all joined in and there followed a mad melee of shouting and shooting, as we all charged through the forest towards the enemy position. I immediately saw that our opposition had made no attempt to defend their position and had not followed the normal jungle procedure of 'standing to' at dawn. They were instead scattered all over the place. Some were washing, some cooking, some standing chatting and smoking in groups; one was squatting down behind a tree with his trousers around his ankles. This was very fortunate, because they were numerically stronger and, had they been better prepared, we would have a much tougher job of it.

'In the event, they mostly fled in disarray with only a handful putting up a fight. One of these fighters started to engage us with a machine gun, from behind a tree, thinking that he was safe. But he did not reckon with our very high velocity SLR 7.62 rifles, or even have time to be surprised when one of our Marines loosed a burst of fire at him and shot him clean through the tree that he thought was protecting him...'

> "Having been surprised the enemy left behind one ton of equipment, one casualty, a Browning automatic rifle, two Garrards, a Browning .45 pistol, an A 156 radio with hand generator and a marked map showing the intentions and positions in the 1st Division of Sarawak. The casualty was winched out of a gash in the jungle in failing light by the skill of Flight Lieutenant Alex Tarwil, 225 Squadron. The equipment followed next morning by the same method. Left without food or equipment in primary forest the enemy had little option but to withdraw in large and small groups to the border.
>
> "One was captured by locals, two more bumped a Gurkha patrol but the bulk walked into the sentries of a Gurkha bivouac alongside the patrol base at Rasau. Here L Company Headquarters had placed itself to be joined by Major Jimmy Liss, OC B Company, 1/6 Gurkhas during the operation. While quietly sipping tea the joint command's peace was rudely shattered by the sharp exchange of fire and collected most of the overs as the enemy was firing high...'
>
> "For the next few days a crop of equipment [and weapons] varying from a tommy gun to a two inch mortar, and a noisome collection of enemy bodies continued to appear in or near the neighbouring river; burial details in the Borneo heat were decidedly unpleasant as 6 Troop and the Mortar Troop discovered."

Tac HQ closed at Lundu and Operation 'Indian Chief' came to an end with a confirmed total of four IBT killed and two captured but the number of wounded or missing in the journey back to the border must have been considerable and will never be known.

Shortly after this operation a patrol of Recce Troop, led by the ubiquitous Sergeant Howe, while looking for contacts in the north Sempadi forest, surprised a group of three Chinese terrorists who were foolish enough to run on being challenged. Two were killed and one mortally wounded. A number of contacts were subsequently arrested, striking a further blow at the chain of supply.

Rukham

The subsequent lull was cut short when there was information of a further incursion, this time from the border in 4 Troop's area, near Biawak.

On 21 March reports reached Lundu of tracks in the forest near Kampong Rukham. Sergeant Howe's tracker team was flown in and was soon hot on the trail of a party of

40 IBT. The third incursion was under way. Following close, the tracker dog failed to point until too late and the enemy camp was bumped without warning. In the ensuing fire fight the enemy used light mortars. It lasted about an hour, during which the patrol became separated. Half under Corporal Harris reached the patrol base unscathed at about 2000 hrs. They were picked up by helicopter at first light and the first sweep quickly located Sergeant Howe and the rest of the patrol; one Iban tracker had a wound in the shoulder and Marine (S) Rendell had lost his 510 radio set.

With the patrol reunited a follow-up commenced, led by Lieutenant Peter Montgomery, with a mixed Troop from the Mortar and Recce Troops, and Second Lieutenant Christie-Miller with 5 Troop. Tracking proved difficult and the bulk of the enemy reached the Gunong Gading with our Troops in hot pursuit, only to be called off when L Company was relieved at Lundu by the 1/6th Gurkha Battalion. It transpired that the enemy suffered casualties in the exchange with Sergeant Howe's patrol and some had headed for home. The local Dyaks had also taken a hand and shot dead an IBT who invaded the sanctity of their basha. Among the debris recovered had been a Company Commander's pack – once again the contents included a marked map, as well as diaries – some compensation for the loss of Marine Rendell's radio.

On 25 March '64 L Company embarked in the minesweeper HMS *Puncheston* for the journey to Kuching, providing them with the first relaxation and fresh air that many had for two months.

Chapter 8

Consolidation

Kuching; Brigade Reserve, Padawan and a taste of 'Claret'

July '63 to April '64

Consolidation

Kuching

> "The time 1000 hrs, 8 January 1964; the place Kuport, Kuching, Sarawak; LST *Frederick Clover* swings her stern out into the stream and with a single bow line holding her into the wharf, begins to turn, slowly at first and then with gathering momentum. The stern moves dangerously close to the little Kampong on the opposite bank but the Pilot, well versed now in the art of manoeuvring these ungainly craft, holds her to the swing until the moment comes to let go for'rard and we are once more heading for the open sea..."

The description of the departure of 3 Commando Brigade Signal Squadron for Singapore heralded the relief of the final elements of Brigade Headquarters by HQ 99 Gurkha Brigade under Brigadier 'Pat' Patterson, who became Commander of West Brigade and of operations in the first three Divisions of Sarawak.

Derek Oakley – G3 Int

'My two and a half years in Brigade Headquarters had been due to finish in October '63, but news came through from the UK that my relief, Mickey Roche-Kelly, would be delayed. Although I was given no reason at the time, it was presumably because there was not another Army Staff Intelligence course for him until October, which meant he wouldn't arrive in Singapore till Christmas. This was what was called 'the exigencies of the service'. It was something of a shock both to me and to Pam as I had been hoping to be home with the family and spending Christmas with them. There appeared to be nothing I could do about it despite some protestations. I'm sure Pam, sitting in Clacton with a horde of children did not take kindly to the news. As for me the novelty of Sarawak and the jungle was wearing off as I had seen so many other people repatriated. In the end I volunteered to stay in Sarawak thus relieving anyone else of coming over and being away from their families too.

'It therefore befell me to have a second successive Christmas in Kuching, but it was made palatable by being with a large number of friends. As with the previous year it was a wonderful Christmas, plenty of food and drink, a quiet existence as 'confrontation' as it was called, was at a bit of a stalemate. There were plenty of invitations out and I spent Christmas Day with Dick and Dorothy Morris in between being duty Ops Room officer.

'I cannot recall when Mickey arrived in Singapore but he certainly didn't come over to Sarawak. He was probably settling his family into accommodation in Singapore, a pleasure I had not had three years earlier. However the New Year celebrations went on until I left Kuching by RAF Argosy on 8 January. There was no shortage of parties, one memorable one being at the home of Roy Henry, then Head of Special Branch and later to become Commissioner of Police in Fiji.

'I started my turnover to Mickey on the 9th and he flew over to Sarawak on the 13th [as the liaison officer in Kuching] leaving me to do lots of shopping, drink crates of Tiger and Anchor, say goodbye to many, many friends culminating in leaving by air for UK on 21 January, reckoning that with my fortieth birthday only two years away, I would never see my beloved Far East again. How wrong I was! I arrived in UK the following day just a week before Pam's birthday. Even my flight home was not without incident as we were diverted because of fog to Manchester airport, but after a couple of hours on the ground flew down to Stanstead where my father was waiting. We had a family reunion in Holland-on-Sea that evening where the seven of us were together for the first time in many, many months.'

Semengo

On arrival from Lundu towards the end of March, L Company spent a fortnight with Commando HQ in Semengo Camp. With the 5th Malay Regiment deployed in Serian District and 1/6th Gurkhas in Lundu District, 42 Commando was now consolidated, with companies forward in Bau and Padawan and a company as Brigade Reserve at Semengo. It goes without saying that we were hospitably received but we were also an eyesore – we were 'jungly'. Clothes that have been repeatedly washed by local methods, spread on rocks in a running stream and pummelled by willing hands with stones and minimum soap, are less than clean, unpressed and quickly threadbare; above all they smell, a fact to which any wife who greeted her returning spouse in Singapore would readily testify; if you had a dog it would not recognise you. We were, in short, a Regimental Sergeant Major's nightmare. A rifle company on active service located in 'barracks' is in any case a contradiction; it was therefore with mutual respect but relief that two weeks after our arrival we exchanged locations with M Company at Padawan.

Among M Company's subalterns was Ian Uzzell, back in the Far East after completing his officer training, while retaining his enthusiasm for all things that flew…

Ian Uzzell, Acting Lieutenant – OC 9 Troop

'I joined 42 Commando in April 1964. I was posted to M Company (Captain Hugh Poyntz) and was given command of 9 Troop with Colour Sergeant Pothecary as my Troop Sergeant. The unit was already deployed in Sarawak and was based at Semengo

Camp, close to Kuching Airport. All new arrivals to the unit had to do a jungle acclimatisation course which was run by the Recce Troop Commander, Lieutenant Peter Montgomery. During one training session he was asked about snakes. He replied that we would never see a snake in the jungle. I did not want to contradict him in front of the course, but I had seen a good number on my previous visits to Borneo, and in Malaya. As he was telling us this I noticed two of his team hammering at something with their shovels. They bought the subject of their attention to us – it was a large, fat, very poisonous pit viper. Peter looked at it, turned to us and said "You *seldom* see a snake in the jungle". I was happy with that statement.

'Life in Semengo camp was very different to my previous tour. We spent time training and working with RAF Whirlwind 10 and Belvedere helicopters. We were introduced to 'tree descending gear'. This is a harness with 200 feet of nylon tape designed for use by parachutists who land in the canopy of the jungle and use the gear to get themselves down from the trees. In our case its use was for getting us into small clearings from a hovering helicopter. It was great fun but I am left with a scar on my left hip from the rope burn I received from descending too fast. Because the pilots knew of my desire to become a helicopter pilot I became a fair target. They would climb as I descended on the tape so that as I reached the bottom I would still be thirty feet above the ground, and they would proceed to dunk me into the tops of trees. I also had a chance to practice 'wet dinghy drills' in Bau Lake, the location of K Company (Major Alex Higson).

'On this occasion as I got myself into the strop at the end of the winch I was towed round the lake at thirty knots trying unsuccessfully to water ski with bare feet. On days that were not busy I could occasionally get a flight to various company locations, and managed to do a recce in an Auster. I also flew on an air resupply mission in a Hastings, escorted by Javelin aircraft; I lay on the floor looking out of the open doorway, to see how it worked from the airborne end.

'We had both an Officers' and Sergeants' Mess, and even a thirty metre rifle range. On Sundays we would invite guests to a curry lunch in the Mess. Following the lunch we would relax outside with a view over the jungle towards the thirty metre range. Visitors would often tell us that they could hear the sound of bagpipes coming from the jungle. All 42 Commando Officers would look puzzled and state that they could not hear anything other than normal jungle noises. It was, of course, 42 Commando Pipe band rehearsing in the area of the range.

Pangkalan Amo

'My Troop was despatched by Belvedere helicopter to Pangkalan Amo which had been attacked by insurgents from Indonesia. We had to set up a defensive perimeter and operate a patrolling programme. We arrived and set about clearing an area around the village and erecting defensive measures such as panjis – sharpened bamboo stakes.

Having set it all up I decided to check our field of vision at night by putting everyone in their stand to positions and sending up a few para-illuminating flares. We moved to our positions in the dark and a voice behind me said "Where are you, sir?" As he said that I felt a sharp pain in my back and yelped as his bayonet stuck into me. The voice continued, "Oh, there you are!" Another member of the Troop reported hearing suspicious noises in front of us. I put up a flare and we all watched as a group of ducks waddled past our position. The rest of the 'stand to' was uneventful and our arcs and fields of fire were proved to be sufficient.

'A couple of days later we were informed that some of the Indonesians, who had just arrived in the village with rubber from over the border, were in the group that had attacked the village several days earlier. We searched their packs of rubber and found that they were smuggling over 2,000 vials of penicillin inside. We arrested them and they were sent to Commando Headquarters for further investigation.

'After a period of uneventful patrolling I was informed that we would be relieved by a platoon of Gurkhas. I asked if I could remain behind for a few days to familiarise them with the area and was given permission to do so. I stated that I had plenty of rice and if they could assist me with ration pack meat I could cater for myself over the few days. We cooked in a communal area and I could see admiration in the eyes of the Gurkhas as I put two of my ration pack packets of curry into my meat. What I had not realised was that they had given me curried mutton. My first mouthful made me realise my mistake, but as I had prepared it in full view of the Gurkhas I had to eat it. It was three months before I ate another curry.

'I was later asked to lead an ambush patrol into an area and act as a diversion by making my patrol's presence known whilst the ambush patrol moved into their designated position in secrecy. We made a point of visiting a nearby village before moving on to our night time stopover close to the border. We moved in silently and set up our sleeping areas and sentry posts. No one spoke; everything was done by hand signals. At about midnight we were woken by a shout of "I signed for it! I signed for it!" It was one of the members of my Troop having a nightmare. We woke him and silenced him but we never found out what it was that he had signed for. We returned to Semengo camp on the following day – which was my twenty-first Birthday. I was invited to the Sergeants' Mess for a celebration drink but made the mistake of wearing my 40 Commando tie in a 42 Commando mess. It was ceremoniously cut in half.

'One sight that I will always remember from my time at Semengo camp was the thousands of fruit bats flying to their feeding grounds shortly before dusk. The sky was full of them from horizon to horizon.

'Our tour came to an end in June and shortly before we left for Singapore I was informed that I would be returning home early from 42 Commando in order to take a flying aptitude test and subsequently undergo helicopter pilot training.'

Padawan

The area that elements of M Company had occupied since January had proved to be somewhat of a backwater in operational terms, though their patrols had been as physically demanding as any in the unit. Known to local expatriates as 'Little Switzerland', in the Borneo heat Marines had dubbed it 'Buchenwald'. The area was a narrow extension of Kuching District, stretching to the border; it was reached by road and track as far as the river that borders the agricultural settlement of Padawan, where stores were unloaded and humped across a narrow footbridge.

The founder of the settlement and of its associated mission school was Archdeacon Howes, who retained a hut in the enclave and was a periodic visitor. He kept himself mostly to himself on his visits but was very willing to talk about the local tribes. The difficulties of movement in the jumble of steep hills and rivers had left this comparatively small area with a number of differing dialects and customs – for one group rats were a delicacy to be savoured.

It was not country that would support any substantial incursion but might provide a safe route for courier or a sanctuary for fugitive or small party. There was one border post, Sapit; a winding fortress, on differing levels and on a ridge overlooking the border; it was taken over initially by 6 Troop. The rest of the Company effort was directed towards providing an internal presence in a diverse area that included a number of Kampongs populated by people of Javanese descent and grouped around the precipitous Gunong Baang – not an easy task…

> "The steepness of the country made all patrols a test of endurance and the scramble course would be viewed in comparison as a cross country stroll. A rate of advance of 100 yards in one hour was not uncommon."

Maybe this aspect of Padawan had influenced the decision to use the location for the introductory jungle courses, run from time to time by Lieutenant Peter Montgomery of Recce Troop. It was to become the initial training ground for Second Lieutenant Martin Read, who joined 42 Commando in mid-March; on arrival he found the unit with a full quota of officers and was posted to L Company, where he joined 6 Troop at the border; he was on a learning curve that would end in Sabah.

April '64 also saw the introduction of plans for cross-border operations under the codename 'Claret', already referred to by Keith Wilkins with K Company at Bau. Contemporary with the unsuccessful bid to take out an anti-aircraft gun, had been other bids based on intelligence gained. A bid to ambush a track across the border from Stass, where 6 Troop had previously served, was successful. Towards mid-May the Troop was relieved at Sapit by 5 Troop (Second Lieutenant Duncan Christie-Miller) and went into training. The ploy hatched at Padawan was to be launched from 6 Troop's old base at Stass…

Martin Read, Second Lieutenant – 6 Troop

A Drop of 'Claret'

'I was fortunate to be selected as part of the unit's very first cross-border operation, which was undertaken in great secrecy. The plan was to set up an ambush along a track, running between two villages and was thought to be used regularly by Indonesian soldiers. Our approach was through difficult secondary jungle; however, we identified the track and finally settled on an ambush location – albeit far from ideal…'

The Patrol Commander, Lieutenant Paddy Ashdown, had been looking for a position with a clear field of fire, sited some eighty to 100 yards from the track and preferably on raised ground, in order to hinder any attempt at counter attack. The vegetation and in particular the long grass denied him any such option. He had therefore settled for a straight stretch of track which allowed some field of fire.

'Half the Troop would man the ambush one day, with the other half protecting the exit route and camp. We were prepared to maintain the ambush for up to two weeks.

'There was considerable inter-village traffic, but no army personnel. The ambush lasted in the end only six days as, in spite of our very best endeavours, our cover was blown by a small village girl and her dog! The dog approached a member of our main killing group wagging its tail and was followed by the girl. We withdrew immediately, but the principle had been established.'

There were to be many more such patrols, some successful, some abortive and some much larger, but for the time being 42 Commando was at the end of its current tour in Sarawak…

Final Score

> "Last blood went to K Company, when a patrol from 1 Troop led by Corporal Edwards apprehended an IBT in plain clothes near the patrol base at Bukit Knuckle. On the next day 42 Commando handed over to 1st Greenjackets and embarked for Singapore in the now veteran troopship MV *Auby*.
>
> "The innings was over and there to see us off was Brigadier Patterson, Commander 99 Brigade. It was the second time we had served under his dynamic command, as many Brunei veterans will appreciate. We were also treated to a fly past by Squadron Leader Trevor Price and 225 Squadron with whom we had worked and lived so closely…"

The departure of 42 Commando in early June '64 left Pat Gardner on the staff at Labuan, but otherwise, for the first time since the Brunei insurrection in December '62 – eighteen months before – there were no Royal Marines units or sub-units on Brunei/ Borneo territory. The respite lasted about six weeks.

6 Troop, 42 Commando at their patrol base in Sapit before being withdrawn for the first 'Claret' operation. The bottom photograph shows Lieutenant 'Paddy' Ashdown (right).

Chapter 9

East to Sabah

Kalabakan, Tawau and the Serudong

July ’64 to May ’65

East to Sabah

East Brigade

When 40 Commando returned to Borneo in July '64, it was to Sabah and under the command of the Malaysian 5th Federal Infantry Brigade (East Brigade); with the Commando went 79 (Kirkee) Commando Light Battery RA; opposite them on the neighbouring Indonesian islands and visible to their OPs and patrol craft were elements of the Korps Kommando, the Indonesian Marines, 'erstwhile guests' of the Corps in less belligerent times.

40 Commando

The Commando's correspondent described the task and area from East to West...

> "The operation is much more amphibious in nature than have been the unit's previous tours, because of the vast river complex lying to the west of Tawau. The border cuts Sebatik Island across the middle, parallel to and four degrees north of the equator and then crosses open water north of enemy held Nunuken Island, before travelling mid-stream up the river Trusan Tamba, then south of the river Serudong and so on westward out of the unit's area of responsibility."

Dick Sidwell, Captain – Adjutant

'In June 1964 I joined 40 Commando in Burma Camp at Ulu Tiram in South East Johore. Lieutenant Colonel John Parsons was the CO and Major Cliff Bye was the Second-in-Command; I was appointed Adjutant.

'In mid-July the unit moved to Sabah to relieve 1/10th Gurkhas who were based at Kalabakan near the port of Tawau. When the CO called on Brigadier Ibrahim bin Ismail of East Brigade in Tawau, he was aware that the Brigadier was a Malaysian but was somewhat surprised to find that the Brigadier had been one of his students nine years earlier, while Colonel John was on the Directing Staff at the Staff College at Camberley.

'The Brigade Major was a British officer and anything connected with cross-border operations had to be channelled through him as the Malaysian Government could not give approval for any such operations and the Brigadier should know nothing about them.

'Kalabakan was the centre for the logging industry where the logs were delivered by trucks and were tipped into the river. At the riverside the logs were made into rafts and floated down the river to the shipping, almost entirely Japanese, lying off Tawau. The Indonesians had recently attacked Kalabakan…'

The attack, which had been at the end of December '63 on a Malaysian infantry company headquarters, had shown their current ineptitude and had caused considerable casualties, leading to the arrival of 1/10th Gurkhas. A large scale combined operation had been mounted to trap the assailants and by the end of March '64, ninety-six out of the original raiding party of 128 had been killed or captured, including twenty-one Indonesian Marines and two of their leaders. The bulk of the remainder were understood to have struggled back across the border but a few were known to be still at large.

'…Soon after arrival the Commando HQ moved into newly constructed wooden buildings above the river at Kalabakan and we were accommodated in relative luxury. In October Lieutenant Colonel Parsons handed over command to Lieutenant Colonel John Taplin and as Adjutant I often accompanied the new CO during his visits by Malaysian Army 'Alouette' helicopter to forward locations. One of these was the Tawau Assault Group…'

Tawau Assault Group

> "The Tawau Assault Group [TAG] consists of elements of 40 Commando under the command of Captain C G Bellamy. The Royal Navy, the Royal Malaysian Navy and the police manned an assortment of boats which include the air-conditioned luxury yacht *Petrel* – flagship of SATAG of course – several minesweepers, local police launches and the occasional frigate. This Group patrols the intricate and not very accurately mapped, crisscross system of rivers and swamps. The police launch, which is usually placed a few yards on the friendly side of the border, is the frequent target of Indonesian machine guns set up on Nunukin [sic] Island, south of Sebatik. Through field glasses the enemy on Nunukin can be clearly seen going about their daily training and return fire from the police launch on one occasion was seen to cause a certain amount of consternation. For political reasons this firing was purely in self defence."

The three companies were rotated between Operational HQ at Kalabakan, forward patrol bases on the Serudong River and the tented camp of the Administrative HQ at Bombalai, where the 'resting' company formed a brigade reserve. For foot patrols on the river line, the going was compared unfavourably with the average for Sarawak, 1,000 yards an hour being quoted as a norm. Bombalai appears to have had its drawbacks as a rest place from more arduous patrolling; kills recorded included '173 rats, fifteen snakes (including several cobras), thirty-eight scorpions and several large hairy spiders.'

A 'Raging Silence'

More important enemy contacts were limited to scraps of information, otherwise there existed what the locally produced newspaper described as a 'raging silence'. One such 'sniff' alerted B Company (Captain Jasper Bacon) to the existence of a basha camp in his area of jungle…

> "At dawn the following day a section under Sergeant Costley was sent to the area and after a long trek, which included the crossing of a deep river gorge by a single high tree trunk made slippery by the morning rain and of the hacking of a way through supposedly impenetrable jungle with parangs, they approached the camp.
>
> "Before the section could close in for the capture, one of the Indonesians, who had been doing his dhoby in a nearby stream, gave the alarm and bolted for the jungle but was shot before he got very far. His friend or friends also made a break for the jungle and managed to evade capture but the hunt continues. The body of the shot man was recovered, together with weapons, clothing which included Indonesian uniforms and other equipment."

Elsewhere a party from 'C' Company, led by Lieutenant Andrew Keelan, was seeking excitement by climbing Mount Kinabalu, Borneo's highest mountain, while in December there was finally an opportunity to break the 'raging silence' and take the action to the enemy…

R A M Seeger, Lieutenant – OC 6 Troop

'In late summer 1964 I was drafted to 40 Commando (based at Ulu Tiram near Johore Bahru) for a two-year accompanied overseas tour. In fact I was already in the Far East on a home service tour with 1 SBS. This anomaly had been caused earlier in the year by my section being suddenly and secretly moved from Poole to Singapore to work there with 2 SBS, the resident Singapore based section.

Raid on Sebatik

'I was lucky enough to take part in a cross-border action against the Indonesians on the night of 8 December 1964. It must have been one of the first offensive cross-border operations undertaken and was certainly 40 Commando's first. Up till then we had been limited to reconnaissance only.

'At this time I commanded 6 Troop in B company which was operating along the Serudong River. Commando HQ was at Kalabakan some miles inland from the coastal logging town of Tawau. The task we were given was to attack an Indonesian Observation Post on Sebatik Island.

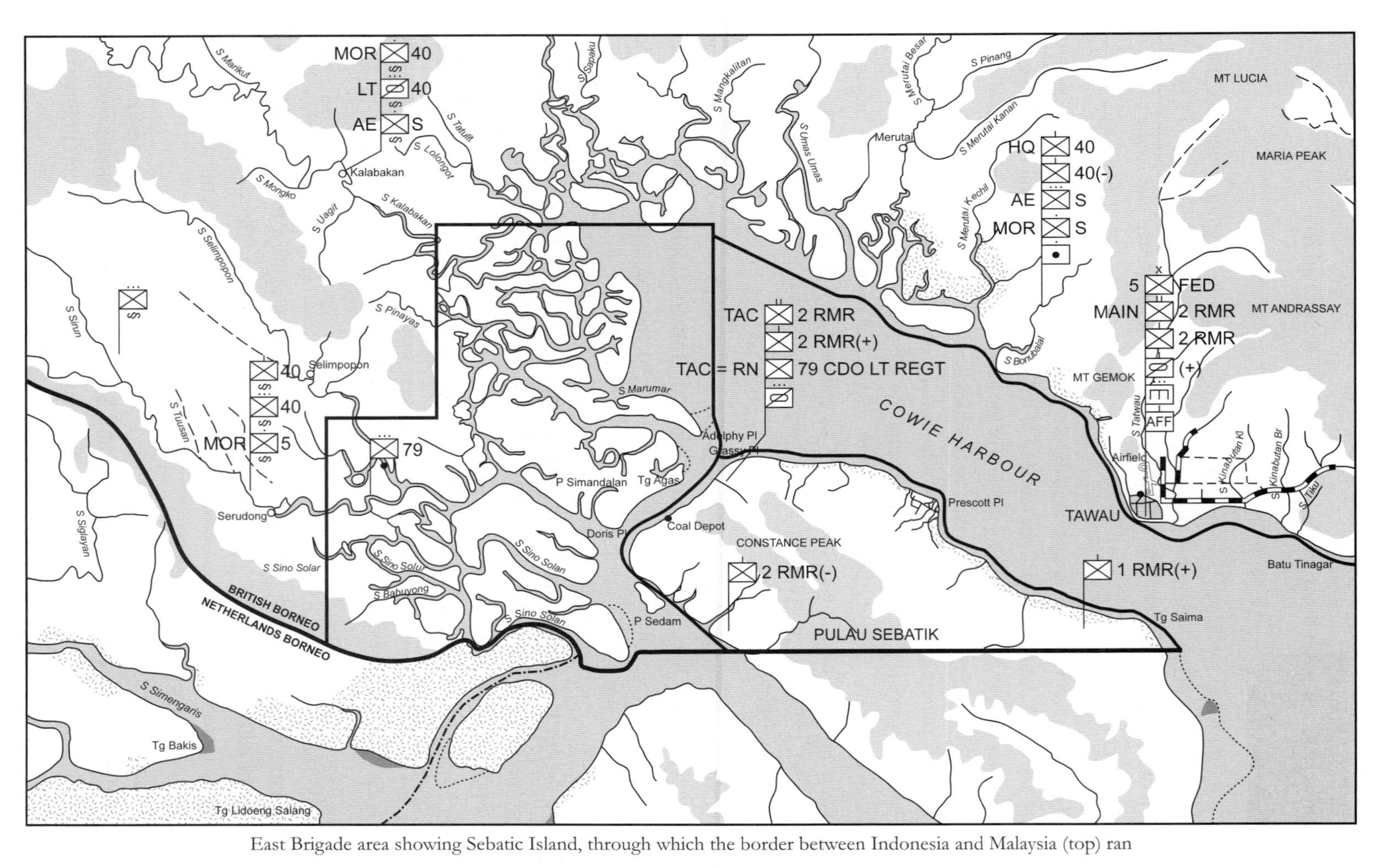

East Brigade area showing Sebatic Island, through which the border between Indonesia and Malaysia (top) ran

'Sebatik Island runs North West/South East and lies south of Tawau. It is in the middle of a large bay and is split diagonally by the border which runs West/East from the mouth of the Serudong River to the open sea. South of Sebatik Island is Nanukan Island. At the time of the raid this had a large Indonesian Marine base on it.

'The OP was 500 yards over the border by the mouth of a river. It was manned by some four to six Marines from Nanukan [sic]. They were quite open in their activity and lived in an atap hut at the back of a small beach. Resupply and roulement were by small boat. There were no obvious defensive measures like earth works, wire or trenches but the jungle and mangrove reached down to the water's edge on both sides. To the west it was less dense and a narrow sandy strip only thinly covered by trees and scrub ran for about seventy-five yards before petering out into thick vegetation. This offered an alternative landing point from the sea and an indirect approach to the position.

'Counter observation on the OP was maintained by a Security Forces patrol boat permanently anchored midway between the island and the mouth of the Serudong. Earlier in the year too, 1 SBS RM had carried out a clandestine reconnaissance of the position. Two men had swum into the shore from an assault boat and crawled up to the edge of the hut. The choice of the OP as an objective under the new operational policy therefore was a natural one. The task was given to 'B' Company and the Company Commander – Captain Bacon, directed me to select a fifteen man raiding party from my Troop. 'I made my selection and immediately began an intensive programme of inflatable handling and close quarter shooting. The pretext for this departure from normal jungle patrolling was viewed with some scepticism by my Marines. It was clear that something untoward was in the offing. The training took place mainly in the

This was the Sebatic Island target.
40 Commando's raid landed on the beach (left) and approached the target (right).

Royal Marines on a typical river patrol in Sabah

Commando HQ location at Kalabakan but a rehearsal sortie by inflatable boat was run from the company base on the Serudong River.

'The attack plan was a simple one. A parent craft would be provided by the Tawau Assault Group – a water borne river and sea patrol force drawn from Support Company. The craft would be the Group's floating HQ (or flag ship) – a medium sized patrol boat. It would simulate a routine move from Kalabakan to Tawau and under cover of darkness launch 3 inflatable Geminis at the North West tip of Sebatik Island. The inflatables would then paddle round the edge of the island and along the shoreline to the border. One inflatable would wait here as emergency support. The other two would move forward into Indonesian waters and beach at the end of the sandy strip. Once ashore the patrol would close silently onto the hut and kill any enemy found there.

'If they were fired at while still approaching the landing point they would abort the raid and return under outboard engine power to the parent craft. Once the boats were beached however, any enemy reaction would be counter-attacked and fought through to a finish. The support inflatable would start its engine as soon as the shooting started and could, if signalled, reach the enemy position within minutes.

'The cover for the raid was the inevitable one – a water borne border patrol, broken down engines and an accidental drift onto the enemy beach.

'The parent craft left Kalabakan late afternoon on the night of the raid. On board were members of the Tawau Assault Group (commanded by Lieutenant Woodham), the unit doctor and a medical assistant. With the support Gemini were Captain Bacon – as the overall operational commander, a signaller for communication to Commando HQ and the parent craft, a coxswain, a GPMG team and several riflemen. With the assault Geminis were myself, my Troop Sergeant – Sergeant Costley, and the other thirteen picked Marines from 6 Troop. These included Marine Allen with the GPMG, a close quarter assault group with SMGs under Corporal Tomlin, and a stand-off/cut-off group of two riflemen – two of the Troop's leading scouts who were both good rifle shots. Torches had been fixed to their SLRs as a simple night vision device for accurate shooting. As the leading man on the approach, I carried a number of M26 grenades.

'The three inflatables reached the border without incident. There were whispered goodbyes and good lucks and the craft separated. After watching the assault Geminis disappear into the darkness, Captain Bacon checked the readiness of his support craft and then settled down to wait for the planned H-hour. To his surprise and alarm, shooting began long before this – within about fifteen minutes of the assault boats' departure.

'I had beached my boats at the planned beaching point and was part way along the sandy strip when an automatic weapon suddenly opened up on my half left. It fired high and the rounds passed harmlessly over the heads of the patrol. For the moment there was stunned silence and then the patrol returned fire. I shouted out directions to spread out left and assault forward. Sergeant Costley and Marine Allen moved up from the rear to give supporting fire from the right flank. At this point I stumbled and fell. I later found that a bullet had gone through the flesh of my elbow but whether my fall was caused by the shock of this or a mangrove root I could not say. In the dark proximity of the action it would just as easily have come from our own fire as the enemy's. I moved forward across several patches of open ground. Fire was still being exchanged and although it was night I experienced sensations of colour and brightness and a curious feeling of treading air. Suddenly the shape of the hut loomed into view. I stopped and crouched in the cover of some trees. I gave a warning shout of "Grenades" and threw two M26s at the front of the house. Sergeant Costley and Marine Allen, who had been moving parallel with me on the flank and were now thigh deep in water, heard the shout and took the only cover open to them. They submerged under water with their weapons held aloft. Even then some of the extreme pieces of grenade fragmentation hit their bodies.

'Marine Allen opened with his GPMG as I followed up my grenades. I walked forward firing my SMG, changing my magazines rapidly so a continual stream of 9mm preceded me to the front of the hut and its immediate surrounds. There was a camp fire burning and the flames of this lit the darkness and enabled Allen to fire specifically at moving enemy. The remainder of the patrol had been held up by the narrow approach and surrounding vegetation. Now, with a sudden rush, they caught me up and fanned out across the beach. Two enemy dead were sprawled out near the fire hit by grenade, SMG or GPMG. Another body was spotted by the hut. A fourth man had been seen stumbling, possibly hit, into the outer darkness. There was not the time to search for bodies or examine injuries. Following shouted orders to return to the boats, the patrol retraced their steps at speed. They scrambled into the inflatables, pushed out to sea and started the motors. As they drove clear, defensive mortar fire from Nanukan began to fall on the OP. Captain Bacon greeted the two boats with relief and then led the last leg back to the parent craft.

'The return voyage to Kalabakan was a relaxed and carefree one as the raiders celebrated success with cans of Tiger. The medical team cheated of major injuries of interest seized upon Seeger's elbow and made what they could of this. Next day, as a culminating touch, the GOC – General Hunt – visited the Commando and talked to the patrol. As a result of the operation, I was given an MC and Sergeant Costley and Corporal Tomlin an MID.'

Shortly after this raid 40 Commando was relieved by 42 Commando who arrived in *Bulwark*; the change-over was completed by helicopter direct from the ship to locations, the unit planning for which is the responsibility of the SOO. Major Bill Mansell, who had joined 42 Commando in mid-1964 as SOO, was a 'batch mate' and had on several occasions cheerfully told me of his intention to take over L Company. Just before the Company left Padawan in June, I had been sent to Cibu in the Philippines to witness a US Navy amphibious exercise; when I returned Bill Mansell was commanding L Company and I was SOO. There were some delays to schedules during the Commando's change-over but these were due to unserviceability of aircraft; deployment was completed on 14 December and 40 Commando was home for Christmas.

42 Commando

The initial deployment saw forward HQ and L Company (Major Bill Mansell) at Kalabakan, K Company (Major Alex Higson) and rear HQ at Bombalai, and M Company (Captain Hugh Poyntz) on the Serudong river line. Sections from Mortars were deployed at Kalabakan and on the river line. The unit contribution to TAG was provided by Support Company HQ (Captain Nigel Martin) with Recce and Anti-tank Troops. As with 40 Commando, the rifle companies were rotated at intervals of about six weeks.

Despite the increased involvement of the Indonesian Army (TNI) and the substantial build up elsewhere along both sides of the Sarawak/Kalimantan border, the relieving unit was to have perhaps less contacts in Sabah than had its predecessor. Notwithstanding, the political and physical geography of the area was unlike any other in Borneo and continued to demand more than usual versatility from the resident unit. There were also some new initiatives.

Kalabakan

Serving the work face of the Wallace Bay Company's logging operation, Kalabakan had a jetty on the river and a dirt track road through the forest to the logging area; there was an accommodation camp at the twelve mile mark and a local Kampong named Brantian. The occupants of the camp were largely Indonesian and a potential problem, whereas the dwellers in the Kampong were indigenous and the subject of a 'hearts and minds' campaign that included regular surgeries provided by the unit's Medical Officer.

The HQ defended camp was sited on the edge of the town, on the side of a hill and some 300 feet above the river. There were four scout cars on inventory and a handful of unit vehicles had been brought up by river, which also provided the main supply route. Scout cars were not new to Commando units but were notoriously temperamental to maintain; they were used for night patrol of the logging track. The work load for vehicle mechanics was testing; in addition to the scout cars and unit vehicles, there were outboard engines, charging engines and water pumps to keep serviceable.

The company at Kalabakan provided patrols, guards and manned one outstation at the so-called 'Neck' position on the river approach. The area west of Kalabakan had been cleared of population and among the initial patrol tasks had been that of putting up marker balloons to aid in artillery registration, no easy task given the paucity of information on the local maps…

> "They became adept at putting them up but were not so good at placing them in the right place. Even if the balloon was in the wrong place, at least the gunners were able to give it an exact 'fix' for the patrol… Only the major rivers are marked, there are no contours and so no hill features are shown and only the grid lines are accurate. On one occasion a shoot had to be cancelled because some of the local Murut hunters had neglected the curfew regulations and had strayed into the target area. When they returned the local police Corporal gave them one of the fiercest 'rockets' ever and the threat of two years' imprisonment and a $2,000 fine next time…"

At the end of January '65, Lieutenant Colonel Peter Whiteley relieved Lieutenant Colonel Ian Gourlay, who, along with his SOO had come to the end of his overseas tour.

Serudong

Initially the company on the river line was deployed to three bases one of which contained Company HQ and a section of Mortar Troop. Later, in order to reduce the number tied up in guarding and maintaining patrol bases, one base was shut down and demolished.

In addition to other patrols there were those providing protection for detachments from a Para Engineer Squadron who were constructing Landing sites in selected locations to the west of Kalabakan, including the area of forest known as 'The Gap'.

To provide additional support a single 105mm gun from 145 Battery was deployed to Serudong Laut, which housed Company HQ, a Mortar section and a Rifle Troop. Spotting the fall of shot in primary jungle is impracticable without a spotter aircraft but, with practice and some coaching from the gunners, we are told that patrol leaders claimed surprisingly accurate results in providing estimates from their own primitive sound ranging equipment – by ear.

Following standard practice each patrol base was fortified and during the hours of darkness protected against surprise by trip flares and 'Claymore' mines that had to be set before dusk and made safe shortly after dawn. As we saw in the case of Corporal Murphy at Serikin in 1963, this delicate task had its risks and was normally undertaken by a practiced NCO; at 6 Troop the devices were controlled by electric circuit that was to be disconnected at dawn before any movement took place…

> "At dawn Stand-to on Thursday 11 February; while disarming a Claymore mine set up as a booby trap in Troop location deep in the Sabah jungle, Sergeant Peter Davidson accidentally set off the mine and was killed…"

Sergeant Davidson left a widow and two small girls.

*

In April, towards the end of the tour in Sabah, it was K Company's turn to be on the river line and they claimed that the last fortnight was the most interesting of the whole period…

'Everyone was looking forward to getting back to Singapore and the wives, families and creature comforts which are synonymous with the Island but interest was turned towards the South, where there seemed to be an increase of Indonesian activity. The first force to leave Serudong Laut to combat this [incursion] included 1, 3 and Recce Troops, with some of Company HQ and 145 Battery.'

Sergeant Edwards later wrote in the Corps Journal of the sequel…

'…We were in K Company location in Serudong Laut. I had just finished getting my briefing from the Company Commander, Captain Peter Montgomery. After four months of slogging and patrolling with little to show for it, I didn't feel very optimistic of our chances this time.

'Three days later we arrived on the river and were intent on reorganising ourselves when a sentry reported a knocking sound to the south. I was just about to tell him that, if we were in the middle of Piccadilly Circus and he reported hearing a bus…

"Let's take a look anyway. You never know", said Second Lieutenant Tucker and off we went with Marine Harding, the Iban scouts (Rum and Baccy) and Corporal Robert's section. The knocking became steadily louder. It was definitely on the river and it gradually became clear that it was somebody chopping.

'*Better go steady*, I thought, slipping the safety catch off, butt into the shoulder. *Stop, listen, advance*. The leading Iban scout pointed to enemy footprints of five men only two hours old, and at the same time the noise of shouting and laughing and the sound of a radio could be heard. *A catchy tune, sounds like the Beatles*, I thought. At my signal for all-round defence the GPMG moved to cover the opposite bank, riflemen melted into cover with not a sound save that of the Beatles… As we camouflaged out, my mind went back to Lympstone and crawling round Woodbury Common, Who would have thought then that we would now be in this position?

'I checked Harding over silently; he nodded and away we crawled through six inches of mud as the tide was out. We edged along trying desperately to keep the muzzles out of it. Every sound seemed multiplied tenfold. The scratch of equipment, the clink of a rifle sling seemed to carry for miles and our belaboured breathing somewhat like a Hoover working on a carpet. The knocking was louder now, or was it my knees?

'*Must get closer; can't see much at the moment*, I thought. There was a lump swelling in my throat, it must have been my heart; anyway I swallowed it. Captain Montgomery was right, in front of me was a platoon or so of the enemy loafing around the river washing off their leopard type shirts and hanging them up to dry, their packs and rifles stacked on the bank.

'We watched silently for ten minutes before going to fetch Second Lieutenant Tucker. As we photographed them the shutter sounded like a dustbin lid being dropped. I lined up my twelve bore shogun on a big, fat soldier who I took to be a Sergeant Major, but this was only in fun as we were a recce patrol. We had to get back with the information as soon as possible. One of them dived into the river and swam towards us; it was absolutely imperative that we got back with the news soonest. Who said anything about running?'

Sergeant Edwards' account stops there; though there is some disparity as to whether this was the second or third day of the patrol, either then or in a later follow up, surprise was lost…

'On the second day of the patrol 1 Troop met an apparently large enemy patrol face-to-face. After an Iban leading scout had shot his opposite number, the enemy went full astern with their wounded man and despite a spirited charge by Sergeant Edwards and his men no further contact was made. This excitement rounded off an otherwise eventless tour.'

For his initiative, coolness and professional skill, Sergeant Edwards was mentioned in despatches.

Bombalai

The tented camp, ten miles from the logging port of Tawau continued to house the rear HQ; under the command of the Second-in-Command (Major John Owen), the location included 'B' Echelon under the Quartermaster (Captain Norman Thackeray) and a resident rifle company in rotation.

The area featured a factory and the offices of Borneo Abaca Ltd (BAL) under the auspices of the Commonwealth Development Corporation; it ran five local agricultural estates growing Abaca (hemp – from which rope is made), Cocoa, Rubber and Oil Palm; there was also some logging for clearance and replanting. Much of the labour, as at Kalabakan, was of Indonesian extraction, while the fringes of the estates contained camps housing both Chinese and Indonesian squatters. It was therefore comparatively easy for infiltrators or fugitives to disappear into the community and some of the raiders from the attack on Kalabakan were still believed to be at large.

The resident rifle company was primarily concerned with this internal security issue and the Company Commander was the military member of a local security committee that included civil, police and special branch representatives. On the day after their arrival, K Company, alerted and guided by a local manager, were able to arrest two fugitive IBT – a rare opportunity that was not to be repeated for some months.

During this first occupancy, each Troop in turn was flown by helicopter to one of the landing sites that were being constructed in the Gap and from which they carried out a patrol in this deserted area…

> "Step from the landing site into the cathedral-like atmosphere of virgin jungle; 200 feet overhead the treetop canopy cuts out much of the light and there is little undergrowth. Unfortunately the area is also mountainous so, though there is little obstruction from vegetation, the terrain is heartbreaking and boot wrecking. Here in the Gap is the really worthwhile patrolling – right up to the border."

Wallace Bay and the Waterways.

The Tawau Assault Group (TAG) had become something of an institution; Support Company Commander was now rejoicing in the title of SOTAG, second only to SNOTAG (Senior Naval Officer TAG). Initially his headquarters had been aboard the patrol yacht *Petrel* but when the yacht went in for maintenance, SOTAG was housed ashore at Tawau in the so-called 'TAG House'. There was a full recorded list of visitors and signals to Commando HQ which sometimes left the recipients with a suspicion of doubt over which Headquarters was thought to be the senior.

After arrival in January '65, 145 (Maiwand) Commando Light Battery RA had augmented TAG. The task remained one of watching the Indonesian Islands, the Bay and the waterways. The dangers came from the occasional burst of machine gun fire or from engine failure that led to some frantic paddling to avoid drifting ashore on the wrong side. There were no casualties.

In addition to TAG, observation was kept on the Indonesian Islands and on their movements by elements of 2 SBS from Singapore and 1 SBS from the UK, who were then operating their own 'roulement' programme.

The river Serudong lay within Sabah territory, with the border to the south; further south was a river that could not be observed from Sabah territory, a situation that involved Second Lieutenant Martin Read in a further cross-border operation that bordered on farce...

Martin Read – OC 6 Troop

'My second cross-border patrol was in the Sabah region, and on the grand scale of things, also contributed little. There was keen interest to know the amount and type of Indonesian boat traffic using the river that ran south of the border and below the Serudong River. The idea was to make a deep penetration to high ground overlooking the river, to find a tall straight tree, shin up it to above the canopy level and establish an OP.

'The operation did not get off to a good start. The initial border approach was to be by inflatable Gemini craft up one of the many estuaries. Unfortunately coming straight out of the jungle and terra firma, our planning had overlooked the possibility of tides, and we managed to end up 100 metres from our landing point on a falling tide. We soon discovered that the mud was in excess of four feet deep – the length of our emergency paddles – and so we ended up like sitting ducks. Fortunately the Indonesians had not considered such a venture and we were left unscathed, sitting out the mid-day sun, waiting to be lifted off by the rising waters and deposited on our beach-head.

'To undertake the feat of climbing a 200 foot tall tree, we had been given a set of spikes, used by telegraph pole repair men. Now these spikes, strapped to the inside of one's legs, may have been excellent to climb telegraph poles with a diameter of thirty to fifty centimetres, but to find a tree, tall enough to get up above the canopy, was going to require a diameter in excess of three metres. The technique required the use of a line holding one's upper body to the tree which you flipped up every time you took a step upwards. This proved impossible and hence no OP was established; but we returned safely and with a better knowledge of tides!'

Last Minute Contact

By 29 April '65, L Company was the company in residence at Bombalai, from which it was due to depart for Singapore at noon on the following day…

> "About a mile east of Bombalai Camp, surrounded by a road complex, lies a piece of swampy hornet-infested secondary jungle, about 1,000 yards long by 400 yards wide. To the South and West it is surrounded by rubber plantations. Abaca plantations border the Eastern edge. To the North, on top of a small hill overlooking much of the ground, is a Chinese sawmill and a few houses. A stream and pipeline run into Bombalai from through this jungle.
>
> "At eleven o'clock on 29 April reliable information was received that 2 IBT were in hiding at a small hut somewhere in this patch…"

Major Bill Mansell carried out a discreet recce of the area with the aid of air photographs and advice from the estate manager. A force of about 100 was available from the Company, an attached Mortar section as well as from the Assault Engineers and the Para Engineers, who arrived from Tawau; a Combat Tracker team was also requested and provided, while the Malaysian Recce Regiment agreed to provide road stops. South and East borders were rubber plantation and to the north on a small hill were a Chinese saw mill and some houses.

Andrew Jackson, Marine S3 – Attached to 6 Troop

'…A plan was conceived for a Cordon and Search and orders were developed and passed down through the afternoon of 29 April.

'That night was going to be dark with a new moon so the movement to set up the cordon would have to be well planned and secrecy was very important. The cordon was to be in position by first light when the sweep would start. The approach was to be from three directions. 4 and 6 Troops, including myself, and the Assault Engineers would start at 0300 hrs through the rubber. This group was to move on a compass bearing till meeting a pipe line and then follow that to the swamp. VHF communications were to be used on this operation and I was carrying an A41. 5 Troop were to leave next and follow the Tawau road. The sweep party of the Para Engineers, with the Combat Tracker Team as reserve, were to leave at 0545 hrs when the cordon would be in position.

'All went exactly as planned and the cordon was in position with no gaps (just!). At the correct time the sweep began…'

> "Twenty minutes later the Para Engineers ran into a hornet's nest and simultaneously two IBT broke cover opposite 4 Troop. On being challenged they turned back. One was shot dead. The Combat Tracker Team followed up and found a small camp, well stocked with supplies, about thirty yards away. Then they too ran into hornets."

'...The second IBT escaped amongst all the confusion and disappeared into the scrubby jungle. My early reasoning to become a signaller and in the chain of command was well justified during this operation; standing in the weak first light amongst the rubber trees, I could listen on the radio to the action going on and understand the situation. The others in the Troop could only guess at what was occurring from the initial shots and the screams of the men stung by the hornets; it felt good to be able to keep my Troop Commander, Second Lieutenant Carter, well briefed, which was my job, as well as let those around me know what was going on.

'By 0900 hrs, after all trails had been unsuccessfully followed up, the second IBT could not be found. It was thought essential that the cordon remained in place but L Company had to leave to catch their flight to Singapore. The East Brigade reserve was called in and a Company of 8 Royal Malay Regiment took over from us. I always remember their very starched, pressed OGs and the way they stepped around the mud puddles as they relieved us. Their demeanour was so different from the jungle experienced Royal Marines of 6 Troop at the end of a long hard operational tour.'

L Company's move to Singapore was duly completed. Two weeks later they were joined by the rest of 42 Commando, who handed over to the 1st Gordons. At about the same time the missing IBT, in wretched condition, gave himself up to the Police.

Chapter 10

Company Signaller

First Commission; Signal Troop, 42 Commando

1964/65

Company Signaller

Andrew Jackson joined the Royal Marines on 1 January 1962 at the age of sixteen; after training at Deal and Lympstone, and earning his green beret in the freezing winter of '62/'63, he joined Course number S3/2 '63, the second basic signaller's course of that year.

On completion he was posted initially to 43 Commando at Plymouth, where the Commando Signal Troop assigned him the role of Mortar Troop radio operator, in which role he later embarked in HMS *Bulwark* for exercises in North Africa…

Andrew Jackson – Marine S3, Signal Troop

'By now I was earmarked for 42 Commando in Singapore, which would be my first commission abroad. Another first for me was the long distance flight, when I was flown home from Libya to the UK, by the RAF, to ensure I would be able to leave on time for Singapore.

42 Commando

'The journey to Singapore entailed another very long flight, again by courtesy of the RAF; it took twenty-four hours to cover the thousands of miles, stopping twice – at Bombay and Gan; the transport aircraft of the time was the four engine propeller driven Britannia. On arrival at 42 Commando in Royal Naval Air Station (RNAS) Sembawang, we found that the unit was in Borneo and we would have to wait to join them. As young inexperienced Marines, during the evenings we were provided with a guided tour of the nearest local village, Nee Soon, an experience we found rather different from a walk round the villages of Devon or Hampshire! We were soon on the move again to join the unit in Sarawak. This time our transport was an old coastal steamer MV *Auby*, where we found living accommodation somewhat basic; an interesting few days at sea, in hot fetid mess decks, went by before we joined our new unit.

'The next few weeks were spent jungle training at Padawan, where 'new joiners' learnt how to fight in a tough and demanding environment of dense and sometimes impenetrable jungle. The main health problems were 'foot rot', leptospirosis – an illness contracted through cuts or abrasions by bathing or washing in water that had been contaminated by rats' urine – and other diseases caused by drinking untreated water. Use of a Millbank bag and of water purifying tablets was drummed into us and we were to be glad of that in the future. We learnt how to move, live in and exploit the jungle. We learnt that if you used soap, or smoked, you could be smelt for miles; we learnt how to use the noises and sounds of the jungle for our benefit and safety. It was a fascinating course that would stand me in good stead on patrols, but taught me little of how to communicate in this difficult environment. That skill I would learn for myself and from the Signal Troop NCO's.

L Company

'I was one of the signallers assigned to L Company, a position I would hold for some time. The signals corporal for that company was Corporal 'Perry' Mason, from whom I learnt a great deal in the coming weeks. The Commando's tour in Sarawak was coming to an end and it had achieved much over the past months, epitomized by the efforts of the Signals Troop (Captain Ray Frost) in providing forward communications. The Troop had created precisely cut and configured VHF aerials, known as 'Yagis', and had greatly extended the range of the VHF radios. This expertise in physics and radio wave propagation and the creation of these odd shaped and high gain aerials, was to crystallize in the unit's next operational tour. There was a quote made at the time – "No limit to the shape of aerials to come, nor to the range of the A41; thirty miles? No problem!"

'In June '64 we returned to Singapore, where all enjoyed a period of leave. I felt something of a fraud taking leave after only being in Borneo for a few weeks, especially as one of my squad mates, Marine Paul Howes, who had joined the Commando straight from training, had been awarded a Mention in Dispatches for his efforts with 5 Troop at Lundu. However, that feeling was very fleeting!

'In July the Commando returned to training and the Signal Troop practiced radio procedure, Morse code, aerial mast and wire erections, line laying and battery charging, all vital to providing effective communications. We also received our first batch of General Purpose Machine Guns (GPMG's); forty-six arrived to replace the Bren guns. The training culminated in Exercise 'Horse's Neck', with 42 Commando and 145 Battery RA embarking in *Bulwark* for an amphibious assault in the area of Mersing on the South East coast of Malaya, supported by air strikes by Sea Vixen and Buccaneers from HMS *Centaur* and HMS *Victorious*.

Celebrations and Riots

'Although somewhat early, to fit into the year's tight schedule, we enjoyed an all ranks Tercentenary Ball in one of the large hangars at Sembawang to celebrate the Royal Marines 300th anniversary (1664–1964). It was enjoyed by all, with good food, drinks and entertainment by the local Rock and Roll/Twist band the 'Crescendos'. I remember it well as I won a prize in the large raffle, which I don't do very often! Amongst all of this the Commando was looking forward to a deployment from Singapore to Hong Kong in *Bulwark* for exercises and a 'run ashore'.

'The country also celebrated with the 1st Anniversary of the creation of Malaysia. This supposedly joyous time became soured as disaffected political groups used the occasion to stir up trouble and riots ensued. The gravity of these fluctuated and appeared to concentrate in the Gaylong area of Singapore. There was arson and rioting and unfortunately several deaths. The causeway to Malaya was closed and curfews imposed; UK military personnel living in the community known as 'outliers' were brought into barracks and patrols were initiated to protect foreign nationals.

'In reaction to all of these troubles, 42 Commando was designated as 'spearhead unit' on stand-by in case the problem spread. The unit was also on high alert for riot duty and we quickly learnt to form 'The Square', deploy the barbed wire, show the banners and prepare to use tear gas. Communications were planned and rehearsed for our reaction to enable them to be dovetailed into the local police forces networks. In September 1964 the unit was stood down as the riots died away – as also did our chance of a 'run ashore' in Hong Kong!

'Instead we prepared for Exercise 'Dark Night', another amphibious assault exercise, this time landing from *Bulwark* onto the North East coast of Malaya. The unit was now well versed in operations from the Commando Carriers and the Signals Troop went aboard into their second home, 4K2 mess deck. The exercise went well, the only mishap being the accidental dropping by a Wessex helicopter of the Command Post trailer with the headquarters VHF and HF radios installed; it was quickly replaced with stand-by radios ready for just such an emergency

'We returned to Singapore in the LPH for more training, some going back to basics while training for the Tercentennial Parade on the exact date of the Corps' 300 year birthday. This was followed by a dinner dance at the Goodwood Hotel in Singapore. On 6 November, Captain Philip Reed took over the Signals Troop.

'The Troop was soon under pressure with Operation 'Tin Can'; reports had come in of Indonesians infiltrating the islands off Mersing. The Commando was ordered to sweep the area to capture or kill the insurgents. There were several islands and the unit spread out with the assistance of HMS *Manxman*, *Kent* and two Minesweepers. Helicopters from *Victorious* were also used to fly sections onto the islands. After several days the area was declared clear and no insurgents were found.

'On return to Sembawang, I joined others in the Troop learning to use the A510 radio, a man-portable set developed by the Australian forces. It was an HF radio constructed as two small boxes, one the transmitter and one the receiver, connected together by a multi-wired cable. It was powered by a dry battery in each box and had the facility to use voice, with a strange horn-shaped mike, or Morse code with the very small key that you could strap to your leg. It could use plug-in crystals to provide fixed

HF frequencies or it could be free tuned. You could fix a small vertical aerial to the set or use a wire cut to the required length of the frequency you were using. It was much lighter than any radio the Marines were normally issued with and was ideal for patrol work in the jungle.

'These radios were also to be used by Combat Tracker Teams. Their communications would either be an A41 VHF radio if the initial contact was near one of our bases, or by A510 HF set if the tracker team had to work deep in the jungle. One problem made this arrangement unpopular; if the team commander wished to contact his headquarters, the signaller would have to stop to rig up a wire aerial to communicate on HF and therefore delay any follow-up.

'In December we left for Sabah in *Bulwark* to take over from 40 Commando. I deployed again with L Company, who were initially based at Kalabakan with 42 Commando Tac HQ. The unit settled in with communications established to the sub-units, and rear links to the Commandos Rear Headquarters. There was quite a large contingent of signallers at the location which contained the Unit Communication Centre (Comcen), from which operated several radio links, including the Unit Command Net (UCN), Brigade Command Net (BCN), Force Command Net (FCN) as well as the local Company Command Net (CCN); Signal Troop HQ and the Line team were also based at Tac HQ.'

Kalabakan

'The camp was a rambling shanty town of tin roofed wooden buildings mainly built on the side of a steep hill. Below, at the bottom of the hill was the logging company headquarters. The winter months are the Borneo rainy season and the many inches of rain falling at this time often caused the camp road ways and local environment to become a muddy quagmire. At one time the Sergeants' Mess was in danger of sliding down the hill, but strenuous efforts to rebuild were made by RSM W J Thomas, which led to the opening of a new mess – 'The Kalabakan' – with a well attended cocktail party.

'The elevated position of the camp did, however, improve communications. The height assisted aerials were further improved by the use of carefully cut and shaped 'Yagi' aerials that have already been discussed. There were two C42 VHF radios in place for this net, with one operating and one as a stand-by. These were backed up by WS62 HF radios sets, as the VHF radios were not guaranteed to work the long ranges to the outlying companies and patrols. Adjacent to the landing strip were defence positions and the Signal Troop had the task of laying lines out to these locations and installing telephones.

'The BCN was manned by a detachment of Royal Marine signallers from 3 Commando Brigade HQ and Signal Squadron. They used a higher powered HF radio set just being delivered to the Corps and called the C11. This transmitted voice or Morse code, used whip or wire aerials and was powered by twelve volt wet batteries which took time and effort to keep charged. These types of batteries were also used by the detachment of Gurkha signallers working their radio back to the Force Command Headquarters in Labuan. They were sending higher classified information to the rear using Morse code, most of the time transmitting and receiving five figure groups which contained encoded text, some sent as 'Formal Messages' – messages that are formalised by a releasing officer and are assigned a date time group. They had to be tracked by the Comcen staff and the radio operators through the radio network like registered letters through the Royal Mail. If they were awarded a high priority by the releasing officer and were very urgent, they had to be sent and delivered very rapidly.

'I was part of the watch-keeping team on L Company radio net that communicated to the foot patrols, providing local security. As resident Company, each Troop spent a week on patrol, a week at the NECK position on the river and the third week on camp duties. Occasionally I carried out watches on the UCN to relieve other signallers. The time on radio watches passed fairly uneventfully in Kalabakan; it was easier getting out of a mosquito net at 0400 hrs in a balmy night to go on watch than it was later in my career in North Norway at minus fifteen degrees in the snow. My only personal excitement – if you can call it that – was being stung by a scorpion one day when off watch. My foot was fairly sore for a day or two. Christmas 1964 was celebrated in the camp with an attempt to concoct the usual trappings of an 'at home' Christmas on a very wet day. Christmas lunch, beer and good cheer ended, I remember, with myself and fellow signallers having difficulty getting up the steep, very muddy road to our 'basha'.

'At the end of January L Company deployed to Serudong and took over the border defensive positions from M Company. The Company location was fairly large and besides the Company HQ had a Section of three inch Mortars and one 105mm howitzer. These not only provided more fire power but also more manpower around the camp.'

Serudong River Line

'I deployed with 6 Troop (Second Lieutenant Martin Read) to a location on the Serudong River closer to the border. It was a well protected camp with its own landing pad. The location had one sandbagged bunker, which acted as the Troop command post and radio 'room'; as the resident signaller I was lucky enough to sleep there. Communications to the Company HQ was by A41 VHF radio, with a well constructed high gain 'yagi' aerial attached and positioned high in a tree, next to the command post. This enabled VHF communications back to Company HQ at Serudong, albeit on a restricted channel. Also installed was another A41 set for communications to any local patrols that went out from this location. I also installed an A510 radio, the lightweight Australian radio set, to

Marine Andrew Jackson's living accommodation and signals centre

ensure I had HF backup to the Company HQ. I rigged a wire aerial across the camp for this radio, giving me good frequency coverage.

'The living accommodation in the bunker was dank and dark, so I wallpapered the sandbag walls inside with new cut open sandbags to improve the inside appearance. For an operating position, I fixed up a table on one wall and raised a sleeping ledge on the opposite wall, giving me a seat and stowage space underneath. My radios were installed in ammunition boxes in a space made under the tin roof, with a weight attached to the microphone lead of my main VHF radio, causing it to drop back into a stand-by position after use. Mindful of the need for a blackout at this tactical site, I rigged up a small torch bulb, powered by an old A41 battery to give me a light at night. Outside my door was a dartboard . The established rule of a ration of two cans of beer a man per day was upheld at the location and many ingenious ideas were invented to keep them cool, but without much success; it was best to drink them when issued as they would only get warmer. Having said that, I could keep several cans inside my 'basha' and they stayed cool, which was very useful when I celebrated my twentieth birthday in this location.

'All the other huts on the site were ramshackle affairs, floors lifted off the ground to keep dry in the torrential rains, with poncho, plastic sheet or rattan roofs and makeshift sides. Sticks were bound together and used to make pathways to enable movement around the camp without the ground becoming a quagmire.

The trees over the camp area were not cut down, leaving them to provide sun cover and camouflage from the air. Each hut 'owner' worked hard to keep them water tight and as comfortable as possible. Some huts were built on the hillside, needing careful construction to stop them sliding down; some grew in size and became semi-detached when two man constructions were developed. My own had a ladder going up to my aerials in the trees.

'Life in the camp was either hard work or rather boring. Local patrols were always out; checking the immediate area to ensure there had been no IBTs about. Those who were not on patrol would either be on guard duty or camp chores. Cooking was centralised using ten man ration packs, with some fresh vegetables brought in on the resupply flights with the much welcome mail.

Bamboo canes were bound together to form pathways around the camp

'There was little to do at night as lights were in short supply and as stated there was a very strict black out imposed. I was lucky in my sandbagged accommodation and I remember reading at night or listening to the world service on the A510 set – another perk for the signaller! Whilst in the camp for example, I remember listening to Winston Churchill's funeral on the world service as it happened, thousands of miles away in the UK.

'I have already mentioned that the camp was surrounded by a sandbagged wall for security and protection; further depth to this protection was provided by barbed wire and panjis – sharpened sticks pushed into the ground and pointing down the hill any attacker would have to climb. These were supplemented by trip flares and Claymore mines set up as booby traps at night on the main entrance pathways. Obviously no one inside ventured out of the perimeter after dark and it would be difficult for anyone to make a stealthy approach to the camp without being heard and without damaging themselves.

'Water supply was a constant problem; it was collected from the river at the bottom of the steep hill which dropped away sharply from the camps. Brought up in jerry cans, it was run through Millbank Bags to filter it; purifying tablets had then to be added to all water used for drinking and cooking. There were obviously no showers and one

Panjis, sharpened bamboo firmly fixed in the ground and angled, made an easily constructed perimeter defence along with barbed wire.

got used to having a strip wash in a couple of mess tins of the precious water. I used to supplement my mess tin 'baths' with a dash of Dettol to disinfect any cuts and bites.

'Weapons were always carried while fetching water, as in all operational areas, and the river was some way down out of sight of the camp. Bringing up the water was a daily and difficult chore, a long, hard and hot uphill trek with heavy jerry cans. There was a request for a pump but the Company Headquarters said they had a greater need and it stayed at their location!'

Casevac

'The routine and the peace and quiet of the jungle morning were violently shattered on 11 February 1965 by a loud explosion and screams. I woke thinking we were being attacked, checked my weapon and immediately transmitted on the UCN VHF net "Hello Zero this is two three contact wait out". My first ever report of live action, as I thought, on a radio net. It would not be my last. The camp was quickly roused and took up firing positions. It was then realised that it was not an attack but something much crueler – the Troop Sergeant had been blown up by a Claymore mine, one of the camp's 'booby trap' defences. All the traps were powered by batteries in the command hut, my location. Every morning I used to be woken up to do my first schedule to the Company HQ by the duty Corporal or Sergeant, who also disconnected the electric wires to the booby traps. This morning I had not been woken up for my schedule. On understanding the situation I reported it to L Company HQ and a 'casevac' helicopter was ordered. Meanwhile the medically trained men in the Troop fought in vain to save the Sergeant's life.

'The helicopter came as soon as it could, which was difficult due to very bad weather. As the helicopter flew off there was a very subdued Troop left behind. The Troop Officer then spent some time with me as he answered questions from Company HQ over the radio and was given the details of the inevitable investigation that was to follow. Over the next few days the Troop was visited by many senior officers carrying out that investigation. I obviously became part of that because of the booby trap wiring in my hut. The landing pad, which was certainly busy for a while, was not a particularly big one nor very open, with high trees on all sides; it just about accommodated the Alouette AH4 (SA313) helicopters that carried out resupply to the location.

'There was an Obituary in the April 1965 issue of *The Globe & Laurel* for Sergeant Peter Davidson, echoing our views at the time of how great his loss was felt. Although not with the Troop for long he was a really keen, cheerful and great guy. We were very sad and distressed for his wife and children who had only just flown out to join him in Singapore.

'Shortly after this incident our Troop Commander changed over and a new young officer, Second Lieutenant Brian Carter moved into our luxury accommodation.

An Alouette light helicopter of the Malaysian Forces
on an improvised landing pad constructed with bamboo palings'

He had not been with us long before we were directed by Company HQ to do a long patrol, close to the border to identify a tall tree in which could be built an Observation Post (OP). It was stated that our Troop had to do this work as we had a Corporal Patterson amongst us who was a Cliff Leader (CL), a professional climber. We were not sure about this patrol and wondered whether we had been given the task to take our minds off the 'accident' at our location. We also believed it would be a tall order to find the tallest tree in a dense jungle consisting of millions of trees!

'Anyway off we dutifully went, with me and the new Troop Commander moving and sharing a bivvy as the 'Command Group'. We got on very well together as I taught him the ropes. I carried the A510 and he carried the spare batteries. I did the radio schedules and he made the tea. For my schedules I constructed 'quick into action aerials' when on the move, by creating a 'sloping wire'. It was directional and to be effective had to be cut to the frequency I was using. After checking in which direction the headquarters was from our location, and therefore in which direction I needed the 'gain' (main output) of the aerial to transmit, I created my simple aerial. I did this by bending over a small sapling; I then attached one end of my wire aerial to the tree and then let the sapling spring back. This gave me the height I needed at the 'high gain' end of the wire and I then attached the other end to the radio set on the ground. Usually I had to use Morse code to send the messages back to the signaller at Company HQ, due to the invariably noisy frequencies; messages would either be written down or relayed by voice from the Troop Commander for me to transmit.

'The patrol was very hot and sweaty, with some of the ground undulating and with dense undergrowth. Occasionally our Iban scouts would appear apprehensive and we wondered sometimes if we were on the right or wrong side of the border. Our patrol task forced us to operate very close to the border with the aim of finding a tall tree to overlook 'enemy territory'. Within such dense jungle we had to rely on the compass and the exact positioning of the patrol was not at all easy. The weather was not always good and often the ground was sodden. As ever leeches were proving to be a problem and seemed to find a way to get inside our jungle greens and attach themselves to our thighs or upper body. Finding the 'tallest tree' was also proving difficult because every time we thought we had found it, there was always another in front of us. Many trees were climbed, most with the help of the 'Climbing Spikes'. These were metal spikes with leather straps which you tied onto your boots. These were designed for signallers, amongst others, to climb telegraph poles, with one foot either side of the pole using the spikes to dig into the pole or, in our case, the tree. Second Lieutenant Carter and the CL, Corporal Patterson, did most of the climbing. After much walking, climbing and swearing, a tree was decided on and marked carefully on the map, allowing us to return to the 'luxury' of our base camp.

'Whether it was due to the incident at our camp before the patrol, or whether it was part of a grander strategy, a short while later the Troop was told to dismantle our Troop Location completely and move back to Serudong. This move obviously prompted much action and hard work. I remember we were instructed not to return any excess ammunition so we all took turns in cutting down trees over the landing pad with belts of rounds in the GPMG. We also became well versed in throwing grenades and letting off trip flares. The two inch mortar also had a busy spell, with us letting bomb after bomb go into the jungle! Of course we first obtained permission from Company HQ of the area in which the bombs would be landing. I had to disengage my aerials and lost VHF communications when I took down the 'Yagi'. I then reverted to HF and worked my radio report schedules to Company HQ on the A510 set, working with a Dipole wire aerial. I also found out when I dismantled my sandbagged luxury hut that I had been living with three snakes in recesses in the bags! They made me move very quickly as I disturbed them and they slithered away. I also realised how lucky I had been over the weeks living with them, as one was a Krait, which is very poisonous.'

Bombalai

'From Serudong 'L' Company moved to Bombalai as part of the programme for rotation of Companies. It was good to get back to civilisation with electric lights, flushing toilets, showers and unrestricted cold beer! With the Company settling in to local patrols and camp business, I joined the camp signallers in watch-keeping on the UCN again.

'There were two moments of excitement that I remember; one was that a member of an armoured car crew had a negligent discharge on his fitted point five machine gun. It certainly woke up the whole camp, putting guards on alert as the rounds made holes in the NAAFI roof. The other out of the ordinary event I remember was a visiting Entertainment show one night. I cannot remember the 'Star', but I do remember there were some lovely dancers in the troupe! This quiet routine did not last for long. It appeared that Commando HQ thought 6 Troop should carry out a vital long patrol as evidently we were experienced in them – possibly after our tallest tree hunt?

'The task was to escort some 'Para Engineers' (Royal Engineers attached to the Parachute Regiment) into a new part of the border area to build some landing pads. Second Lieutenant Brian Carter came and saw me and convinced me that, as the two of us had got on well together during patrols, I should join them as his signaller on this 'walk'. Off we went, by helicopter and then on foot. We covered a lot of different ground which always seemed to undulate incessantly. Some movement was in very thick jungle where we had to take turns in cutting the vegetation to make headway. At other times we moved in more open jungle on flat gullies, which were easier walking but could flood with up to a foot of water very rapidly in the torrential monsoon rain.

'There was an abundance of wildlife, with innumerable insects, ants and small mammals on the ground and monkeys and birds in the tree canopy. We were near the border and moved as tactically as possible, stopping and going to cover if we thought the noise of the jungle was too quiet and something or someone was frightening the animals. It was very wet and leeches again were a daily problem. They seemed to be able to get onto our legs through the OG (Olive Green) trousers which were tucked into our jungle boots. Sometimes you would find them fully gorged on blood and very difficult to get off the skin.

'During one night stop I had trouble with the wild life in a different way. I awoke one night with a feeling of great irritation around my head and face. Using a very shaded small torch I checked my head area to find my pillow was being eaten by a foot wide column of ants. I quickly moved it out of my bed space and tried to go back to sleep cursing them, as they had destroyed the one and only luxury I carried, a rubber blow up pillow. On patrol you kept the weight you carried down to the minimum and that was my one indulgence – I missed it for the rest of my tour, being unable to replace it in Bombalai.

'Again I was carrying the A510 HF set with Second Lieutenant Carter carrying the spare batteries. We were now well practiced in working together, always not far apart, both when on the move and when we stopped, built our 'bivvies' for the night and I carried out my schedules back to headquarters. Again, from experience, I used my 'quick into action' directional aerials by using sloping wires attached to saplings. I then strapped the small Morse key to my leg, which it was designed to do, and sent my messages. My Morse code by now had improved, and I was a lot faster. This was to stand me in good stead during my next job at Royal Marines Poole as a signaller in Landing Craft.

'All these patrols proved that the training we had carried out on the new radios (A510) and all the Morse code exams we had taken in Eastney Barracks paid off. Our locations and other information had to be encoded for transmission using a code called 'griddle', if it was believed to be of operational use to the enemy. My communication skills improved on this long patrol – as did my adroitness in flicking leeches off my legs as I transmitted. When we stopped for some time, as we did to build some landing pads, I constructed more effective, complex aerials. These were usually 'dipole' aerials which again were built with specifically cut lengths of wire, frequency dependent, but raised at both ends and broadside to the headquarters. You then had to raise or lower them to search for best effectiveness.

'On this patrol, as normal, I did guard duties as I had no night schedules. It was not thought worth trying any communications at night using the extremely noisy HF frequencies. One night guard I remember well. As was usual when camped in the jungle, we were in an 'all round' defence formation. We had trip flares set out on the best entrances into our area, with a guard lying down observing those entrances. That night we had already been 'stood to' as the Marine on guard duty thought he heard someone moving nearby in the jungle. Nothing was found, so we went back to our bivvies again. When I went on guard, it was not long before I heard noises in front of me. It was pitch black and I strained my eyes and ears to decide what it was. I carefully felt the Bren gun to check the magazine was loaded correctly, held it tight to my shoulder and followed the noise. I did not want to wake the Troop up again unnecessarily but neither did I want to let an enemy closer. At that tense time I was sure I could hear the insects crawling around my area, so dark was the jungle you relied much more on your hearing than your sight. The noises in front of me were a constant rustle of floor debris and, after thinking it through, I deduced that a stalking man would not continue making that amount of noise and more importantly, it was in the direction of our gash pit, where an iguana had been spotted earlier. I decided that it must be the lizard again, but followed the noise until it ceased. In the morning our gash pit was found to have been ransacked.

'This was a great proving ground for a young signaller as some schedules were arranging food parachute drops and the patrol members were not pleased if 'Sigs' failed to get through or got the wrong location! It did at least mean that they were keen to help with aerial construction. Locations were always difficult as the maps were inaccurate and invariably poor on contours and weak on detail. The patrol was supposed to be building the new landing sites (LSs) in certain grid references, but we all wondered whether we got them in the correct positions or not. We either used a balloon to show where the patrol was if needed to be spotted by helicopters, or one of the troops would climb the highest tree to get a view of the area over the jungle canopy to try and check our position. It was very much trial and error.

'The Para engineers we were escorting were good and bad. They were not as good at the 'yomping' as we in 6 Troop were and some of our members quite often had to carry some of their equipment, including saws, axes and explosives. However, once they were in location and had to build LS, they came into their own. They were very professional and effective. They would take the trees down, sometimes by blowing them up, take off the branches and wedge the trees together into a stable level structure for a helicopter pad in amazingly quick time. When we had completed our task, it was from one of the LSs that they had built, that we were taken out by helicopter back to Bombalai. On arrival I remember other Marines in the camp keeping well clear of us as we smelt very strongly after many days on patrol. We threw our sweat soaked rotting OGs away and enjoyed a good shower.

'I carried out one more patrol in the area with 6 Troop, which was a totally different one than the last. This time we were in assault craft and patrolling the mangrove swamp areas and islands along the local rivers. We thought the boats were far easier than 'yomping' everywhere but we soon found it was not so good if you ran out of water, which we did. Pushing assault craft over the river bed, knee deep in mangrove mud is not so much fun. This did allow the odd leech or two to attack us again. Once they had attached themselves to you they were easier to get off with a lit cigarette – if you were not in a tactical area and you could smoke. Otherwise, when tactical, I used a small drop of Dettol which removed them quickly.

'I seem to remember we used A41 VHF sets on these patrols sometimes relaying our messages through other stations on the net. Using the correct call signs was essential so as not to get confused. Fixed call signs were in use, with Zero as the Commando Headquarters, One, Two and Three being the three Company call signs and A and 'B' Echelon using 92A and 92B. Names for personalities were also used on the nets such as 'SUNRAY' for the Commander, at any level, 'ACORN' for an intelligence specialist, 'HOLDFAST' for an Engineer and 'PRONTO' for a signaller. These did not provide much security and in later life I worked with the incumbent Chief Signal Officer to change the Call Signs for the whole Corps.

'We didn't come into contact with any IBTs on our river patrols and the only time we fired our weapons was to try and get a good supper. There was a huge boar spotted on the bank and although we believe we put around 8 rounds of 7.62 into this pig it did not stop. We were amazed at this and also annoyed, as we had missed the chance for some very good fresh meat.

'As the days to the end of our tour came closer, L Company believed they had finished the worst of it, but there was a sting in the tail. The day before the Company were due to fly back to Singapore there were reliable reports of 2 IBT hiding in a small hut about a mile east of Bombalai Camp…'

Andrew Jackson's part in the cordon and search operation that followed and in which one of the two IBT was killed, has been described in the previous chapter. With the departure of L Company on that day, Andrew returned to Signal Troop…

'…Two weeks later the second IBT gave himself up to the Police and at the same time the remainder of the Commando, including myself, now back in the Signal Troop, returned to Singapore in *Albion*. After a 'Clear Lower Deck' a good leave was had by all. The married 'outliers' enjoyed family life again and single Marines, like me, enjoyed the good and bad entertainments of the nation. As usual I had a mixed 'run ashore' with good dinners in fine restaurants, or a few beers in the Britannia Club. Early on during this leave period, the Britannia Club was taken over by 'Royal' from 42 Commando, thoroughly enjoying themselves with the 'Shore Patrols' being very diplomatic for a change. After leave it was return to work and back to IS drills and Amphibious Warfare training. This, after the rigours of the Borneo operations, shows the well known versatility of the Royal Marines.

'There followed one of the largest amphibious exercises at that time, Exercise 'Windy Weather', a two unit, two Commando Ship exercise. Other ships on the exercise were *Victorious* for fixed wing support, and cruisers *London* and *Royalist* for Naval Gunfire support, together with numerous escort vessels, fleet replenishment ships and submarines. It was an imposing fleet on the South China Sea as it moved to the exercise area on Malaya's East coast.

'On return to daily routine in Singapore, I initially worked in the Communications Centre, processing, transmitting and distributing formal messages to the duty officer and staff officers of the Commando. My final role was as the signaller in Sembawang's very own radio station, the SRE (Ships Radio Equipment). My duties when on watch were either to wake up the camp with bright and cheerful music after reveille or soothe them to sleep late at night after the NAAFI. I learnt a great deal about music and enjoyed working as the camp DJ; it was a world away from the hot, fetid jungles of Borneo and a quiet relaxed end to what had been an exciting eighteen months on my first tour in a Commando.'

Chapter 11

Return to Sarawak

Sibu, Serian and Measures of 'Claret'

January to December '65

Return to Sarawak

Mid-West Brigade

The build up and the arrival of reinforcements, including units judiciously diverted from training or on passage to Hong Kong, led to a requirement for an additional Brigade Headquarters. 3 Commando Brigade HQ was therefore called forward from Singapore to Sibu, where they were to establish a Mid-West Brigade, which was to control the 2nd and 3rd Divisions of Sarawak and free West Brigade to concentrate on the 1st Division.

The Brigade was now commanded by Brigadier Leslie Marsh and had under command a battalion of the Royal Malay Regiment (RMR), a Gurkha battalion and the Gurkha Independent Para Company. The Headquarters opened at Sibu on 17 January '65, with the operational HQ in the requisitioned Teacher's Training College and the rest of the main HQ in a 'basha' camp by the airfield and alongside the offices and Helicopter Park of 845 Royal Naval Air Squadron (RNAS). The supply chain was largely by air back to Kuching, where elements of 'B' Echelon were therefore stationed.

Brigade Signals

At the time of this deployment the Brigade Signals Officer was on leave in UK and the Assistant Brigade Signals Officer (Lieutenant Sam Pope) carried out the recce and the initial deployment of the Squadron. He writes of the signals environment and of the contribution of the RM Signals Branch…

Sam Pope, Lieutenant – Assistant Brigade Signals Officer

'The importance of communications to the success of British Forces in a campaign conducted over such vast distances and difficult terrain is self-evident. In 1963 tactical communications in use by the Army were heavily influenced by the requirements of NATO in Germany. Most equipment was designed to be fitted in vehicles and man portable radios were not expected to cover much more than a few miles of open country. Thick forest and mountain ranges were a combination not envisaged by the arbitrators on requirement specifications for military radio equipment. As these people tended to be very largely officers of the Royal Signals, a Corps which seldom operated further forward than brigade headquarters, it was not surprising that considerable ingenuity was often in demand to achieve adequate communications within 40 and 42 Commandos when deployed to Borneo.

'Fortunately the Royal Marines have not suffered from the demarcation between Royal Signals and the regimental signallers of the Infantry. As ever, the Corps Signals Branch was predominantly trained and equipped to operate from brigade down as far as the rifle company, so the problems with which they had to cope in Sabah and Sarawak could be taken on board with some confidence. The Branch's tenet that improvement in communications should always be sought had to be constantly applied, with enthusiasm.

'The laying of line by signallers with B Company of 40 Commando and the development of the Yagi aerials by Signal Troop of 42 Commando are but two examples of the determination of signallers to improve communications. The Yagi was an ingenious Royal Marine invention that was so successful that it was soon to be found in every Army or Royal Marine unit within the Sarawak's First Division.

'There were few if any periods when RM Signallers were not deployed somewhere in the main area of operations with the Brigade Signals Squadron or with the Signals Troops of the two Commandos; some signallers were also attached to the SBS teams and others deployed from the LPH to provide communications for helicopter control, often a long way up country.

'In the Signal Squadron all NCOs would have served previously in the Signal Troop of one of the Commandos as would most of the Marine signallers. One particular instance, well known to signallers at that time, suitably demonstrates the style of the Branch. Every evening/afternoon the US Forces in Vietnam sent a C130 aircraft down the length of their area of operation with VHF re-broadcasting endless logistic reports. This would seriously interfere with the unit command net of a particular unit, probably 40 Commando. One day a very American voice came through on the command net to say "You limeys get off the air! Don't you know were fighting a war up here?" Quick as a flash the Marine S3 replied "So are we – and we're winning ours!"

*

During the two months at Sibu the Headquarters Defence Section had one call-out to help defend a village location under threat of an attack. The Section was led on that occasion by Lieutenant Pope. Though the attack did not materialise, a series of accidents left them stranded for ten days at Long Jawi before they could be lifted out by helicopter. One of these accidents, involving a helicopter of 845 Squadron carrying a patrol of the RMR, gave Surgeon Lieutenant Commander Mends and his Medical Section a more difficult task…

'The crash occurred up country in almost inaccessible jungle. Two helicopters flew the Doctor, Wardmaster and SBAs to the spot and winched them down to the crash scene. Here they worked under very difficult conditions and managed to extricate one survivor who was flown to Sibu hospital, but regrettably died on the way. By nightfall they had recovered all but two of the dead before darkness compelled them to evacuate the spot and they were winched up into the helicopter and returned to Sibu, wet, dirty and very tired'

'The following day an SBA returned and was again winched down and to his horror found that torrential rain had swept away the helicopter wreckage and the remaining bodies. He left the spot and continued to the village of Kaput where he gave medical attention to the local Iban villagers before returning to Sibu. The missing bodies were later recovered.'

On the 22nd March, HQ 19th Infantry Brigade from the UK relieved HQ 3 Commando Brigade as HQ Mid-West Brigade. Of the turnover by the Brigade Signals Squadron, Sam Pope had this to say...

'As the only subaltern in the Squadron, when the Army's 19th Infantry Brigade came to relieve us, I was astonished to find no less than five Royal Signals officers lined up to take over my duties. The solution was to put a Royal Marines signals corporal in charge of each Army officer; this worked remarkably well.'

40 Commando

Dick Sidwell – OC B Company

'For its next tour in Borneo 40 Commando was to operate for five months in Sarawak First Division as part of West Brigade under Brigadier Bill Cheyne; we were relieving 1/2 Gurkhas with HQ at Serian on the road south from Kuching. We always enjoyed taking over from Gurkhas as they left large stocks of rum to be drunk only during inclement weather! The advance party arrived in Serian on 8 July 1965 and B Company team moved straight out to Pang Amo by helicopter that night. The Gurkha base was a defended hill top situated fairly close to two kampongs, one Chinese and one Malayan; they were between two and three miles from the Indonesian border. There were several footpaths but no vehicles or large boats could reach these kampongs, either from Serian to the North or Tebedu to our West. All movement of men and supplies had to be carried out by helicopter or parachute.'

Pang Amo

'The Gurkhas had done a remarkable job in clearing all the trees and most of the undergrowth on the hill; they had established three rows of concertina wire around

Aerial view of Pang Amo's fortified base for B Company, 40 Commando for five months.
Bottom centre – helipad; centre left – 105mm pack how; Large light area – galley, dining room and canteen; Centre right – two inch mortar pits.

the site and had set up a series of Claymore mines and trip flares. They had dug a command post and communications centre into the side of the hill, a gun pit for the 105mm pack-howitzer, two mortar base plate positions and a number of trenches dug well into the hillside with effective overhead cover. Everyone was accommodated in two rows of atap shelters, nicknamed Park Lane. These shelters were screened by sandbags on the outer side and provided protection from the sun and from all but the heaviest rain. As time went by most of the shelters were lined with material from damaged parachutes, but there was no protection from mortars, so the trenches were very close to the shelters.

Captain Dick Sidwell, the 'Squire of Pang Amo' commanding B Company 40 Commando, returning from patrol with Pang Amo base camp in the background

'There was a helipad suitable for the Commando Sioux helicopters and RAF Whirlwinds. Further down the hill the ground was levelled to provide a volley ball pitch and a parking place for visiting helicopters. There were three entrances to the site through the barbed wire, each of which was covered by sentries twenty-four hours a day.

'The Company advance party flew in a week before the main party and the two Troop Commanders, Second Lieutenant John Chester, 5 Troop, and Second Lieutenant Jonathan Thomson, 6 Troop, went on patrols with the Gurkhas up to the border area. The Gurkha Company Commander, a British officer, took me to the two local kampongs which were longhouses with many pigs and chickens scratching an existence underneath them. The Malays in Kujang Tembawang were not unfriendly but were not accustomed to white faces and kept their distance at the early stages; the small kampong at Pang Amo was Chinese who were mainly traders and handled all the local produce and also some rice and pepper brought over from Indonesia. Quite a lot of the pepper belonged to the Indonesian officer in Peripin, the kampong immediately opposite us. We were advised to watch the Chinese carefully as they could be providing shelter for CCO who crossed from Indonesia. In practice we were never aware of any CCO in our area and I believe the Border Scouts and local labour would have told us if there were any strangers in these kampongs.

'There was room for only two rifle Troops at Pang Amo, together with an Australian Gunner detachment manning the 105mm pack-how and a mortar section lead by Sergeant Binnie from Support Company manning two three inch mortars; four Iban trackers joined us in August and two Border Scouts visited on a regular basis. Simon Pack relieved John Chester in early August but Simon left us in September to join Recce Troop; he was relieved by Second Lieutenant Bob Edwards. The other forward Companies were A with Major Dickie Grant at Plaman Mapu about five miles to our East and C Company with Captain John Weston at Tebedu about six miles to our West. Like us A company relied entirely on resupply by air but there was a road from Serian to Tebedu.

'The task for each of the forward locations was to dominate the tracks leading up to the border with Indonesia and to prevent any infiltration by CCO from Indonesia. This was to be achieved by laying frequent ambushes. We were not authorised to cross the border other than in close pursuit if we had been attacked. On only one occasion was anyone killed in an ambush and sadly it was an old man returning at night after curfew from a day's hunting.

'Soon after our arrival at Pang Amo we were told to plan possible raids over the border but these were classified as Top Secret. I discovered several years later that although the 'G' staff at West Brigade knew what was being planned the 'Q' staff were not told. This explains why our request for special equipment including bergens which would have helped with the loads that were being carried on ten day patrols was not approved.

'The daily routine at Pang Amo started with a dawn stand-to at 0530 hrs and was followed by a small clearing patrol checking the perimeter of the base and immediate approach. On most days one of the Troops would be out on patrol while the other was providing sentries, working on the defences and improving the amenities. These patrols would last between three and seven days, and included laying ambushes on tracks used by the locals. At the early stages much time was spent recording the layout of these tracks and noting how much they were being used. This was not as easy as it may appear, as the maps of the area although printed in 1965 were based on aerial photos and were very basic in their detail. Contours were not accurate and anyhow, because much of the area was secondary jungle, visibility at ground level was restricted. We refer glibly to the border between Indonesia and Sarawak, whereas in practice you could only guess roughly in what area the border would run.

'The locals practiced 'slash and burn' on any reasonably level ground, leaving only burnt tree stumps and a layer of ash. These areas could be of sizes varying from two to ten acres and were planted with rice and tapioca for a few years before being allowed to return to jungle which took over very quickly. Leading a patrol through these areas was a slow job and could involve a lot of cutting which created unwanted noise. If you ran into a bamboo thicket it was best to circumnavigate it; this involved compass work and careful pacing. It was very easy to misjudge your position after doing this several times! What a difference GPS would have made!

'The Second-in-Command, Captain David Hunt, had a full time job in keeping the perimeter of the base clear of secondary growth to ensure clear lines of fire; he was able to recruit a few local labourers for this work whom he also used for removing rubbish and burning it outside the perimeter. Repairing and replacing the bamboo structures and replacing the atap leaves was a continuous routine as everything rotted quickly especially during the rainy season; even the hessian on the sandbags rotted after only a few months. He had to ensure that our water supply from the stream was correctly filtered and sterilised before being pumped up to the galley and showers.'

Supply Drops

'The base was resupplied with almost all its requirements by parachute every eight to ten days. We were always told when an aircraft was due but we dreaded the sound of the approach of any RAF Argosy aircraft which would be dropping one ton containers; they were very inaccurate and the parachutes were frequently caught up in the jungle canopy and took many hours to recover. The much preferred alternative was the RNZAF Bristol Freighter which dropped the smaller parachutes accurately and often within the perimeter. Every now and again these parachutes failed to open and the possibility of a load of bricks, sand and cement free falling on us was daunting. Luckily this never actually happened and after about two months David Hunt, with help from Malaysian Army Engineers, was able to build a galley with a concrete floor and a set of very efficient showers. Items such as mail, eggs and fresh meat were delivered by one of the unit's two Sioux helicopters on an almost daily basis. The pilots, Lieutenants Roger Learoyd and Nick Wise were our most welcome visitors. About once a month I was flown back to Commando HQ for an 'O' Group and Roger Learoyd enjoyed practising auto-rotation and used to switch off his engine just above the jungle canopy; needless to say I did not enjoy it.

'We normally received as many as twenty parachutes or eight one ton containers in a single drop. During each drop we had to secure the landing zone in case any Indonesians came into the area having been alerted by the overflying aircraft, and to prevent any looting by the locals. We had difficulty on one or two occasions when

RAF aircraft arrived late in the afternoon as we had to secure a large area and recover the supplies before dark.

'I remember one morning that the schoolmaster in Pang Amo kampong sent me a note in pigeon English asking whether he could have some 'jems' for his family. It took some time to discover what it was that he wanted, but apparently one of the local labour team who handled the rubbish had found a small tin of jam from our ration packs and showed it to the schoolmaster who decided he rather liked the jam. At the end of our five months we had all got very bored with the ration packs in which many of the meals were hydrated so as to reduce the weight that we had to carry on patrols.'

Body and Soul

'We received a steady stream of visitors. Quite early in our tour we had an Army doctor who wanted to visit the local population to take blood slides as a check on malaria so we had to provide escorts for him. He was followed by a senior Army Medical Officer who wanted to study our medical facilities; quite simply all we had was Leading Sick Berth Attendant Edwards who proved to be outstanding and handled our casualties splendidly. The Army were not used to the Naval Medical Service wherein real responsibility is placed on junior ranks. The unit doctor, Surgeon Lieutenant Alastair Thom, was exactly the right man for the job and we all had great faith in him. I do not know if this is a good example of his medical expertise but the reassurance he gave was memorable. One Marine while out on patrol had a leech crawl up into his penis; this not only worried the Marine but also caused us all great apprehension. When I spoke to Alastair about it he got on the radio and sent an 'opdem' [operational demand] for a gross of condoms. I commented that I wondered how we could keep the condoms in position so he quickly sent a further 'opdem' for a gross of small rubber bands.

'A Chaplain occasionally visited us and it was the RC Padre, Father Jim McCormack, who helped us all in so many ways. He was a remarkable Christian. A Dentist visited once to deal with any problems. He finished quite quickly but he was left with us for three days as there was no helicopter to pick him up. He then went to the kampongs and removed a number of teeth from the locals.

*

'There were two Border Scouts deployed in our area and they would clock in fairly frequently to report what was being carried across the border; they provided the only source of information in our area. Brigade intelligence reports would cover the whole brigade area and bore little relevance for the particular forward areas.

'About once a fortnight I held a petty sessions for the locals making use of an interpreter. I interviewed volunteers who wanted to become Border Scouts or to join the Malaysian Rangers, pregnant women who begged for a helicopter lift to Serian and many locals asking for favours, mainly food. One of our local labour force asked me to stop our men throwing empty aerosol mosquito repellent tins out with the rubbish as once in the fire the tins exploded and frightened them.

'As the months passed so did the standard of our accommodation and amenities improve. We obtained two kerosene fridges in which to store our butter, fresh meat and chicken; any spare space was used for cans of beer. Malaysian Engineers laid a concrete floor on the galley, dining area and the showers. Corporal Northover did excellent work for us; I cannot remember whether he was an Assault Engineer or a Carpenter, but he added a number of refinements.

'Each Troop Commander developed his own method for his Troop to carry rations, filtration kit, water, ammunition and radio batteries. On ten day patrols it was the radio batteries that caused most problems as they were so heavy. Jonathan Thomson ordered from Hong Kong some small packs with a zip fastener along the top and waterproof lining which proved to be excellent as they enabled you to keep one set of dry clothing and socks for use overnight. I used mine for the rest of my service. We tried to get a few bergens but our request was turned down by Brigade staff. When in thick jungle you could only move quickly if you moved in single file and it would have been really useful to have some form of walkie-talkie so that you could keep in touch with both ends of the column.

'It was towards the end of August that we started to carry out cross-border patrols, known as Claret operations. Infantry battalions were not at that stage authorised to take part and only Gurkha, Parachute and Commando units were.'

Operation 'Kid Glove'

'Our first operation was called 'Kid Glove' and was launched on 28 August with Simon Pack leading 5 Troop and Jonathan Thomson leading 6 Troop; Bob Edwards with Colour Sergeant Fraser in charge of a section of Recce Troop and two signallers set up a rebro [rebroadcast] station on a ridge near the border. We took two days on the approach to our target, which was Peripin, where we had been told an Indonesian unit was based alongside the river. We cut through thick jungle and established our laying-up position from which to set the ambushes around Peripin which was now within 800 metres. Our mission had been remarkably vague *'See what you can see around Peripin but don't get involved in a protracted fire fight'*. On the following day I sent Jonathan Thomson with three Marines to recce forward of our base. He reached a position where the jungle ended and the recent 'slash and burn' had started. He thought he could identify a sentry position though it did not appear to be occupied at the time.

'The next day 6 Troop moved forward to establish an ambush, while 5 Troop moved round to the West to take a close-look at Peripin. In early afternoon a fire fight broke out and 6 Troop moved forward to support 5 Troop. They could see the Indonesian position from where a machine gun, armalite rifles and mortars were firing. Jonathan called up the FOO [Forward Observation Officer] who was with me at Company HQ and over 100 rounds of 105mm were fired to cover the withdrawal of the two Troops. Two Marines in 5 Troop had been injured and Lance Corporal Young of 6 Troop was hit in the back where a bullet caused the belt of GPMG ammunition he was carrying to explode.

'Both Troops pulled back to Company HQ where the SBA was able to patch up the wounded. The company moved quickly back to the border following a track regularly used by the locals. It was almost dark and the enemy did not seem to be following us up closely so we continued for a further hour in the dark to a landing site that had been cleared recently. At first light the next day the wounded were picked by helicopter, and the Company and the rebro station worked their way back to Pang Amo. Lance Corporal Young was evacuated to Singapore for further treatment.

'What had we achieved on this operation? We had located the Indonesian positions beside the river and not only had we surprised them but we had hit them hard in their own base. They had experienced the effect of over 100 artillery rounds and we believe that at least six of them had been killed. It was interesting to note that a round from one of our self loading rifles [SLR] had lifted one of the enemy right off the roof of a basha; an armalite rifle may be a lot lighter to carry but it was not as effective as the SLR.

'What did we learn? If attacking a defended position which was surrounded by open slash and burn areas as well as jungle, two under-strength Troops may not be sufficient to cover their withdrawal effectively. It would have been much more difficult for us if the enemy had followed us up more closely.'

Operation 'Spring Onion'

'The second Claret Operation was 'Spring Onion' and it was launched on 9 October '65. The target was again Peripin which we now knew was occupied by a platoon of the Indonesian Army and which had a 12.7 AA gun as well as 51mm mortars. This time I took 3 Troops; 5 and 6 Troops and also 2 Troop with Second Lieutenant Ian Binnie from A Company at Plaman Mapu and a rebro party. Our packs and the heavy rebro equipment were flown to a landing site near the border by a Whirlwind shuttle. Each man was carrying rations for seven days, water, filtration bags, radio batteries and ammunition. Three Troops and Company HQ moving in single file through the jungle in heavy rain made slow progress and it took two days to reach our harbour position on a long ridge above a track approaching Peripin. Early the next morning 6 Troop moved closer to Peripin and took up an ambush position. During the morning an aircraft flew over but we could not see it. We assumed that we had been spotted by the enemy and we heard heavy automatic and rifle fire close to us; we remained very quiet but nothing else happened. Several days later I was told that it had been a RNZAF Bristol Freighter that had accidentally crossed the border and the Indonesians opened fire on it. I withdrew 6 Troop to our harbour position for the night.

'Next day I moved 5 Troop into another ambush position and sent a small group forward on a three hour recce but they found nothing to report. That evening a signaller with 2 Troop which was securing our harbour position had an accidental discharge while cleaning his rifle. I felt sure that people in Peripin must have heard it as we were so close. I decided to stay one more day and sent 6 Troop to relieve 5 Troop in the ambush position. One or two locals were heard on the track but otherwise nothing happened. On the eighth day of the patrol we withdrew back across the border and after picking up the rebro team went back to Pang Amo.

'What had we achieved on our second Claret operation? The answer can only be 'nothing'. We saw no enemy but did hear some locals. More than likely they sensed that we were there and our presence would have been confirmed by the accidental discharge. Perhaps if our presence had been reported to the Indonesian Army they decided to sit tight in their defensive positions having been hit so hard a few weeks earlier.

'What lessons did we learn? A column of nearly eighty men moving in single file in close jungle could only make very slow progress and could be noisy. It was almost unmanageable through lack of short range communications. I decided that I would never take more than two Troops at full strength if operating near Peripin in the future.'

R A M Seeger – OC 'D' Company

Operation 'Freefall'

'By the time 40 Commando came back for its third Borneo tour in late summer 1965, cross-border operations were routine affairs. The war had escalated considerably. This time the Commando was based at Serian in Sarawak and I had a company location on the border by a small village called Kujang Sain.

'My company (D Company) had been specially formed to match the positions we were required to defend and was made up of numbers 1 and 2 Troop from A Company, a section of mortars from Support Company and a variety of specialists in my company HQ. Our base was on a hill top, well dug in and surrounded by barriers of wire and mines. A nearby position had recently been attacked and partially overrun by the Indonesians so we were not inclined to take chances. My in-camp daily routine usually began with a digging session in the cool of the morning before breakfast when we deepened and expanded our underground living quarters and work areas.

A general view of the Base Camp at Kujang Sain, close to Indonesian border, from where D Company, 40 Commando operated during Operation Freefall

'Operation 'Freefall' took place between 6/10 September '65. In this operation, which I proposed and planned myself, I took the company across the border from Kujang Sain and 'fire assaulted' an Indonesian army base by the village of Apuk. We surprised the enemy and raked the position with rifle and machine gun fire. Mortars and Artillery completed the assault and covered the subsequent withdrawal. Indonesian casualties seen to fall during direct fire were estimated to be nine killed and seven wounded. Our own Troops were unscathed.

'On the morning of 6 September a selected Company HQ, 1 Troop (Lieutenant Taffinder) and 2 Troop (Second Lieutenant Binnie) moved south from Kujang Sain along the border to a point where it hooked west into Indonesian territory. The ground here was high and steep, offering good communications and defensive fire positions for a fighting withdrawal. For these reasons it had been chosen as a forward base for the operation. 3 Troop (Lieutenant Linn) from A Company at a nearby location (Plaman Mapu) had secured it the day before and would hold it until our return. We spent a relaxed night guarded by the 3 Troop sentries and then at first light on 7th September, bade goodbye and stepped across the border into unknown jungle.

'We were carrying rations for seven days and an average supply of ammunition. Riflemen had 3 magazines and a bandolier, GPMG teams 400 linked rounds, and

A mixed group of D Company Headquarters and 1 Troop, enjoying a beer after Operation Freefall. CQMS Wilson is standing third from left.

every man a grenade. Jungle gear had been cut to the minimum – a parachute cloth sleeping bag, a poncho, a spare pair of socks, a face veil, water bottle, a mess tin, personal sundries and a generous supply of mosquito repellent. Each Section carried two water bags and a small machete. Faces were heavily streaked with camouflage cream and personal equipment organised into the 3 lines. The only 'documents' carried were identity discs, blank notebooks and clean maps. Lavatory paper was unmarked and each man had a plastic bag for sweet papers, spent matches, cigarette ends and food wrappings. Our cover story was a routine border patrol whose commander had got lost.

'Intelligence reports had indicated an Indonesian position at Apuk but there were no firm details. Information on the ground was meagre and had been gleaned from inadequate air photographs and maps. Our first task therefore was to find the enemy!

'The first day was slow and tiring. Direct progress proved impossible. There were large tracts of open ground and groups of civilian workers, round which awkward and painstaking detours had to be made – no easy tasks with a line of sixty men. After some searching, a secure and concealed harbour area was found, near to a convenient stream and on top of a small hill. The plan was to stay here for two days whilst a reconnaissance patrol, specially picked for their experience and fitness, identified the location and activity of the enemy.

'The patrol I chose comprised myself, an HQ Lieutenant (Second Lieutenant Wells-Cole), the Company Sergeant Major (CQMS Wilson) and a PWI HQ Sergeant (Sergeant Adamson). For speed and stealth we carried belt order only – water bottles, ammunition and cold rations for twenty-four hours. We were armed with Armalite rifles.

'We soon found ourselves with the same problem as the company on the first day – open or cultivated ground, villagers and workers. The consequent need for cautious concealment, detour and back-track aggravated the job of looking for the enemy camp and by nightfall our information was as inconclusive as ever. Soldiers had been seen moving in the village but we had come across no sign of a permanent position.

'That night it rained hard and we started off again in the dawn, stiff, cold and anxious. There was only limited time left to complete our task. All turned out well, however, and by 0800 hrs the enemy position had been found. It was on an isolated piece of high ground by a bend in the river which flowed past Apuk. Steps ran down to the water from what appeared to be the main entrance. A series of bunkers, communication trenches and Atap buildings clustered round the flat summit. Alongside the river ran a frequently used track leading, it was assumed, to the village. The position was observed for an hour and then, with the ground knowledge gained on the move out, fast progress made back to the company harbour.

'In the jungle everything is relative. To my returning patrol, the company harbour seemed the height of comfort and security. We drank, ate and relaxed, then settled down to plan the company follow-up. It was to be a simple and straightforward affair. Packs would be cached in the stream bed near the harbour area and the company would close on to the enemy's position by the patrol's return route. Near the enemy base they would split, each Troop following its own path on either side of the river to the final assault position. The only complication was the Mortar and Artillery fire which was to come down fast and less than 100 metres in front of the forward sections. By the end of the afternoon preparations were completed. Coded radio messages had been transmitted, 'O' groups and briefings conducted in hoarse whispers, and all weapons and ammunition carefully checked, cleaned and stowed.

'Next morning – 10 September – we set out as planned for the enemy position. As we drew near, a lone civilian was sighted heading towards us through the trees. The lead Scout gave the Danger signal and the sign for an indigenous local. Quickly we faded into the cover of jungle scrub. The local walked unhurriedly past but without apparently noticing anything. Another alarm came from an energetic domestic pig on the left flank.

'300 metres short of the enemy base, a rear Company HQ was dropped off as a withdrawal rally point. A few minutes later the Troops split; Sergeant Adamson and myself led Second Lieutenant Binnie's 2 Troop towards the point we had observed the base from on the day before. Lieutenant Taffinder's 1 Troop went across the river and over un-reconnoitred ground towards a parallel position fifty metres north. Behind the leaders in each file walked GPMG gunners and Energa grenadiers – just in case contact was made earlier than expected.

'Seventy metres behind the planned firing positions and on a slight rise, I dropped off my MFC (Corporal Holland), FOO (Bombardier Livingstone), HQ Signaller (Corporal Hathaway) and a rifleman escort. I myself carried on with 2 Troop to spring the assault. Some fifty metres short of the river and about seventy metres from the first enemy bunker we halted. Second Lieutenant Binnie spread his sections out in extended line. The far left one went slightly further forward with the Troop Sergeant – Sergeant Preece and Sergeant Adamson. Weapons in the aim and safety catches off, we settled down to wait for H-Hour.

'We watched a bathing party walk out of the front entrance of the enemy camp down to the river. Other movements could be clearly seen in the position. Then just before H-Hour a large well built Indonesian soldier began to climb the steps to the camp. Unable to resist this target, I opened proceedings with a single shot from my armalite.

'The soldier catapulted forward, hit by the simultaneous fire of a 2 Troop GPMG and a dozen or so SLRs. The other weapons on the south side of the river raked the bunkers, sentries and moving personnel at the edge of the camp.

'North of the river 1 Troop were still on their approach in a long single file. They had been having difficulties with the unknown ground and a large open gap in the trees and only the Troop Commander and one GPMG team were in position. The remainder broke into a run firing on the move.

'As the Troop's second GPMG team crossed an exposed gap they saw three enemy thirty metres to their right coming down a ridge from the camp. They opened fire and killed them but not before one had tried to throw a grenade. Luckily for the gunners, it hit the back of the leading enemy and exploded against him.

'The CSM who should have been at the rear HQ but had accompanied 1 Troop, directed a newly joined young Marine (Marine Porter) with an energa, to fire at one of the forward bunkers. With satisfaction he saw it score a direct hit. Second Lieutenant Wells-Cole who had stayed where he had been told at the rear Company HQ watched with interest as enemy return fire began to burst through the jungle trees above his head. Ahead of them in the forward HQ, the MFC and FOO had brought down white phosphorous markers and were giving their corrections for a close engagement of the enemy.

'The first shot went down at 0953 hrs and two minutes later, I gave the order to withdraw. Now reluctantly the sections began to pull back. There were small sharp explosions from enemy grenades and two inch mortars. Just too late machine gun fire began to kick up the earth where the Troops had lain. Machine gun fire also followed 1 Troop back across the exposed gap. On target, our 105mm shells and 81mm mortar bombs began to burst amongst the enemy fire positions.

'The transition from days of silence to sudden uninhibited noise was startling. Men called out or talked in excited release, commanders shouted orders, radio operators tried to make themselves heard and a vengeful Marine from 1 Troop (Marine Kennedy) shot the pig that had caused alarm on the way in.

'The CSM (who had hurried back to his post) checked the company through the rear HQ and saw it shake back into the discipline of jungle silence and single file. I moved up into the lead and two Assault Engineers (Corporals Finn and Cudbertson), fired the Claymore mines they had rigged to cover the withdrawal. The mortars and artillery fired their final shots and, except for the heavy breathing of men moving at speed and the squelch of jungle boot in mud, all was quiet again.

'I expected a follow-up. Shouts and noise of movement had suggested a sortie from the camp but nothing developed. We reached the border without interference and by the end of the afternoon were back in Kujang Sain.

John Weston, Major – OC C Company

Operation 'Stonehouse'

'The operation took place on 16 September '65. The target was an Indonesian raiding base on the south bank of the river Sakayan in Kalimantan, about five miles south of the

Lieut Mike Taffinder (seated centre) wih members of 1 Troop, D Company, 40 Commando at Kujang Sain after taking part in Operation Freefall in September 1965 during cross-border operations.

Malaysian border. This was the base from which raids had been launched into Sarawak, in particular those on the police post at Tebedu, where 40 Commando were now based. The strength of the enemy at their base was not known exactly, but was believed to be at about platoon level, with additional mortars. This was the section of the border where the Indonesian army was most frequently apparent, so that reinforcement of the base might possibly take place.

'To ensure sufficient force to cope with the task we decided to use the whole Company, with 7 Troop (Second Lieutenant Barry), 8 Troop (Lieutenant Milne-Hume) and 9 Troop (Lieutenant Trotman); I would be in command and an artillery FOO would accompany us. Two 105mm howitzers would be at Tebedu in direct support; as we moved off, one of these was flown to a fire position just short of the border.

'Shortly after dawn the Company was flown to a landing site close to the border and set off on foot for the target, avoiding main tracks and paths and keeping as quiet as possible. The route turned out to be easier than expected and, after selecting two layback positions for the return, the Company arrived at a hill-ridge, close to but above the river valley – out of sight of the target but in a position from which we could hear sounds of activity. A small recce party went forward to select positions on the river bank for the firing party; immediately afterwards the firing party moved into position. Due to limited space the size of the party was reduced to one rifle section, the GPMG groups from each of two Troops, the four energa grenade launchers and one M79 grenade launcher.

'As we were getting into position, two women with their washing crossed the river to our side, saw us and shrieked. This alerted the enemy who opened fire. We had by then identified their base and selected individual targets. We opened fire and continued for about two minutes until there was no sign of life. Amazingly, some men whom we had not previously noticed popped their heads up to see what all the fuss was about. They were also shot.

'The firing parties then withdrew through the covering force, 7 Troop, to the first layback position on the hill-ridge. At this point mortars in base-plate positions well to the rear of the enemy base opened fire with a few rounds, but caused no casualties. After confirming that everyone was clear and ready to move, we moved by stages to the second lay-back position, two Troops moving at a time, covered by the third. There we remained overnight in a position of all round defence.

'There had been some ineffectual enemy machine-gun fire during the move but no casualties had been caused. From dusk the enemy fired mortars in what appeared to be a 'sweep and search' programme. Once their bombs were falling well clear of us, we replied with fifteen rounds of 105mm HE on what we estimated to be their base-plate position. There was no further enemy fire.

'At first light next morning we set off for our base at Tebedu, again moving tactically. For the final stage from the LS at the border, we were lifted by helicopter, arriving at about 1030 hrs. During the Operation we suffered no casualties; we could not say what the enemy casualties were, but later reports from local people said that thirty-two graves had been dug and that the raiding base on the Seaman river had been abandoned.'

Major Weston was later awarded the Military Cross for his part in this highly successful and clearly copybook operation.

Dick Sidwell – OC B Company

Operation 'Angel's Kiss'

'Our third Claret operation was Operation 'Angel's Kiss'. Company HQ with twenty-two ranks of 5 Troop and nineteen ranks of 6 Troop set off on 1 November using a RAF Whirlwind helicopter to ferry us to a new landing site prepared a few days earlier and also dropped off a section under Second Lieutenant John Barry to set up a rebro station on the border. For eight hours on the following day we moved forward very quietly to NE of Peripin where we harboured. 6 Troop laid an ambush for two days on the main track leading from Peripin to the 'slash and burn' area, where they had seen a sentry position, probably one from our first operation. They had to keep off the track itself because local workers were likely to use it to get to their crops. A section from 5 Troop carried out a recce to the east of our position and reported that there were no locals in the fields and it looked as though the paddy crop had not been tended for several weeks.

'The next day 5 Troop relieved 6 Troop who returned to the company harbour site; everyone was very wet and cold and not looking forward to yet another uncooked meal. That night on the evening schedule the CO radioed that he understood from Brigade HQ that Peripin may have been abandoned by the enemy and we were to get close to Peripin to see whether this was true.

'Early next morning I left one section of 6 Troop in company HQ with the FOO, Captain Brian Kingshead RA, the signallers and the SBA, Edwards, at the harbour position while I joined Second Lieutenant Jonathan Thomson and two sections of 6 Troop for a close recce of Peripin. It was at this time that Marine Hall developed appendicitis and had to be taken back to the landing site for evacuation. Later in the morning I ordered Second Lieutenant Bob Edwards with 5 Troop to move up behind us to a position from where they could support 6 Troop and secure the track to the North where it left the 'slash and burn' area and entered the jungle. This area was a series of low ridges at right angles to the track about 150 yards from crest to crest. The leading section was guided by Corporal Danells as he had been there before. In the meantime Jonathan and I crept forward onto the next crest about forty yards in front of his two sections so that we could have a close look at Peripin. To start with there was no sign of any movement in the enemy 'basha' area but after a bit we saw an Indonesian soldier cleaning his high black leather boots and another eating. The enemy had not abandoned their base.

'Then suddenly the machine gun that Jonathan had placed on the main track to the East and rear of us fired a short burst; fire was quickly returned by the enemy and mortar bombs began to land on the reverse slope of the ridge on which we had been sitting. The pair of us ran back very fast to the section covering us. Jonathan picked up his other section while I went on to where 5 Troop should have been waiting for us as I had no radio set and so was unable to find out what exactly was happening. I then found that 5 Troop had never reached that position; I assumed that the firing that I heard to the East was 6 Troop and it was they who had called down the artillery fire. I could see that the 12.7 AA gun was firing on fixed lines straight up through the agricultural area. Avoiding this fall of shot I headed back towards my HQ where I found 5 Troop.

'I discovered later that two Indonesian soldiers had left their base and walked up the track to their sentry position and when within ten yards of 6 Troop's GPMG gunner he shot them both. Almost simultaneously about six enemy opened fire on 5 Troop as they crossed over a ridge to our rear. Bob Edwards, Corporal Danells and eight Marines were under direct fire so they ran back to the ridge where the rest of the Troop had taken up fire positions; Marine Kelly was hit in the back of his thigh and had difficulty walking. A second Marine had a slight wound on the lip. Several mortar bombs fell and Danells was hit on the temple by a piece of shrapnel and he fell. Lance Corporal Dignam ran back to pick up Danells who was lying in the open. [For his bravery Dignam was awarded a Mention in Despatches].

'Bob Edwards contacted the FOO who quickly brought rounds of 105mm on to the enemy and the mortar firing ceased. Bob pulled his Troop back along the track as he was aware that some enemy were moving round to outflank him and he wanted to get his two injured men to the Company harbour position where the SBA could tend their wounds. Because the condition of Danells was so serious 5 Troop set off via the main track to the border hoping to reach the landing site about 3,000 yards away to enable a helicopter to pick up the casualties before dark. Sadly Danells had died by the time they reached the landing site.

'Jonathan called for adjustments to the 105mm fire as 6 Troop withdrew to the company harbour position and then acting as rear guard followed 5 Troop and Company HQ back over the border. The company was ferried back to Pang Amo by one RAF Whirlwind helicopter. At last light when there was only the rebro team, Jonathan, two Marines and me left on the ground the helicopter pilot left us without warning and it took us over six hours to walk back to Pang Amo in the dark.

'What had we achieved and learnt on our third Claret operation? We found that the Indonesians were still occupying Peripin and that they patrolled their side of the border and had a sentry position which was occasionally occupied. We were able to get very close to their base without being detected but, once alerted, their reaction with defensive fire was quick and tracks were likely to be covered by mortars and machine gun fire. We had killed a number of the enemy and probably wounded others. As Company Commander I was fortunate to have as Troop Commanders two Second Lieutenants who used their initiative, manoeuvred their sections tactically and did not hesitate to call for fire from supporting arms.

'Once we were all back in Pang Amo it was good to know that David Hunt had been in contact with Commando HQ arranging the removal to Serian of Corporal Danells and the wounded Marines, and the return of the visiting Troop who looked after Pang Amo while we were away. He arranged the immediate replenishment of the 105mm and our own ammunition supplies.

'We continued to carry out regular patrolling of our area for the next few weeks but 'Angel's Kiss' was the last of our cross-border operations from Pang Amo. 40 Commando was relieved by the Argyll and Sutherland Highlanders in the last week of November. B Company were flown back to Serian and then moved by road to Kuching, from where we embarked in the LSL Sir Lancelot for Singapore; it was on board this LSL that we enjoyed our first really good meal and a comfortable bed for five months. Once again we were very fortunate to be back in Johore for Christmas.'

Chapter 12

Royal Marines Aviator

845 Naval Air Squadron; Sarawak, 2nd and 3rd Division

March '64 to May '65

Royal Marines Aviator

845 Naval Air Squadron

M J (Mick) Reece, Captain – Detachment Commander

'As a person who, latterly, frequently fails to recall what he had for breakfast, the 'invitation' to jot down my recollections of Confrontation as a Royal Naval Wessex helicopter pilot some forty-four to forty-five years later is, in 2009, a greater challenge than the conflict itself. Fortunately, pilots, providing in their dotage they can find them, have one great memory aid; namely, their logbook. Their otherwise curt and bland entries listing the type of aircraft, airframe number, with whom one was flying, a brief note of the mission, the hours flown can, even now, stimulate memories and, above all, the logbook has the supreme benefit of providing accurate dates. For me, as an inexperienced and newly trained Whirlwind Mk 7 pilot in 848 Naval Air Squadron, my journey to Borneo started in Autumn 1963 at RNAS Culdrose when I was invited to attend an operational conversion course to fly the Wessex Mk 1. With a number of enthusiastic, but equally inexperienced, colleagues we were destined to form 706 *Bulwark* Flight and join HMS *Bulwark* the following March for transit to the Far East where we would reinforce and join 845 Naval Air Squadron. At the time the Wessex Mk 1 was the largest and most powerful helicopter in the Royal Navy's inventory and was already deployed in the Far East with 845 Squadron. The challenge to master a new and more complex gas turbine aircraft was in itself demanding and exciting. However, with all the benefit of hindsight, although a considerable improvement on its predecessor, the Whirlwind, the Wessex was a helicopter designed for low level operations in a temperate climate and, as I will describe later, was to manifest many technical, engineering and aviation limitations in the tropics. Secondly, unlike – I understand – the majority of operational ground and aviation deployments today, we had no specific-to-theatre training or even advice.

'706 *Bulwark* Flight formed immediately after Christmas leave in January 1964 for an intensive but conventional UK training period. Fortunately, the weather was not quite as bad as the previous and infamous winter of 1963, but tropical it certainly wasn't. I cannot speak highly enough of the maintenance ratings. They worked marvels to prepare the aircraft not only for an intense series of training exercises away from Culdrose but also for their imminent embarkation and deployment to the Far East.

The majority of the ratings had no previous helicopter, let alone Wessex, experience. They also had to squeeze in less popular – for them – military distractions such as living in the field and small arms training. All these activities were encompassed in a whirl of exercises throughout January and February in such unlikely tropical locations as Bodmin Moor, Dartmoor, Salisbury Plain, Larkhill and a detachment to Portland for SS11 and machine gun firing at Lulworth. As befits a Naval Squadron, there had to be an Admiral's inspection to assess its fitness for an operational deployment. The inspection was conducted by Rear Admiral Percy Gick and his staff. It should have taken place on Bodmin Moor but appalling weather confined us to a corner of Culdrose airfield. I recall supervising maintenance ratings erecting a large marquee – standard issue to squadrons at the time – and serving a two star meal for the Admiral prepared on field cookers. I often wonder what would have happened had we failed. In two months 706 *Bulwark* Flight worked exceptionally hard to create a skilled team that would not flounder when thrown into the deep end of Borneo. It is hard to remember now how little helicopter, let alone Wessex, experience the Flight had when it formed at Culdrose.

'As befitted our mission to the Far East, HMS *Bulwark* sailed on 7 March 1964 from Plymouth in freezing conditions for a helter-skelter passage, with a company of 43 Commando and a battery of 29 Commando Regiment RA embarked. No time to stop at Gibraltar, and the briefest of halts passing Malta. I recall I flew to Halfar airfield to collect the mail. All too quickly the heat and sands of Libya were on the horizon for a short work-up exercise. Exercise Sandfly in North Africa proved a valuable and essential initiation into the Commando Ship assault role, remembering also that the flight deck crews and ship's amphibious assault organisation were equally inexperienced. I suspect few would care to repeat those chaotic days on the Flight Deck.

'Even now, two events stand out from that frenzied exercise. Firstly, a three ton lorry was driven to as remote a location in the desert as we could find and, we thought, many miles from any habitation or person. The following day, before it was enthusiastically rendered unroadworthy by our SS 11 missiles and machine guns, we noted that it had been jacked up and the four wheels and tyres had mysteriously vanished. The second more unfortunate event was that the forecast strong onshore wind rose dramatically during the exercise impaling all four LCAs on the beach and it proved impossible to extricate them. Not only during the exercise did we have the distraction of delivering survival rations to the crews but, in the end, I had the sad task of winching them off the craft and returning them to the sanctuary of *Bulwark*. Following a by now familiar pattern, there was insufficient time for a measured recovery operation because the ship had to dash for Suez to comply with its booked transit through the canal. So, we left Libya with a rather sad three-tonner, minus its wheels, in the desert, four equally sad landing craft on the beach and a company from 43 Commando ashore, under the command of Captain 'Jungle' Baizley, with an initiative test to find its way back to UK – no doubt, there was a plan. I cannot recall what happened to the Battery and its guns. I presume there was another plan. I understand that the LCAs were eventually recovered by Malta Dockyard.

HMS *Bulwark* sportily waves goodbye to HMS *Albion* after their handover in Aden

'HMS *Albion* was waiting gleefully to greet us in Aden, and judging by the graffiti on the aged aircraft, which were transferred to *Bulwark*, our predecessors in 845 Squadron were very happy to be going home. *Albion* also very kindly transferred her Landing Craft. While in Aden we officially threw off the mantle of 706 *Bulwark* Flight to be integrated into 845 Squadron for passage to Singapore. Meanwhile, in the hangar our new and relatively smart camouflaged Wessex were trying to ignore the recently acquired veteran aircraft scarred with much improper advice from the old Squadron.

'The speed of the voyage was maintained with only a brief stop in Singapore. Lieutenant Commander 'Tank' Sherman, our new Commanding Officer, greeted his replacements and confirmed our future deployment. Half the squadron (with many pilots and ground crew waiting to go home) was already deployed in Sarawak supporting military operations in both the 2nd and 3rd Divisions, the other half would remain embarked. The Squadron would change round approximately every three months. And thus, a few days later, off the coast of Sarawak, the squadron reorganised and split once more. During my time in 845 Squadron it was never reunited.

'In April, 1964, the Borneo half of the Squadron, eight Wessex and a Hiller, was deployed in three detachments at Sibu, Nanga Gaat and Simanggang to support counter insurgency operations throughout the entire 2nd and 3rd Divisions of Sarawak. Sarawak has been aptly described as a giant jungle covered prune! It is a vast area, similar in size to Wales, mostly mountainous and almost entirely covered in jungle. It is very hot and wet with early morning low cloud and afternoon thunderstorms as constant problems. For aviators, and no doubt the Troops on the ground, it also had the major limitation of not having any accurate maps. Most of our maps were all white with only the significant rivers shown. Even so, they did have the odd helpful remark annotated by the Royal Engineer surveyors such as *"ere be dragons"*!'

Simanggang

'My first deployment was to the small airstrip at Simanggang in support of the 2/10th Gurkha Rifles. It had a treasured bonus because the pilots were privileged to live in the Gurkha's Officers' Mess and I was allocated a most splendid Gurkha orderly.

'On our arrival we found the detachment's morale particularly high having just successfully fired the first (and probably only) French made SS 11 missiles against an identified Indonesian target. It transpired that a patrol from A Company, 2/10th had recently been ambushed and the CO resolved to destroy an enemy camp on the ridge overlooking the 2nd Division and, in particular, Simanggang. The assault by A Company was supported by Field Artillery and two 845 Squadron Wessex firing SS 11 missiles at a large cave near the top of the cliff and below the enemy camp, which had been identified as an enemy OP. One of the aimers was Lieutenant David Storrie RM. I believe a total of eight missiles were fired although, I understand, not all functioned according to the French sales specification; quite possibly because they had been stored for some time in less than ideal conditions in the detachment location. Even so, the missile firing, combined with the artillery support, enabled the Gurkhas to capture and destroy the enemy camp.

'My own introduction into Borneo operations was less auspicious. One of my first missions was a resupply sortie to a company base some forty-five miles from Simanggang. One of my passengers was a goat with the most attractive markings and, even now, I recall with embarrassment that my only thought was for its security within the aircraft. Unfortunately, having landed at Jambu, the company base, my Wessex went unserviceable and I was obliged to stay the night. The menu choices offered by the most hospitable Gurkhas that evening were snake or goat!

'Operating close to or on the border the Gurkhas patrolled aggressively. They had a number of contacts and we were frequently employed flying machine gun strafing

A Wessex Mk1 of 845 Naval Air Squadron operating over deep jungle, showing the navigation problem that pilots had in locating targets and landing sites.

sorties with the aim of interdicting identified enemy approach or escape routes. On a few occasions, following a contact, I was tasked to recover enemy bodies and transport them to Simanggang. I confess that looking down from my lofty and detached cockpit perch and witnessing sodden corpses being tossed into the cabin of my aircraft, I could not but reflect how wretched and insignificant our enemy appeared and, particularly, how diminutive.

'After two productive and enjoyable months supporting the Gurkhas from Simanggang, we were relieved by the RAF in early June 1964 and our small detachment joined the main 845 Squadron base at Sibu airport. Sibu, the capital of the Third Division, is a large town of mainly Chinese population, sitting on the Rajang River, the main water artery of the Division. The squadron was crammed into bungalows near the airport, some three miles from Sibu town. From Sibu and our forward operating base at Nanga Gaat, our helicopters endeavoured to support one battalion and a succession of companies patrolling in the SAS role to cover an area of some 25,000 square miles.'

Nanga Gaat

'115 miles to the East of Sibu lies Nanga Gaat, at the junction of the Baleh and Gaat rivers. 845 Squadron had first moved to 'The Gaat' in November 1963, and constructed landing pads and accommodation behind a bungalow, which belonged, as did the land, to the Temmonggong Jugah, The Paramount Chief of the Ibans. By April 1964, the Gaat was already a legend in Sarawak for its unique way of life, the close association with the Ibans, the relaxed dress, the Anchor Inn, the premiere of *From Russia with Love* and the unparalleled hospitality. Although there were others, two of its most distinguished and successful Detachment Commanders were Royal Marines, namely Lieutenants David Rowe and Tim Donkin. Progressively, the base was extended and significant improvements made. Notably, a substantial 240 volt generator was flown in and installed by HMS *Bulwark*'s electrical department. There was soon more electricity available than could be absorbed by the small village that had grown up, consisting of the Jugah's family, Gurkhas, Surveyors, Malays, Border Scouts, coolies and 845 Squadron itself. Deep in the eastern half of the Third Division, the Gaat became the very centre of the 'Hearts and Minds' campaign.

'The relations with local Ibans developed to the extent of embarrassing friendliness cultivated by longhouse visits, income for the coolie party employed at the Gaat, medical services provided by the resident RN Sick Berth Attendant, coupled with the knowledge that any serious medical cases would always be flown to hospital at Kapit or Sibu. This call on our humanitarian services was graphically illustrated in June 1964 when a cholera epidemic struck isolated longhouses in the vicinity of Nanga Gaat. I and many others had the distressing task of flying pitiful patients to the nearest, and overwhelmed, 'cottage' hospital in Kapit. I have to confess it was relatively easy sitting up in my elevated cockpit, isolated from the disease and filth of our weak and often dying passengers. However, I had the most profound admiration for our air-crewmen who with great compassion carried these poor souls into and out of the aircraft and consoled their equally distressed relatives. There is no doubt that, thanks to our intervention, many lives were saved. Nevertheless, the majority of aero-medevacs appeared to be women having difficulty in labour. Mercifully, no child was born in our aircraft but there were some close shaves, so much so that at Sibu some air-crewmen took a short course in midwifery.

'The colourful character of Nanga Gaat and the nights at the Anchor Inn will be remembered by all that served and stayed there. But it must not be forgotten that it was from this jungle site that the majority of the squadron's operational sorties were launched. These tasks increased throughout our stay until over 300 hours per month were being flown by the three Wessex and, later, one Whirlwind based there. The jungle covered mountainous terrain was almost entirely uninhabited except for the occasional longhouse and the isolated military patrols, whose very presence depended on 845 Squadron. Trees, which soared to a height of 200 feet made landing sites hazardous and difficult to locate after transit flights, where three to six thousand foot mountain ranges, poor weather and inaccurate maps presented a continuous challenge. We soon

[illegible]

845 Squadron refuelling in the field aided by local labour

Part of the 'Hearts and Minds' campaign was the evacuation of serious medical cases from kampongs. Here an Iban is being lifted out, accompanied by his typical baggage.

became familiar with our 'long haul' military support operations to isolated bases and confined clearings, or, occasionally, the wisps of smoke from a smoke grenade rising from the canopy. One piece of foresight, for which we were grateful, was that our aircraft had been equipped with a 200 foot winch, twice the length of the anticipated need in UK.

'Both detachments not only supported major units working in the Third Division but, in particular, developed a special relationship with, successively, the SAS, the Guards Independent Parachute Company, the Gurkha Independent Parachute Company and an Independent Company of the 2nd Battalion Parachute Regiment, whose four man patrols, alone in the jungle for two months at a time, we admired so much. Transit distances to the border sites from the Gaat were frequently sixty to seventy miles. From Sibu, aircraft supported all military activity in the Western half of the Third Division and the transit distances were even greater. It was not uncommon on Troop lift or resupply sorties for the aircraft to be flying for four or five hours non-stop away from Sibu.

'Aero-medevac cases from all over the Division to Sibu hospital were also a regular feature of the Squadron tasks both by day and night. These mercy missions were too numerous to record in detail, but probably the most celebrated case was in August 1964, when Kumbang, a fifteen-year-old Iban boy, was flown out of Entabai at night after a harpoon had pierced and passed through his head during a night fishing expedition. Kumbang later returned to his longhouse apparently none the worse for his experience and the harpoon was presented to the first pilot of the aircraft, Lieutenant 'Cosh' Kennard, Royal Navy, who also received a Queen's Commendation for the operation. Shortly after the cholera epidemic had subsided, the first rotation occurred and I returned to *Bulwark* and, in August, flew in support of 42 Commando for an exercise appropriately called 'Exercise Horse's Neck'. In the event, the Squadron's involvement was abruptly halted after two days and we were redeployed to meet the first reported Indonesian incursion into Malaya in the Pontian area. A few weeks later large numbers of Indonesian Paratroops landed in the Labis area and four Wessex and a Hiller were deployed to support the 1st Battalion New Zealand Regiment and the 1st/10th Gurkha Rifles. 270 hours were flown and the prompt reaction and deployment of the Troops given by our aircraft was a major factor in the success of that operation. However, I was not involved and shortly afterwards was back in, by now, a familiar Sarawak environment for the remainder of my tour.'

Meeting Demand

'Looking back, there was an understandable and constant demand from our military customers for us to fly the limited number of aircraft we had to their maximum potential and beyond, carrying the maximum number of Troops or stores over excessive distances. This demand was matched in equal part by the squadron willingness to do and even, with hindsight, exceed their best. I apologise if, for a moment, I must get technical but earlier I mentioned the limitations of the Wessex Mk 1. Its performance was woefully inadequate for the demanding hot and humid Borneo tropical conditions and some of these characteristics were only learned through bitter experience and numerous incidents 'on the job'. For example, it was not possible to hover at or near the maximum permissible all up weight. The maximum all up weight was the designed maximum weight the airframe and transmission was permitted to carry under any circumstance. A planned 'hover' weight was calculated from a combination of the fixed airframe weight and the variables of fuel and payload, temperature and altitude, but must never exceed the maximum all up weight. It was soon apparent that the text book para for calculating hover performance in tropical conditions were far too optimistic. After a few incidents, and many more frights, the need to review our operating procedures became abundantly apparent. For example at Simanggang and Sibu it was possible take off from the airport runway at maximum all up weight using a rolling take off to gain translational lift. This technique was used for sorties when sufficient fuel would be burned off in transit to enable a safe and controlled arrival at the planned destination. This is of course how airliners operate today (with much computer assistance) but in Borneo, heading for a confined area landing, such calculations were paramount, and there was inevitably a steep learning curve.

'Of necessity, as well as amending the templates for our calculations, we developed procedures of checking full power and establishing a free air hover before making cautious approaches into jungle destinations. These necessary checks were only possible because we were not threatened by an enemy equipped with surface to air missiles; sadly, a privilege our successors on current operations in Iraq and Afghanistan do not have. At Nanga Gaat, not having the benefit of a runway, a technique was developed to position the fuelled aircraft on a small hill overlooking the site. The passengers would walk up the hill to embark before the helicopter dived off to gain translational lift. I doubt this procedure, which proved most effective, was ever committed to a text book and certainly would never have gained official sanction!

'The maintenance record for the detachment ashore became a byword throughout the Far East. In July 1964, for example, there was not one day with less than seven out of the eight helicopters serviceable and an overall serviceability of ninety-five percent was obtained with a flying rate in excess of sixty hours per month per aircraft. The consistent high serviceability was by no means because the aircraft never went unserviceable, quite the contrary, but was achieved by prolonged hard work on the part of the maintenance teams coupled with high priority stores backing. Every major component change was performed ashore at some time and small maintenance teams found themselves dotted over the Third Division salvaging aircraft, changing engines, etc., often working under difficult and unpleasant conditions and displaying the utmost resilience and initiative. For example, the strain on expensive Wessex hours meant we were obliged to use a piston engine Hiller (later to be joined by two Whirlwinds), for the smaller payload tasks. The Hiller had obvious limitations and was recovered to Sibu under a Wessex on no less than three occasions, once from the headwaters of the Baleh some 200 miles from Sibu. Tragically, the aircraft was eventually lost together with the pilot endeavouring to support Royal Engineer surveyors on a mountain peak.

'When 846 Squadron, flying Whirlwind Mk 7s, was withdrawn from Sabah and disbanded we managed to acquire two of their aircraft. These two aircraft were considerably more limited in the Borneo environment than the Wessex but proved tireless workhorses, taking on the frequent essential but low payload sorties, which had been proving a drain on the Wessex hours and maintenance support. I note that for the last six months of my tour I was actually flying more Whirlwind hours than Wessex on such tasks, which included VIPs, Commander's reconnaissance and even delivering Father Christmas to the Sibu hospital. Not only was the Whirlwind more primitive in capability but these sorties were back to basics in a number of ways. Rarely did the payload permit the luxury, for me, of an air-crewman. Therefore, refuelling from pre-positioned forty-four gallon drums using a hand pump and doing my own servicing became the norm and a race against time before the passengers returned having enjoyed their iced chilled drink and impatient to move on to their next stop.

Sadly, we even lost one of these Whirlwinds. It suffered a hydraulic failure and crashed on the very next sortie after I had delivered it to Nanga Gaat. Mercifully, the pilot on that occasion was not injured.

'The high operational tempo in Borneo, well in excess of peace time projections and, no doubt, carefully prepared graphs by the procurement boffins, created a tremendous drain on the provision of spare parts. I suspect similar pressures and sacrifices are being experienced today to meet the demands of current operations in Iraq and Afghanistan. It is to the Royal Navy's credit that the stores support during Confrontation was superb. We were aware, although selfishly not too upset, that this was at the expense of the Wessex Mk 1 anti-submarine squadrons back in UK, who were severely restricted on flying hours. From the smallest of components to complete engines, these were flown out commercially within hours to eventually be united with one of our poorly aircraft at Sibu or Nanga Gaat or even on a river bank or in a clearing.

'I referred earlier to the technical limitations of the Wessex Mk 1, some of which were overcome, some we just learned to live with. The helicopter relied on an extraordinary AVPIN starter, in which a highly combustible liquid was ignited by a starter cartridge to spin the gas turbine so that it could itself be started. These starters were highly unreliable and became coked, well inside their planned maintenance schedule. This was embarrassing and frustrating until one bright spark decided to pickle the starters in Pepsi Cola at more frequent intervals – problem solved. Another unusual problem, unfortunately not solved during my time, was the windscreen wipers. These were hydraulic and the seals were no match for the tropical heat and humidity. They had the unhelpful and blinding habit, when flying through a tropical rain storm, of smearing hydraulic fluid onto the windscreen. This meant that thereafter, even when the rain had stopped, it was impossible to see ahead. As our maximum speed was some 100 knots we suggested, to no avail, that Jaguar might be able to provide a cleaner and more reliable electrical alternative. Another unforeseen problem concerned the impact of heavy tropical rain storms on the rotor blades. Inconveniently, the rain would literally strip the protective rubber coating from the leading edges and even split open the metal blade tips. Either event would cause violent vibration and precipitate an uncomfortable emergency landing. It follows that we tried to avoid severe rain storms whenever possible, inspections schedules were rapidly revised and the experts at home were invited to develop more resilient materials as a matter of some urgency.

'In contrast to my short spell in the Second Division, no positive enemy contacts were made in the Third Division of Sarawak during our stay. However, our helicopters enabled one battalion and special companies in the SAS role to control over 25,000 square miles against the triple threat of border crossing, sea incursion and internal subversion. In particular as I have already said, we developed a special relationship with the SAS, the Guards Independent Parachute Company, the Gurkha Independent

Parachute Company and an Independent Company of the 2nd Battalion Parachute Regiment.

'I believe, without exception, we all admired the professionalism of these remarkable men who patrolled in such a vast area of primary of jungle for one to two months at a time, isolated and entirely reliant on our support. However, without in any way degrading the standards and accomplishments of the others, the unit that stands out in my memory was the inimitable Guards Independent Parachute Company. Not only was their organisation, patrolling and administration highly professional but they had *style*. The Company included such highly individualistic officers as Robin Dixon, who had won a gold medal as a member of the Olympic Bobsleigh team, Algy Clough of Clough Oil, who, I recall, even on patrol judged it necessary to carry a chequebook in his hip pocket, and Lord Patrick Beresford. It was not uncommon for us to include with the standard resupply sorties a hamper from 'Fortnum & Masons'. I even witnessed certain Patrol Commanders on return to Sibu from a two month patrol, take a shower at the airport before catching the next Borneo Airways flight en route to Singapore or Hong Kong. They returned just in time to meet up with their guardsmen and lead them back into the jungle.

'Naturally, as one would expect in the military support role flying over the Borneo jungle we had our aircraft incidents. Nevertheless, we were stunned that after a relatively successful run in 1964, we should suffer a series of major accidents in February, March and April 1965, resulting in the loss of five aircraft, three pilots, two air-crewmen and twenty-one soldiers. However, in spite of these disasters, the entire Squadron reacted with magnificent resilience; any temporary impact on morale was quickly dissipated by the demands of tasking and by ever present hard work.

'When I returned to UK at the end of May 1965, 845 Squadron aircraft both ashore and afloat had flown 10,000 hours since HMS *Bulwark* left Plymouth. At the time, that figure was probably a record for a British helicopter squadron, and represented a maintenance and flying effort for which all members were justly proud, though the cost was high. During my time ashore, the Wessex Mk 1s, Whirlwind Mk 7s and Hiller aircraft flew 6,064 hours including fifty-four night sorties; they lifted 32,629 passengers, 3,224,285 pounds of stores and 903 aero-medevacs. I am pleased to report that these achievements did not go unrecognised and the Squadron was awarded the coveted Boyd Trophy, presented annually for the finest contribution to Naval Aviation. The citation of the Flag Officer Naval Air Command, Vice Admiral Sir Richard Smeeton, is a fitting summary of a remarkable commission in 845 Naval Air Squadron. It said:

> "By their operations and exercises both ashore and afloat, 845 Squadron set a standard of efficiency in Borneo unsurpassed by any other Squadron deployed there and made a considerable contribution to the defence of Malaysia. They earned the praise of all.

Their flying was of the highest order and the enthusiasm and professional ability of the maintenance ratings enabled the Squadron to achieve an outstandingly high serviceability rate and the distinction of meeting every demand made upon it."

'I am proud that in some small way that I was able to play my part in 845 Naval Air Squadron's contribution during Confrontation.'

The Royal Navy helicopters operated rather a long was away from their mother ship at Belaga, 200 miles up the Rajang river in the Third Division.

Chapter 13

Lundu Finale

42 Commando; Mainly 'Claret'

December '65 to May '66

Lundu Finale

When 42 Commando returned to Sarawak in December '65, it was to the Lundu District of First Division, a task then allocated to a battalion group or its equivalent.

For the first time the Commando deployed with its own Air Troop (Lieutenants Cameron and Gregson), equipped with two Sioux helicopters and based with Commando HQ at Lundu – a location described by their Chief Petty Officer Artificer as 'a pretty little village nestling at the foot of an ominous looking mountain and perched on the banks of the dirtiest looking river I have ever seen'. Of their contribution the unit correspondent wrote…

> "Since coming to Sarawak the team has proved its worth several times over. They may not be able to move a combat tracker team at short notice, but for medevacs, recces, visits and for small urgent resupplies these aircraft are ideal."

Tom Seccombe, Captain – M Company Commander

'I joined M Company in September 1965 as Second-in-Command to Mickey Denyer. The unit was preparing for its forthcoming tour of duty in the First Division of Sarawak where we were to form part of 99 Gurkha Brigade. Bob Mylne was due to join the unit to replace Denyer, but as his posting was delayed, I was told that I would take the Company to Borneo. I was coming new to the jungle and clearly had a lot of catching up to do as two thirds of the Company had a previous tour under their belt.

'While Denyer was still there, I managed to get a place on the Jungle Warfare Course at Ulu Tiram which I attended with four subalterns from the unit, two of them M Company Troop Commanders. This course was absolutely invaluable; it was extremely well run and the course instructors, mainly ANZ, were all men of considerable jungle experience and all too mindful of their responsibility for instilling jungle know-how into people who would very soon be commanding on active service. I remember thinking that I did not see how any putative Company Commander, coming new to the jungle, could have coped adequately with his new responsibilities without training of his sort – in the coming months this view was confirmed! It also gave me a first-hand impression of the abilities of two of my future Troop Commanders, including the exceptional navigational skills of Mike McMullen which were to prove invaluable in the coming months. Of the unit's preparation for the tour I can remember little, apart from the fact that once we were deployed, it was obvious that a great deal of it was inadequate.

'At this time the unit was commanded by Peter Whiteley, with John Owen as Second-in-Command, and Mike Robinson was adjutant; K Company was commanded by Gerald Ferguson, I think, who was shortly to be relieved by Mike Halford; Jack Smith commanded L Company. The unit clearly had some experience as far as the Headquarters was concerned, but little or none at Company Commander level. Four of the newly arrived intake Troop Commanders were all from the same YO batch and they were first class – very fit and lively (at times almost too lively) and were to take readily to the jungle environment.'

Operational Recce

'The unit's recce of our future area of responsibility in Sarawak duly took place and I was told that I would be taking M Company to Bokah in the east of our area; L Company on my right would be at Biawak and K Company on the extreme right flank by the sea at Sematan.

'As I have indicated, the course at the JWS had given me a certain measure of confidence in my ability to operate in the jungle and, about ten days before the advanced party arrived, something else occurred which was to add to that confidence. HQ 99 Brigade contacted 42 Commando and said that the unit we were due to relieve 2/2 GR were carrying out two final cross-border operations from Bokah and Biawak, and they thought it would be a good idea if the Commando sent two officers, who would be operating out of these bases, as observers on these two operations. Within twenty-four hours of the unit being informed of this, I and an officer from L Company, who was going to Biawak, were in Kuching; the following day I was flown into Bokah, practically at first light. I then found that the company that we were taking over from was not in fact to undertake this particular operation; it was instead to be carried out by another company flown into Bokah.'

Separan River

'The aim of the operation was to ambush the Separan River some two days march over the border. Brigade intelligence had known for some time that the river was in regular use by Indonesian forces for Troop movement and re-supply. I met the Company Commander who was to carry out the operation, Len Lauderdale, who amongst other things told me that his FOO had injured himself and would I undertake the necessary gunfire direction should it be needed. I had no option but to say 'yes', wishing at the same time I had paid more attention during courses at Larkhill. I could see that the bombardier and the gunner of the FOO's signal party were also not too enthralled by the idea.

'We spent the whole of the first day getting up to the border – more about this later – and 'bivvied' on our side of the high ridge that delineated it. Lauderdale had already given his orders for the operation before I arrived, not that I would have been able to understand them, because they were all given in Gurkhali; I was able to spend a couple of hours discussing it with him in the evening. We were just about to move off the next morning, when a Sioux helicopter dropped off a replacement FOO at a small helipad about 400 metres below our position. Great relief all round! The FOO who had been dropped off was in fact to accompany me on nearly all my Claret operations. He was of Portuguese descent originally, I think, from Goa – a very tough egg, not only extremely good at his job, but a most capable jungle operator. I always felt all the better for having him with me. The approach down to the river that first day passed off without incident and I was interested to see the Gurkha Company's routine on the march.

'The next day proved very lively. We got down to the river just before midday and took up an ambush position on the track by its side. Almost immediately an Indonesian patrol walked into our right flank and a fire fight ensued. After the initial confusion, which Len handled very well, we were left with two wounded – one badly. Quite obviously we could not remain there once we had been bumped and we withdrew carrying the wounded and covered by our own gunfire. After about an hour Len summoned up a casevac helicopter, the company having cut a very rudimentary LS. How the pilot got in and out I will never know, but he did. It was a remarkable piece of flying which I am glad to say was recognized as such by the powers that be. It may be worth saying that throughout our tour we were supported by this particular RAF squadron, and they never once failed us. I mention this because I have often heard the RAF in Borneo being compared unfavourably with the FAA helicopter squadrons. All I can say is that this was not my experience.

'The company got back up to the border the following day, to be met by their Colonel and the Brigadier commanding 99 Brigade, Bill Cheyne, whom I found most impressive. This operation was very useful to me, as I was able to see Len handling his company in a variety of circumstances, some of them under fire. I was able to see gunfire support being used and to observe the organisation of the helicopter casevac.'

Bokah

'Back at Bokah I had a short time to wait before the advance party, which included the three Troop Commanders, arrived. I used this time to pick the brains of the resident Company Commander (Jeff Ashley). Bokah was not a hilltop border fort – as was Biawak and the fort on my left flank, belonging to another unit to the east. Instead it was set back a day's march from the border, presumably to provide defence in depth should an incursion take place between the two forts. Conditions therefore were not as primitive as in the forts which were literally carved out of the hill, on or very near the border, very heavily defended by machine gun emplacements and mines etc., and with no attempt at concealment. These very strong company bases were General Walker's solution to combating Indonesian incursions in strength. Up to the Spring of 1964, it had been a platoon Commander's war, now it became a Company Commander's war with company strength, cross-border operations mounted from these forts.

'Although a high proportion of Bokah was underground and in the same sort of bunkers used in the forts, some of it was above ground in atap huts. It stood in a large clearing, partly natural, partly man made, on the fringe of the jungle forest as it ran down to the river, surrounded by wire and protected by all the usual defences. Machine guns were sited for all round defence, and also covered the helipad about fifty metres outside the perimeter. A high watchtower in the centre of the base gave a very good field of sight right up to the jungle edge. The river leading down to Lundu (where Commando Headquarters was established) ran close to the base to the north with a track by its side leading down to the Bokah village, with its resident Border Scout a few hundred metres away. There was virtually no contact with the village, except for the girls who came to do our laundry. Resupply and Troop movement was invariably carried out by helicopter and the river, because of its vulnerability to ambush, very rarely used, although the Charwallah's men and stores came up that way without suffering any ill effects.

'The base normally held about 120 men, although the population fluctuated. This included a 105 Gun detachment and a Sapper section who were mainly engaged on construction work and the provision of clean water. General Walker when he had set up the jungle fort chain, had insisted on splitting up the artillery at his disposal into penny packets, with guns in most company bases along the border interlocking with flanking bases – a decision in contradiction to Gunner's doctrine which favours concentration! These guns were used to support Claret operations and, if the operation demanded it, additional guns could be flown into the mounting base. They were also used for what was termed 'harassing fire' over the border, usually at night. I don't know to what extent it in fact harassed the enemy but certainly it initially harassed me by keeping me awake half the night!

'During the turnover, before the main body of the company arrived, all the Troop Commanders were taken out by their opposite numbers on familiarization patrols on our side of the border. This included visiting the villages and getting to know the border scouts in our area. When the change-over was complete and the company had arrived, these patrols continued and I used to attach myself to them as I felt inclined. They served two purposes; to enable me to get to know the area and to give me some idea of the capabilities of the individual Troop Commanders. I had by this time been told that I was to keep the Company for the duration of the tour; because no second in command was provided, this meant that I had to name one of my four subalterns to do the job. It was bad luck on the one I chose – they were all of equal seniority – as it effectively tied him to the base when he much rather have been out in the jungle commanding a Troop.'

Planning and Procedures

'Claret' was the term used to describe all cross-border operations into Indonesian Borneo (Kalimantan). The principal aim of these operations was to pre-empt similar Indonesian incursions by pinning them inside their border and forcing them into a defensive, rather than offensive posture. Because of their extreme political sensitivity – remember that at no time during Confrontation did a state of war exist between us – such operations were governed by strict guidelines, the most important of which, from a Company Commander's point of view, was the need for meticulous planning, briefing and rehearsals; above all on no account should any soldier/Marine taking part be captured by the enemy! Rather easier said than done. This latter guideline prompted me to tell my company that on all Claret operations I would not re-cross the Border without every member of my Company, be they alive or dead. In retrospect this was a rash promise which on one occasion I was nearly unable to honour.

'It was quite obviously implicit, or I considered it to be, that the Company Commander should personally lead all Claret operations. I suppose unless my memory is very much at fault, I was to lead seven or eight such operations, all of varying length and strength. Originally the guidelines had stipulated the depth of any incursion into Kalimantan, but these had since been relaxed, and patrols of up to 15,000 metres in depth were sanctioned – although this distance would have been out of range of our covering 105's, whose maximum range was about 12,000 yards – and at a Troop strength, which, after my first Claret operation, I increased to two full Troops plus. The greater strength, the better I thought, although it significantly increased the problems of control. Seventy men with two metres between them extended over 140 metres and odd things can happen.

'On one occasion I was at about number eight in the Company when I saw a single file of men approaching the column from the right on, as the Navy would say, 'a steady bearing, closing'. Just before shouting 'Enemy Right', I recognized the leading man as one of my senior SNCO's. He was in fact the leader of the last section of the whole Company. How he got there was and still is a complete mystery. On another occasion a man simply disappeared from the middle of the Company, being missed at the hourly ten minute halt. He had been there at the previous halt, so he had been missing for anything up to fifty-five minutes. As was the drill, a shot was fired which was answered almost immediately from what appeared to be very close by. Over the next two hours the answering shots became fainter and then stopped altogether. Five days later, he walked into Biawak, about fifteen kilometres away. I had sent the rest of the Company back to Bokah when we got to the Border and spent four days there with about twelve men, hoping that he would find his way back into our area. I was within three hours of being ordered back to base by the CO, so I was saved from having to break my promise. That he was able to find his way home was due to the fact that we had issued every man with a cheap compass which, although not suitable for any detailed navigation, could at least be relied upon to point north.

'In our area we had the usual mix of primary and secondary jungle, and the going varied considerably on both sides of the Border. The whole territory was crisscrossed with innumerable streams and small rivers which slowed up progress considerably. These streams could become literally impassable for a few hours after heavy rain. The Separan River, which I had visited on my first cross-border operation with the Gurkhas rose so much in the rainy season that it became almost impossible to define its normal course. Although we made several attempts to reach it, I was never able to do so again during the time I remained at Bokah. A characteristic of operating in the jungle which will be known to everybody who has done so, is that you are never dry. Perspiration, rain and a crossing of streams ensured you were wringing wet for a high proportion of the time. Everybody carried a dry set of kit which he would put on at night, thus ensuring reasonable comfort, but there was always the thought that the discarded wet clothes would have to be put on at the start of the following day.

'One of the mantras which had been dinned into everybody in our pre-deployment training, and indeed at the JWS, was that we should never ever use jungle tracks and trails for fear of ambush. In theory this was absolutely correct, but in practice it was very seldom possible. I remember on one occasion listening with disbelief at the time given me to reach a certain RV. I think it was one and a half days. We reached it alright, but had I not used tracks or trails, it would have taken me four and a half days, and the operation could not have taken place. Ignoring this rule placed a high premium on the jungle craft and alertness of your point Marines.

'Quite often we had Iban trackers with us, but I think only on our side of the Border. We also had an Infantry Patrol dog whose task theoretically was to warn us of enemy presence. He was an Alsatian called Rinty, and I have never felt sorrier for any animal. His size, weight of fur and tender feet made him quite unsuitable for this kind of work. The poor beast was always snagging his coat on bushes and boughs, or treading on thorns, causing him to yelp most of the time. He was, however, good for the morale of the Company, because they could see somebody having an even worse time of it than they were. His handler, a Private in the HLI, was devoted to him, but this devotion was at some cost to himself, as he had to carry rations for the dog as well as for himself. Eventually Rinty went down with some nameless canine tropical disease and had to be casevaced.

'The business of rations etc. leads me conveniently to the question of kit. The lightweight Jungle Fighting Order, as issued, was totally inadequate for our task. For a patrol of anything up to ten days, you had to carry a considerable amount of food, clothing and ammunition, and we soon acquired a variety of kit more suitable for our needs, including a large pack, patterned on part of a scale of kit long out of service. These packs were copied and made up by firms in Hong Kong and Singapore. Basically I didn't care what anybody looked like or wore, providing he carried the necessary food and ammunition the length of the patrol demanded. The choice of food we could also leave up to the individual. It was possible to choose from the normal twenty-four hour ration packs, composite rations from the larger packs, Malaysian Army rations, or even Gurkha rations. All these could be made available if required, although the vast majority stuck to the twenty-four hour pack.

'One of the things I shall always remember about this tour was the willingness of those in authority to provide you with what you wanted, provided it was not too outlandish. I remember asking for and receiving three Remington shotguns and a silent Sten gun which was surprisingly efficient – even though I never thought that my OPDEM for a crossbow was taken seriously by anyone but me! The only thing that was in short supply during our tour was 105 shells, and we were constantly advised to use our artillery support sparingly. This exhortation was generally ignored, certainly by our FOOs.'

Command and Control

'Not all the Claret operations were necessarily ordered by Commando or Brigade HQ. If you presented a sufficiently good case for an operation you wanted to carry out, I found that Commando HQ was generally very receptive to ideas, but quite obviously any such plans had to be cleared by Brigade HQ and above (Labuan). If you did get a green light for an operation, then everybody made sure you received all the necessary planning information. The map and air photograph coverage were very good and if you needed additional air photographic coverage, this was arranged reasonably quickly. Good map reading and the ability to interpret air photographs correctly were of critical importance.

'As I've already said, in Mike McMullen I had a map reading genius. In all the work we carried out together, I can't remember him ever making a single mistake and he even evoked the praise of George, my FOO who quite rightly regarded his own map reading skills quite highly. With such a person as Mike in the company, it was difficult not to over work him and his Troop by putting them on point duty too often, but from the Company Commander's point of view, knowing that such a person was leading the company, was a considerable comfort. In this respect as far as M Company was concerned, the leading Troop Commander placed himself at about number five or six in the column and I usually travelled with one signaller immediately behind the leading section. I don't know if this was the correct place for the Company Commander to travel; probably not from an ambush point of view, but the advantage of being close to the front of the column, which could extend up to 150 yards, I thought outweighed other considerations.

'Good communications, it goes without saying, were vital to all Claret operations and they were not always easily achievable, with a border ridge in our area rising to a considerable height. Nearly always we were obliged to put in a relay station for our rear link on the ridge, or immediately below it, for the duration of the operation. This station would of course need to be guarded which added to the manpower bill. Communications on the other side of the border were also not particularly easy and more than once I had to rely on my FOO's radio – Gunner communications, although faced with the same problem as our own, always seemed to work better, as generations of infantry officers have found out over the years!

'A great deal of time and effort went into the planning of these ops and into the rehearsals. It did not matter that certain aspects of these rehearsals were unrealistic; what did matter was that everybody got a good idea of the sequence of events that were going to be carried out. When all your preparation was completed, you presented a plan to the CO for approval. He then, in his turn, forwarded it to Brigade Headquarters with his own recommendations.'

Early 'Claret'

'My first two 'Claret' operations were spent in trying and failing to reach the Separan River. I don't know if those in authority thought we had not been trying hard enough, because they then sent in an SAS patrol to see what they could do. They too failed, I am delighted to say! I then switched my focus to siting ambushes, on what I considered to be likely tracks leading up to our side of the border. These also did not prove productive, although we were able to gain some good intelligence from the locals who wandered into our position.

'I had a particularly good interpreter whose job as a school master had been made redundant by Confrontation. He was also extremely skilled at jungle craft and could read tracks as well as any Iban. It soon became quite clear to me that the Indonesian soldiers we faced were not using the tracks but were tending to remain in what we knew to be quite strongly defended bases; thanks to the questioning of the locals, we had quite a good general idea of where these bases were and all our efforts now turned towards locating their exact positions.'

Sematan

'A little over halfway through the tour I was told that Bokah was to be handed over to 2/10th Gurkhas as part of a rationalization of border posts. I was told that while the Separan River was in flood, the pickings would be slim. This turned out to be spectacularly not the case, as Chris Pike's Company who relieved us were to find out. I hasten to point out that I am not insinuating for one moment that his success would necessarily have been ours. M Company, I was told, was to move to Sematan and be collocated there with K Company. 'This was most unwelcome news. It meant losing my own area just as we were becoming very familiar with it on both sides of the border, and having to share a location with another company which I thought was bound to be uncomfortable. In fact my fears were not justified.

'The Company was comfortably housed in tents on the football field, while I had exclusive use of a bungalow overlooking the river estuary. It was all rather like being moved from Aldgate to the French Riviera. All my subsequent operations were now to be Claret and we no longer had any responsibilities for operations on our side of the border. A road link also existed between Sematan and Lundu which eased the problems of Troop movement and re-supply. The major advantage of this new arrangement was that as M Company were not primarily responsible for the security of Sematan, I could now take the company out at full strength, and not have to leave a Troop behind on guard duty as had been the case at Bokah…'

Biawak

The Border fortress at Biawak stood on a ridge some ten miles west of Commando HQ and the District capital at Lundu, with an uninterrupted view to the East across the trees to Gunong Gading, the focal point of those earlier incursions. The border lay about a mile away to the west and barely half a mile to the South. From time to time it was mortared.

The base had changed significantly since April '64, when it had been occupied by a single Troop of L Company. Rebuilt some 400 yards away from the original site in the Kampong, it now housed L Company Group, which included four rifle Troops; 4, 5, and 6 Troops and 'Mercer's Marauders' – an ad hoc rifle Troop formed from MT drivers, whose vehicles had been left behind in Singapore as surplus to the requirements of Lundu District; also included were a section of three inch Mortars, a detachment of 129 Light Battery, RA, with a single 105mm howitzer, as well as the handful of cooks and signallers from Commando HQ. Apart from the scale of the fortress, with mortar pits, gun pit, well constructed bunkers and overhead cover, there were other signs of sophistication; local labour had been recruited to assist with camp chores; there was a volley ball court; firing ranges had been improvised and there was a programme by which members of the garrison took four days of rest and recuperation at 'Sematan-on-Sea', where the unit had its own sailing dinghy.

After two months of occupation, despite active patrolling and supporting fire on likely targets at indeterminate times, there had been no recorded contact with the IBT and, as had once been the case at Bombalai, the kills were limited to the 450 rats claimed by the team organized by the Company Sergeant Major (QMS Llewellyn) and his henchman, Marine Rankin.

Some of their patrols had of course been cross-border, though no operational reports have been found. The need for close security meant also that accounts in the articles forwarded to the Corps journal had became increasingly anodyne, though, with the benefit of hindsight, limited accounts of the odd patrol clearly refer to such operations.

In April ’66, L Company Group (Capt Jack Smith) and Biawak would feature prominently in the largest ‘Claret’ operation undertaken by either Commando, A two company operation, code named ‘Lively Cricket’, it involved both L and M Company Groups, was controlled by Commando HQ under Major John Owen and directed by Lieutenant Colonel Peter Whiteley, while temporarily acting as West Brigade Commander.

Reconnaissance of the Indonesian base at Sedjingen was carried out by patrols of L Company, led by Lieutenant Clark; the fact that Sergeant Pearce, on one of the patrols, remained undiscovered, though within five yards of the enemy sentries, testifies to the closeness of the recces and the skill of the patrols.

Tom Seccombe – OC M Company

Operation ‘Lively Cricket’

M Company was to do two more Claret operations of any significance. The first, between the 13th and 16th April, was a two company attack on an enemy base at Sedjingen, code named ‘Lively Cricket’ and the second an operation, rather facetiously code named ‘Herbert Johnson’. ‘Lively Cricket’ was the most important operation carried out during 42 Commando’s tour of duty, and the one with the most lasting consequences, as it involved the loss of Lance Corporal Collins, the ramifications of which went on for many years.

‘The operation involved a fire assauLieutenant on the enemy base to be carried out by L Company operating out of Biawak, and the ambushing by M Company of the main track leading south out of the base, hopefully catching the fallout as the enemy positions were abandoned. The two Companies would RV a day’s march from the target. M Company would be helicoptered into an LZ, again about a day’s march from the RV. This was very much L Company’s area with which they were reasonably familiar; for M Company it was new territory. Once we had reached the RV, M Company would merely tag along behind L Company until we reached the outskirts of Sedjingen where we would carry on south, bypassing the enemy base, into our ambush positions. It all sounded very straightforward!

‘The RV was effected surprisingly easily without anyone getting lost or shooting one another, and off we all set for Sedjingen in considerable strength. D-Day was, I think,

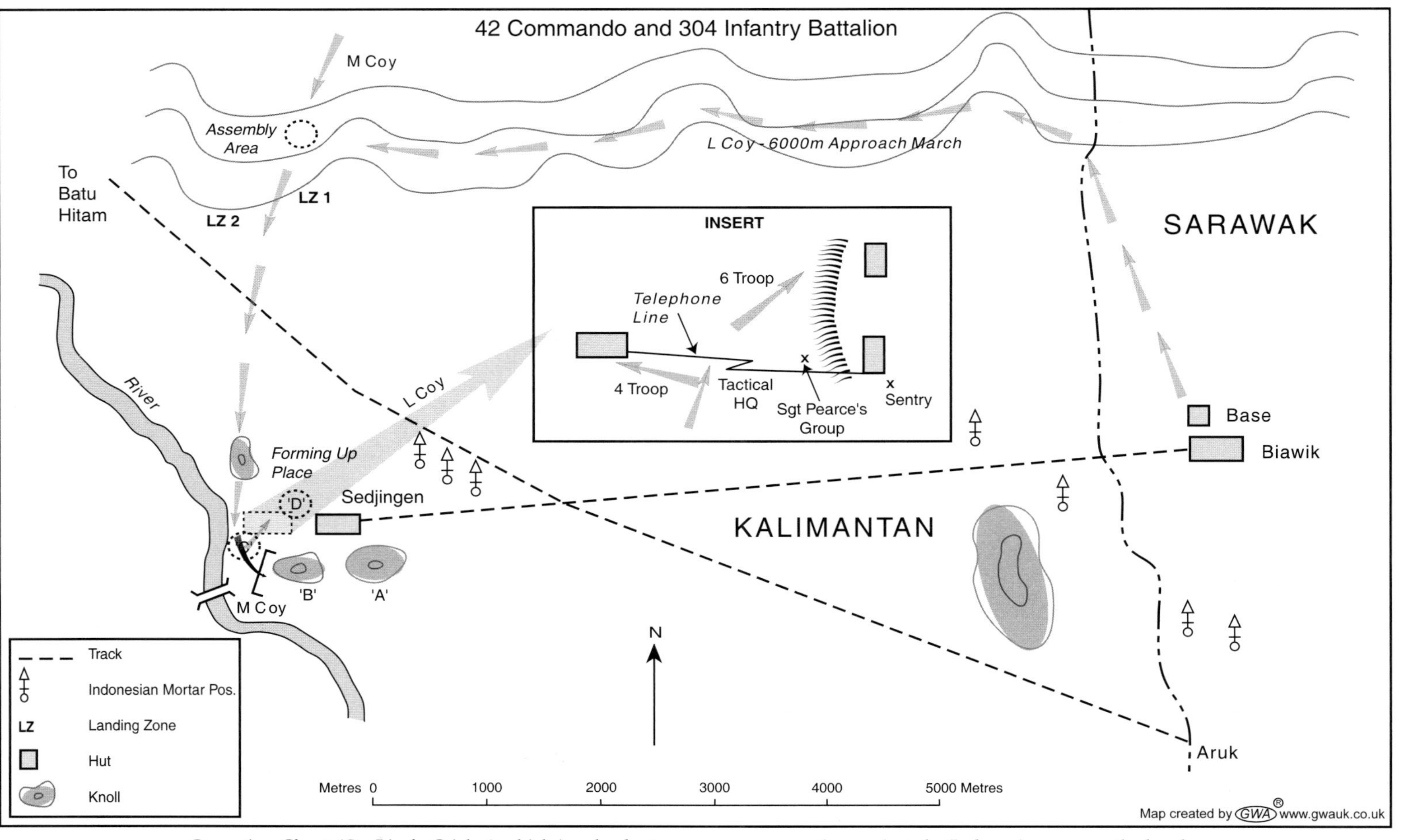

Operation Claret (Op Lively Cricket) which involved a two-company operation against the Indonesians across the border on 16 April and enough time had been built into the plan to enable recces to be carried out by both companies in the afternoon of the day before. I was particularly anxious to get into position in plenty of time, because the air photos had identified a large area of open grassland between the line of my approach and our designated ambush position. Obviously I could not go across this grassland in broad daylight, and would have to avoid it by sticking to the jungle fringe skirting it. By the time we parted from L Company, we were already running late, due to the considerable time it took to bypass Sedjingen, while ensuring that we did not get mixed up with L Company's recce party. I had already identified from our photographs a Company RV that was about 500 yards from my ambush position. We reached this RV late in the afternoon. I had been expecting a single track leading down to it, but was not prepared for a whole network of tracks and paths which complicated the route finding, and added to my sense of vulnerability!

'The Company shook out into all round defence in the RV, and leaving them in charge of my Sergeant Major, I quickly assembled my recce party of about ten men – myself, FOO, two Troop Commanders, two signallers and four protection party. As we came to the edge of the grass field, it had become pretty obvious that we did not have time to skirt it and there therefore was no alternative but to plough straight across it, in full view of anybody who might be watching. It was a most uncomfortable few minutes, but luck was on our side and it brought us directly to the main track out of Sedjingen that we were going to ambush. Both Tony Dunlop of the left hand Troop and Mike McMullen of the right were able to complete their individual recces in sufficient light and we then backtracked across the grass – this time mercifully in near darkness. All the necessary orders were then given, and the Company turned in for the night.

'As L Company's assault was going in just after first light, this meant leaving the RV in darkness to get into our ambush position in time. The track across the grass field which was beginning to resemble a four-lane highway, was proving to be a blessing in disguise; to get into position skirting it, would have taken about three quarters of an hour, whereas we were in position ten minutes after leaving company RV, where, I should have said, we left the Sergeant Major and ten Marines. To say that his party was composed of 'odds and sods' would be untrue, but I had ensured that the ambush party had first call in terms of experience and ability. George's guns had already stood to, furnished with the appropriate ranges, etc. and all we had to do was to wait. Not for long. Almost immediately L Company's attack began, manifesting itself by bullets clipping the trees above us, not quite high enough to be comfortable. Any minutes now, I thought, the fallout of Indonesian soldiers would be pouring down the track into our position.

'Five minutes went by and nothing happened. Then heavy firing broke out behind us. Clearly the Company RV had become involved. The initial heavy firing soon moderated into sporadic shots and I became extremely anxious as to what had happened; needless to say I could get no sense from my Company radio. The unit command net, for a change, was working beautifully and I was able to send off the initial contact report, while the rear link operator was able to give me what news he could of how L Company were faring. As I was fretting about the Sergeant Major in the Company RV, two enemy soldiers were shot at the upper end of the grass field, behind Tony Dunlop's Troop, our only customers so far from the expected direction. Then a great deal of noise, voices shouting and splashing was heard from the river, about twenty-five metres to our front, and it became clear that it was being used as an escape route. We had not had time to recce the river the night before, as had been my intention, and I was left in a quandary. Should I now move McMullen's Troop up to the river bank, keeping Dunlop's Troop on the left in their present position? It meant that I would lose control of the right hand Troop, and would be vulnerable if any enemy came up the track from our right. At the time it seemed it was not a worthwhile chance to take, so we stayed put.

'The noise from the river soon lessened, but it was still possible to hear people shouting to one another all over the whole area to our front. We then heard another burst of machine gun fire coming from the company RV and still no radio contact. My rear link operator told me that a Casevac helicopter had been summoned. Clearly L Company had suffered some casualties.

'George's guns had, as far as I can remember, been firing on the main track to our right and on the river area to discourage any enemy reinforcements coming up that way. We heard a helicopter landing and taking off and then soon after that the unmistakable sound of a mortar being fired; I waited with some apprehension for the bomb to land, which it duly did, not far away. George told me it was still an acceptable distance from us, but when we heard several more mortars firing, I asked him what he could do to try and neutralize them. He then initiated what I think the Gunners call a 'sweeping search', distinguished by its very heavy expenditure in shells. After this had been going on for about half an hour and still no customers to speak of, I began to think about withdrawing. This was only to be done on orders from Commando HQ. I got them on the radio, the Second-in-Command was on the set, as he had been throughout I understand. In answer to my request to withdraw, he asked me to hang on for a bit longer for reasons which he said would become clear later. However, he did say that if my position became untenable due to the mortar fire, I could withdraw at my own discretion.

'Our position did not become untenable and we wound up our ambush and retreated across the now familiar grassland to the RV to be greeted by a grinning Sergeant Major and his party, all clearly in very high spirits.

'It appeared that three quite separate enemy groups had come down from Sedjingen almost in to the Company RV. Obviously this was a preferred 'bug-out' route and quite a few did not make it. Morale in the RV party was understandably sky-high and they considered quite rightly that they had the best of it, rather than us.

'We left the RV and made our way back up the track in the direction of Sedjingen. As we came abreast of the base, John Owen called me up and asked if we would keep a look out for an L Company Marine who was missing. With the benefit of hindsight, I suppose I ought to have taken the Company into the village to try and find him. It would not have been without some danger, but may well have been justified in the light of what was to come. At the time it simply did not occur to me. What did concern me was that we had stayed around a good one and a half hours after L Company had pulled out and I had no idea when and how the enemy would react; so we kept going. We spent a further night out before reaching Biawak the next day, and subsequently helicoptered into Lundu and then by road back to Sematan.

'That very briefly was the part played by M Company in 'Lively Cricket'. In the event, apart from L Company's actual attack, not much turned out as planned. We had been unbelievably lucky in not being detected on D-1 and I had been exceptionally fortunate in having Sergeant Major Hill in charge of my company RV. Could I have achieved a greater degree of success by moving Mike McMullen's Troop up to the river line? Ignoring all other considerations, the answer is probably. Should I have gone down in Sedjingen to look for the missing Marine? Again, probably, but one thing is quite certain, at the time the company would not have thanked me for it!'

L Company had a fierce exchange on the objective, followed by a fighting withdrawal, aided by artillery fire. During the process Lieutenant Clark was killed and two men were wounded; Lance Corporal Collins was missing, initiating a problem which was not fully resolved until his body was repatriated some twenty-six years later, in 1991.'

Tom Seccombe – OC M Company

Operation 'Herbert Johnson'

'We were to do one other major Claret operation during the tour. This time I took the Company at full strength, not far short of ninety men with attachments, on a lengthy patrol to explore quite a large tract of Kalimantan, which had not received any attention before, and to try and locate an enemy base which we knew to be in the area.

'We followed the usual procedure of being helicoptered into a mounting base and from thence moving across the border. Day three saw us well inside the enemy side of the border and by midday we were moving, rather disconcertingly, in relatively open country, for which the study of the air photographs had not prepared me. I was quite confident that I was in sufficient strength to deal with most eventualities, but I was now in country which was not only entirely new to me, but crossing a terrain that progressively became far too open for comfort.

'We passed a number of people working small patches of cultivation from whom my interpreter was able to elicit that the Indonesian army did patrol the area fairly regularly from a base about one and a half hours away, but not in any strength. They were extremely nervous about talking to us and soon melted away. We moved back into the jungle fringe and set a new course in the general direction indicated by the farmers. After about two hours we heard the sound of two mortars being fired, but the subsequent explosions were quite a way off, and I was not able to determine whether they had anything to do with us.

'In late afternoon, still in the jungle fringe, the point section halted the column and I went forward with my FOO to be greeted by the lead Troop Commander, who came back to us with the news that he thought we were very near to an enemy location. We made our way up to the lead scouts, worming the last few yards on our stomachs. They indicated a patch of primary jungle standing in a natural clearing some 200 yards away in which they had seen movement. After examining this patch, both the FOO and I saw both movement and light reflecting from a number of shiny objects, which made me think that somebody might also have been watching us. Just as I was considering this possibility, voices and laughter were heard which, although we could not see anything, indicated that a body of men were moving towards the base and were very near to us. I sent the Troop Commander and one section, still under cover of the jungle, to investigate. Within a few yards they found a very well used track leading in the direction of the base, but no sign of the people who had obviously just gone down it. I put the leading Troop into an ambush position on the track, and sent back down the column for the other two Troop Commanders to put them in the picture.

'It was now getting dark; in the remaining light I moved the Company into a lying up position 200 yards into the jungle and then raised the ambush. We went into all round defence, and as darkness fell, I settled down to compose a lengthy Slidex message to Commando HQ. In it I said that we had, without doubt, located an active enemy base of indeterminate size within range of our guns, and requested instructions. I realised that it was very unlikely that I would be given the go-ahead to attack the base, as it had not been properly recced and there would be inadequate time for proper preparation; any attack would have to go in at dawn the next day, as we could not hang around, in the numbers that we were, without detection. Additionally I could not say categorically that we had not been detected. Later on that night I received instructions to withdraw at first light which is what we did, having resisted the temptation to lob a few shells into the base as we did so. In retrospect, had we bumped the enemy patrol the night before, the matter of whether to attack or not would have been taken out of our hands.

'That really was our swan song. We heard subsequently that talks about a cessation of hostilities had been going on for some time and I hope the raid on Sedjingen had concentrated the Indonesian negotiators' minds somewhat. A 'ceasefire' was in fact declared during the last week of our tour. [Claret operations were terminated on 28 May '66. This did not prevent repeated mortar attacks on Biawak, despite the best efforts of the Royal Artillery sound ranging team].

'On the whole it had been a stimulating and professionally rewarding six months. I was most fortunate in having some excellent Marines, SNCO's and Officers in the Company, whom it was always a pleasure to meet subsequently.'

Chapter 14

Forty's Fifth

40 Commando: Sarawak, Second Division; Air Troop Debut and Last Borneo Tour

May to September '66

Forty's Fifth

Albion's *Argosy*

In early May '66, 42 Commando ended the tour in Lundu District and 40 Commando began its fifth tour since April '63, when the system of 'Roulement' between Commando units had begun; the unit deployed to the Second Division of Sarawak, with Headquarters at Simanggang, the capital. The process was more complex than usual and *Albion* had just completed a ten day shake down at sea, after leaving dry dock…

'Renjer Roulement'

> "After three days back at the base, we sailed for Labuan with about 450 of 40 Commando on board. We went to Labuan first to relieve one flight of 848 Squadron who had by then been working quite unsupported by us for over two months. Time allowed us to swim and sport ashore before going to commence our three day stint off Sarawak.
>
> 'The first two days involved flying 40 Commando to Simanggang returning with the [Malayan] Renjers. This could not be completed in one day owing to a late start for flying each morning due to mist and also to the distances involved. The Renjers settled down well although the Troops spoke little or no English; the only difficulty that arose was over food – do you or do you not eat food if it's been cooked in the same kitchen as pork? – an insoluble problem afloat. One gathers the most devout members went hungry.
>
> 'On the third day we found ourselves carrying out our first – and still the last – roulement using both helicopters and landing craft. The Renjers were flown into Lundu, the most western and the most active part of the Indonesian/Sarawak border, and 42 Commando was brought out. The LCVPs had an exciting run up the very shallow Lundu river to collect mountains of unit stores. The turnover took something like six hours and immediately we did a twenty-two knot dash back to Singapore Naval Base to get in before the Dockyard packed up for the weekend…"

…There followed a trip to Japan with the Commando Brigade band embarked and a leave party from 42 Commando 'led' by Captain Peter Downs.

40 Commando had been the first Royal Marines unit to receive its own integrated Air Troop, though this was its first deployment to Borneo. One of the pilots was Ian Uzzell – now a fully fledged aviator and on his third tour to Borneo…

Ian Uzzell, Lieutenant – Air Troop

Royal Marines Light Helicopters

'There have been Royal Marines pilots since 1911 when Lieutenant Gerrard RMLI qualified as one of the first naval pilots. Royal Marines flew in both World Wars and when helicopters were used by the Navy for assault landing, Royal Marines also started to fly helicopters. They were trained by the Navy and thus wore the Naval Flying Badge. In 1965 Royal Marine units were issued with the small Sioux AH Mk 1 helicopter. The first Royal Marines who flew these helicopters were former helicopter pilots with the Navy and converted to the Sioux at the School of Army Aviation, Middle Wallop. From 1965 Royal Marine Officers and Senior NCOs were trained from scratch by the army and on completion were awarded the Army Flying Badge.

Lieutenant Ian Uzzell with his Sioux AH Mk 1 helicopter taking off from HMS *Albion*

'The Sioux AH Mk 1 was the Westland Helicopter version of the Bell 47G 3B-1. It was a three seat side-by-side aircraft with the pilot in the left hand seat. It was powered by a single turbo-charged Lycoming engine rated at 270 horsepower which it could maintain up to 12,500 feet. It had a maximum speed of ninety-one knots, range of about 300 miles, and could carry an under-slung load of up to 500 pounds.

'The pilots were trained for a variety of roles including: airborne reconnaissance; airborne command post; artillery observation and control; forward air control; casualty evacuation; radio relay; liaison duties and light load carrying, under-slung or on the litters on either side.

'On completion of my course I was to be posted to 40 Commando Air Troop in December 1965. However, one week before I was due to be awarded my wings I crashed due to disorientation during my final night flying exercise in November 1965 and my posting was delayed until I had recovered from my injuries, and completed my final handling test on 2 March 1966.'

40 Commando

'I finally arrived in 40 Commando (Lieutenant Colonel John Taplin) in April 1966 and carried out a theatre conversion course at Kluang in Malaya, to learn about the peculiarities of flying in the hot and humid atmosphere of the Far East; how to land and take off in small jungle clearings and how to navigate over primary jungle. Navigation was made relatively simple in that there was no appreciable magnetic variation, practically no wind, and the cruise speed for the Sioux in those conditions was sixty knots. So we drew the line on the map, measured the bearing, measured the distance in nautical miles – that was how many minutes the flight would take. We then flew the bearing, not having to make any corrections for variation or wind, and flew for the requisite number of minutes. If our destination was not directly under our nose it must be either a short distance to the left or right of the current position. The main problem with navigation was that everywhere looked very much the same – trees, trees and more trees. A clearing was often not visible unless from directly overhead.

'Immediately after the completion of my conversion course, 40 Commando was due to leave for the final operational tour of Borneo. The unit possessed three Sioux helicopters with three pilots. Captain Roger Learoyd (a former helicopter pilot with the Navy) was the Air Troop Commander and Lieutenant Richard Persse and I were the pilots. Our ground crew were primarily Naval Air Mechanics who had all had to complete the Commando Course before joining the unit. The Chief Mechanic was Chief Petty Officer Tetchner.

'We were to fly from Burma Camp to HMS *Albion* for transit to Borneo. I had as passengers Marine Mawby, one of our ground crew, and Fred the hawk, our Troop mascot. My inexperience with the particular helicopter I was flying, combined with the location of the helipad, caused me to over-pitch on take-off, a condition in which the rotor blades start to slow down, and I was forced to land on the road next to the helipad. Having ascertained that there was no damage to the helicopter, I hovered to the parade ground, prepared again for take-off and was soon on our way to join *Albion*.

'Three days later, on 4 May, we disembarked for our flight to Simanggang in the Second Division of Sarawak. My first take-off from a ship also proved to be exciting. The procedure was to lift off from the flight deck, hover to the side of the ship over the sea, move into forward flight when clear and climb away. As I moved out over the water I noticed my rotor revs were decreasing again, but this time I had fifty feet clearance to the surface of the sea in order to pick up forward speed and increase the rotor revs to their correct level. Those watching on the flight deck just saw my helicopter disappear over the edge and rushed over to see if I had crashed into the sea. But no, I was climbing and on my way to Borneo.

'During training we were taught to avoid flying over large amounts of water or over large areas of woodland, in case of engine failure. My first operational flight for my unit was from HMS *Albion* to Simanggang and consisted of a twenty mile flight over the sea followed by a further thirty miles over primary jungle. Over the next few months I would become very familiar with flying over vast expanses of trees.'

Simanggang

'40 Commando's area covered the Indonesian border from a hilltop underground fort at Jambu occupied by A Company (Captain Bob Darwell) in the east, via B Company (Captain David Hunt) at Lubok Antu and C Company (Major John Weston) from Batu Lintang to the border with the 1st Division in the west. Here, at Sungei Tenggang, Captain Mike Gambier was in command of D Company, which was formed of 5 Troop and elements of Support Company.

Lieutenant Ian Uzzell, who served twice early in the campaign as a Troop subaltern, and later as a Sioux pilot

'We were given an area familiarisation in an army Scout helicopter before taking on our own tasking and operations. Our main role was liaison, taking the Commanding Officer and other officers to visit the various Troop locations, taking company and Troop commanders on recce and moving people from one location to another. Other tasks included casevac and medevac, lifting stores from the airdrop sites to the company locations, target registration for artillery and mortars, radio relay, public relations and even filming by ATV.

'The airfield at Simanggang was about a mile outside the town itself and based alongside us was the Unit Dog Team, with both Guard and Tracker dogs. As well as being third pilot, I was also appointed as the Unit Dog Officer, so when I was not flying I was setting trails for the dogs to follow – or acting as a 'villain' for the guard dogs.

Lieutenant Ian Uzzell on Jambu No 1 helipad with his Sioux helicopter

'As well as Fred the Hawk, the Air Troop acquired various other animals which were kept at our location on Simanggang airfield. They were all given the name of Fred by Captain Learoyd and included three pythons, a monitor lizard and a tiny Scops Owl. It was expected of the pilots, if we saw a snake on our way to the airport that we would attempt to catch it and add it to the collection. My closest encounter was with a large green snake which crossed our path one morning. The Land-rover screeched to a halt and I was ejected from the back with the instructions "Go get it, sir!" I chased after it and with a headlong dive just missed catching it by the closest of margins. I was applauded for my efforts, but what they did not realise was that it took great skill to make it look as if I wanted to catch the snake. I had no idea what it was, or if it was poisonous, so had no intention of actually catching it.

'A particular problem that affected our flying in this area was that in the mornings a thick mist would rise from the jungle canopy, making any flying impossible as the Sioux was not equipped for instrument flying and we therefore could not enter cloud. The mist would soon start to rise and give a small clearance of about 100 to 200 feet between the tree canopy and the base of the cloud. Our navigation in those conditions had to be purely by course and time travelled as we could not see the landmarks that we could use when we had full visibility. It was in such circumstances that within a few days of our arrival I was tasked for my first medevac mission.

'Corporal Crowley had become ill during a patrol and needed to be recovered to Simanggang. I was sure that I knew where the small clearing in the side of a range of hills was, but for some reason I could not find it. I flew along the ridge in both directions with no sign of a clearing. Then I managed to establish radio contact with the patrol, and was informed that the clearing was still in cloud. I waited for about thirty minutes until the cloud lifted sufficiently to allow me to identify the clearing. It was small but was approachable from the side; having picked up Corporal Crowley and his large pack I had to turn around inside the clearing in order to fly out and back to base. It was difficult, being my first time in such a tight clearing, but it boosted my confidence in the capability of the Sioux and in my own abilities. On a similar mission at a later date to recover another casualty in the same area I reported that I was flying along the ridge line and would be with the casualty in five minutes. I then heard an American voice relaying my message. Due to the conditions my message was being heard in Vietnam and they thought I was on my way to recover one of their wounded. I corrected them and completed my task

'My next flight was to take Captain Gambier to do the spotting for his mortars. They were based very close to the border and had targets that required to be registered. Although pilots were trained for this task, on this occasion he did the correction of fire whilst I flew the helicopter so that he could get the best visibility of the fall of shot.'

Crossing the Border

'Most of our flights were purely liaison where we would take passengers from one company location to another, or to take Patrol Commanders or Company Commanders on recces. A few days after the medevac, I was sent to B Company location from where my task was to insert an SAS patrol across the border into Indonesia. This meant doing something that none of us really liked, which was to fly two journeys to the same location in unsecured territory. This was necessary as I could only take two passengers at a time with their kit, and the patrol was of four men. The flight had to be at low level – just over the tree tops – and as fast as possible in order to get all the men on the ground and away from the landing point as quickly as possible. Flying so low made the navigation much more difficult. I later had a further mission into Indonesia from D Company location, when I had to take an SAS Officer to try and make radio or visual communication with one of his patrols, from whom he had not heard for several days. We took a spare radio and 250 feet of string to lower the radio to the patrol if we found them. But we were unsuccessful in locating them. They subsequently returned safely.'

*

'We always had to be conscious of the weight of passengers and stores because of the maximum weight limit of the Sioux. This meant that we had to work out before a flight how much fuel we could put in and therefore how long a flight could last. Each company location kept a quantity of aviation fuel in four gallon flimsy containers. We would carry on our aircraft a large filter (known as a B type filter) so that we could ensure no impurities were put into the fuel tanks. The fuel gauge on a Sioux is not too reliable and so before each flight we would put a dipstick into each tank to work out the quantity of fuel remaining. On several occasions the flight plan would be changed during the sortie itself and on several occasions I had to drain off fuel in order to lift additional passengers.

'If we were particularly heavy, we could not get much more than two or three feet off the ground whilst under full power. If the site was on the top of a hill the procedure would be to launch off the helipad and dive over the side of the hill to pick up forward speed and thus also more lift. It could look very exciting to passengers and those who were watching from the ground. It certainly boosted my confidence in the aircraft itself. The most difficult take-off that I had to do was in a clearing in the jungle which was completely surrounded by trees 200 feet high. It required a vertical landing and a vertical take-off. Landing was not too difficult as I was by myself and not too heavy but, having picked up my passenger, the aircraft was very reluctant to climb. The technique was to slowly increase power so that the helicopter rose under control until clear of the canopy. By this time it was on full power and could not rise any further. I then had to very gently coax the aircraft into forward motion without losing any height – or I would hit the trees – but by moving forward I would also lose a bit of lift, so it was a bit of a balancing act. Once a speed of about twenty knots was reached, the helicopter gained additional lift because of this speed, known as translational lift. The aircraft gave a slight shudder as this additional lift took effect, and I, as the pilot, breathed a huge sigh of relief.'

Medical and Casualty Evacuation

'Medevacs and casevacs were not limited to service personnel; we also provided this cover for civilians. On one occasion I went as passenger with Captain Learoyd to collect a woman who was very ill. Not only did we take her to hospital, but also her husband and child. She was placed in the litter at the side and her husband was in the centre seat with the child on his knee and I was in the right seat so that I could keep a watch on the woman. I was not entirely convinced that we could get off the ground, but we did and in a three seat helicopter we successfully carried five people.

'The most difficult medevac that I had to do was to collect a Marine from the side of a hill; he had been injured during a patrol. There were no trees on the site but fairly long grass. I had been tasked to take the Commanding Officer (by this time Lieutenant Colonel Derek Pounds) around the various Company locations and on the way back, collect the casualty and transport him to Simanggang. It was not a prepared landing site and I approached the hill realising that I could only put one skid on the ground. I also

A Sioux with an outside litter rigged for casualty evacuation

noted that I required a very high power setting as I made my approach. I informed the CO that I could not lift both of them from the site and he volunteered to remain with the patrol until I could return to collect him. As he was getting out of the helicopter the aircraft started to shudder a lot and I thought it might be getting into ground resonance. This is a potentially very dangerous situation as it could literally shake the aircraft to pieces. The only way to stop it was to lift off the ground and I could not do that until the CO had actually got out of the aircraft. It seemed to take ages and as he got out he placed his headset in the litter without switching off the microphone.

'I lifted off quickly to stabilize everything and then placed my skid back on the ground so that the casualty could be seated inside. The vibration started again so I lifted off as soon as possible and flew back to Simanggang with the sound of rushing wind in my headset. After refuelling I noticed a problem with the aircraft which meant it could not be flown again until repaired. Luckily an RAF Whirlwind was calling by shortly afterwards and I went with it to direct the pilot to where the CO had been waiting for my return. When the patrol returned to base they told me that they were most impressed by my rescue of their injured companion as I was cutting the grass with my rotor blades whilst the skid was on the ground. The reason for all the vibration was now apparent.'

*

'Sudden loud noises are not what pilots like to hear, particularly when airborne. I was approaching B Company location on one occasion and had just settled into a hover before landing when there was a loud explosion. My first thought was that something was wrong with my aircraft and put it on the ground as quickly as possible. Then there was another loud bang and I realised that it was the artillery attached to the Company firing their guns. I made a request to the Company Commander that they hold off any firing when helicopters are arriving or leaving. Another unwelcome loud noise was the sound of an unfortunate bird hitting the helicopter. This happened to me on at least three occasions, one hitting the rotor mast and another hitting the bubble of the cockpit, luckily not smashing it. The aircraft always had to be checked for any serious damage that the bird might have caused.

'We had other 'Hearts and Minds' tasks from time to time. Partly this took the form of civilian medevacs but also involved dropping leaflets in some difficult to reach areas and on one occasion dropping sweets to the local children in the Simanggang area. We were required to transport the local political officers around the area to visit some remote villages. On a couple of occasions I had to fly to and from Kuching and routed over my old stamping ground of Serian.

'From the air one could see many things that would have been missed otherwise. On one occasion I watched a tidal bore rushing up one of the rivers close to Simanggang, and on another occasion saw a complete circular rainbow underneath my helicopter. Later I was to discover that this effect is known as a 'Glory'.

'Our tour in Borneo came to a close at the end of September 1966. We flew our aircraft to Kuching Airport where we practiced flying with under-slung flags for a fly past before we left. We also had the opportunity to fly over some of the other areas of Borneo and along the coast, until our final flight which was to the docks at Kuching, from where our Sioux would be lifted onto an LSL to be returned to Singapore.

'I had served in Borneo as a Troop Commander and as a helicopter pilot almost from the commencement of operations in December 1962 until our final withdrawal in September 1966. Helicopters played a very important part in the success of the operations there. Movement on the ground was very restricted as there were few roads and travel by river boat was long and arduous; it also depended on the state of the rivers which could flood with amazing rapidity. During the early part of the campaign we only had the Troop lift aircraft, Wessex and Whirlwind 7 and 10, and later the larger Belvedere twin rotor helicopter. The Sioux gave us many more possibilities. It allowed Company Commanders and Patrol Commanders to do detailed recces. It gave the Commanding Officer more mobility to visit the various locations. I suppose it could be likened to an airborne Land-rover as a most useful asset.

'As I left Borneo I got the news that I was to leave 40 Commando and join 45 Commando in Aden to command their Air Troop.'

On the ground soldiering was less rewarding. The Companies had been as busy as ever, patrolling, setting ambushes, improving fortifications, registering targets and building bridges and relationships with the local people. All of which activity had brought no contact with IBT. A handful of CCO suspects or fugitives were apprehended but even these were liable to be quickly released by Special Branch for their own reasons.

Improvement of communications was still demanding. The cover of the Corps journal of October '66 carries a photograph sent by Major Sidwell (erstwhile B Company Command) of two members of 40 Commando Signal Troop, half way up a tall aerial; it bears the caption…

'Up the Pole'

> "3,000 yards from the Indonesian border the Company Commander at Lubok Antu was virtually out of touch with Commando HQ at Simanggang – but the Unit Signals Officer, Lieutenant Murphy, and the Company Signals Corporal, Corporal Paterson, climbed the 120 foot Police radio mast and fitted a special aerial and all was changed…"

The hill fortress at Jambu occupied by A Company (Captain Bob Darwall) also had a strong Signals team; led by Corporal Bert Preston, it also included David Nickisson (later Captain), whose emailed recollections may, perhaps, show a change of tempo if not of priorities…

David Nickisson, S3 – Company signaller

World Cup and Wildlife

'I have many good memories of the deployment and, to quote just one off the top of my head, of the night when England won the 1966 World Cup. We had set up the HF radio – probably the C11/R210 or maybe an A 13 – and the Unit Command Net was broadcasting the match over the VHF C42 link. We then jury-rigged all of the location's telephones (Tele Js) and ad-hoc intercom systems so that as many of the Company as possible could listen in. The hill nearly took off when England won and the local wildlife must have heard us from miles around.

'I also remember the night when a sentry on a GPMG position whose oppo had gone to shake his relief, was joined by a wandering Orang Utan. I was on watch in the CP and the screams, one from the sentry and one from the Orang Utan, were horrifying even to us. The sentry took a dive out of the gun pit and was found some time later, well outside the wire and about 100 feet down the hill. I think the Orang Utan was spotted cowering up in the trees but cannot recall exactly. When the sentry was brought into the CP he was deathly white and the LMA, Tim Holt, had to give him a sedative to calm him down. Unfortunately, while I can still see the sentry's face, I cannot put a name to him.'

Meanwhile the peace process continued, leading to a virtual cease fire, broken in a number of places but not in Second Division, where plans for withdrawal and hand over were well advanced. The process of dismantling some of the defended locations was already in hand, proving the efficacy of the indigenous defences and posing problems for 5 Troop of D Company…

'Panji Problems'

"Before we leave Sungei Tenggang, we will demolish all bunkers and uproot all barbed wire defences, this of course means arduous labour on the part of people not patrolling, The thousands of razor sharp bamboo stakes, which are referred to among other things as Panjis, have been the cause of many casualties among our ranks. There are two methods of plucking these playthings from their hiding place in the wire. The best method is by hand, wearing wiring gloves. The second way is to impale a leg on a panji in the long grass and then to run horrified and white-faced up to the sick-bay, looking like an early Christian martyr. This, incredibly, seems to be the vogue among 5 Troop personnel. In fact, bandaged calves and thighs decorated with stitches are now de rigueur for all working parties in the wire…"

Now under the command of Lieutenant Colonel Derek Pounds, 40 Commando's withdrawal was to be phased…

'Under Way'

"With the departure of A Company for home the withdrawal programme is getting under way at last. Stores are being back-loaded to Kuching by every available boat and vehicle and shortly Simanggang defences are to be levelled and the perimeter wire cut up and buried.

"The present withdrawal plan we hope to be the last. Changes have been frequent and the overall withdrawal a direct contrast from the unit's slick fly into positions from *Albion* when we arrived in early May.

"For the interest of past members of 40 Commando and those interested in train time tables, the four company locations are now in the process of reduction to two for the hand over to the relieving unit at the end of September. 'A' Company left their hilltop fortress in rubble in August and have departed for Johore Bahru. B Company, alongside the river are to hand over to two Malay Platoons during the second week in September, leave one Troop in Simanggang and depart with D Company to Johore Bahru a day later. This will leave HQ and C Company remaining to return to Malaya at the end of September, as the Main Body. Two Malay Platoons will relieve C Company of their hilltop road head position at Batu Lintang.

"Such is the basic detail of the final move of Royal Marines Commandos from Sarawak after [over] three years of Confrontation.

> "40 Commando was responsible under 3 Command Brigade for the First Division at the onset of Confrontation and is the last British major unit responsible for the Second Division and the final British major unit to leave Sarawak. C Company will represent the British Forces towards the end of September in a farewell march past in Kuching."

Postscript

Confrontation was declared to have ended on 12 August '66, a peace agreement was signed in Jakarta on 16 August and 40 Commando's withdrawal went ahead as planned.

Elsewhere CCO and TNI infiltrators were not all willing to comply and incidents continued to occur in some familiar places. On 14 August there was a clash near Tebedu, in which the Queen's Own Buffs had their first fatal casualty. Up in the Fifth Division, where it had all begun, the Gurkhas were still in pursuit of a substantial incursion led by a Lieutenant Sumbi. The pursuit entered the area of Bukit Pagon and ended beside the River Trusan, where Lieutenant Sumbi and his remaining party were captured by 1/7th Gurkhas on 3 September. The pursuers described the going as 'horrendous' though, unlike Rupertforce in 1963, they were aided in their route finding by unit helicopters.

In East Brigade incursions continued aimed at the Kalabakan and Brantian area. These were harried and broken up by 1st Royal Hampshires until they handed over to a Malaysian unit and left for home on 14 September '66.

Chapter 15

RM Special Boat Section

1 and 2 SBS; Sarawak, Sabah and the Straits

1962 to 1965

RM Special Boat Section

2 SBS

2 SBS had been deployed to Singapore in July 1960. Based at HMS *Terror*, initially under Naval command, the Section operated from a large shed next to the Red House Sailing Club and near to the RN Clearance Diving Team. They were also close to the 6th Submarine Squadron, with whom they would train.

With the arrival of HQ 3 Commando Brigade in early 1962, the SBS once again passed under their command. On the operational side, the emphasis was on the reconnaissance of the beaches of Singapore and Malaya. In the event priorities were to be distorted.

In December 1962, at the time of the Brunei insurrection, HMS Albion had been on passage to Singapore with 40 Commando embarked, after exercises off Aden and Mombasa during the change over with HMS Bulwark. When the ship called briefly at Singapore, 2 SBS were also embarked. Captain David Mitchell, who had arrived to take over command from Lieutenant Stewart Syrad, was just in time to sail with the ship.

By the time that *Albion* arrived off Brunei the initial rebellion had been put down in a series of operations by the Gurkhas, 42 Commando and the Queens Own Highlanders. The task now was one of extensive mopping up and when A Company (Major P G Davis) took over responsibility for the security of Limbang, the SBS was initially attached...

David Mitchell, Captain – OC 2 SBS

'Apart from a small number of jungle patrols the SBS role was mostly confined to river patrolling in the Limbang area, using Gemini inflatable and aluminium hull assault craft, and in doing numerous logistical trips. This lasted for some two or three months after which we returned to Singapore.

'After a brief stay we were next deployed to Kuching, capital of Sarawak, for more river patrols, under HQ 3 Commando Brigade and again in support of 40 Commando'

42 Commando relieved 40 Commando in July. A feature of the system of 'roulement', by which units were rotated to and from Borneo, was the work hard/play hard routine that persisted in the 'rest' periods, when units tried to squeeze essential training – amphibious, jungle and weapon – and all the events, sporting and military, of a

peacetime regimental calendar into an often interrupted programme of a few months. When they returned to Singapore in mid '63, the SBS were no exception; their correspondent wrote:

> "The past few months for the Section have been the naval mixture of bustle and rush, prior to and during major exercises and comparatively quiet periods of training in the Singapore area, where sport, notably rugger, has rated supreme.
>
> "The annual exercise FOTEX provided the Section with a chance to practice its pathfinder role and, as the exercise was 100 miles up the East coast of Malaya, there was a chance for members to prove their seaman-like qualities, or otherwise, during the approach which was by MFV. Acquaintance was renewed with HMSM *Anchorite* who was to have carried a team in one phase of the exercise, but owing to certain postponements this was finally cancelled. The exercise was memorable as being one of the few where communications worked well all the time.
>
> "Exercise 'Test Tube' was a tactical beach recce carried out from HMSM *Andrew* by a boat section led by Lieutenant Wiltshire, the new Second in Command ... the exercise involved a fifteen mile approach and withdrawal paddle ... While the exercise progressed the remainder of the Section moved up to Penang Island and, on being joined by the members from the *Andrew*, spent a week practicing non-tactical beach recce and water skiing after work.
>
> "September saw the Section carry out its first local night water descent and it is hoped that many more will follow. The Commandant General visited us during his tour of units out here. He inspected the new store and office and joined the Section in a group photograph..."

David Mitchell (continued)

'In October '63 we were deployed to the Eastern end of the border with Kalimantan – to Tawau, where we were to support the Royal Leicester Regiment. The port of Tawau lies on the northern shore of a large and well protected bay known as Cowie Harbour. On the south side of the bay is a large island – Sebatik Island – which is split more or less east/west by the border with Kalimantan.

'After a brief stay in Tawau we set up a base at Wallace Bay, a timber export point on the north eastern edge of Sebatik Island. From there we were well able to move in amongst the large array of small, mostly mangrove covered islands between Wallace Bay and the mainland and to monitor any possible incursions by setting up covert OPs. The mangrove also extended up the Kalabakan River to the main timber extraction station at Kalabakan itself. The town was also easily approached through the jungle and had already been raided by the TNKU – fortuitously the Manager, Dai Rees, was doing his rounds and thankfully his Burmese wife had the foresight to hide.'

Of this period in Tawau, ending just before Christmas '63, the Section correspondent wrote, if a trifle facetiously…

> "Mid-October saw another of those five minute wonders, when the Section had thirty-six hours notice to move to Tawau in North Borneo (Sabah) to assist in chasing infiltrators.
>
> "We are now operating off the western end of Sebatik Island under command of 1st Battalion Royal Leicesters, with one sub-section embarked in the local frigate to provide an interception force for her radar contacts. For some peculiar reason it seems to be particularly difficult to get that particular sub-section away from the sea and back to the mundane duties of day boat patrols and night ambushes."

David Mitchell (continued)

1 SBS

'In March '64, Lieutenant R A M Seeger and ten NCOs and men from 1 SBS, normally based at Poole, were moved to Singapore to help supply a continuous SBS presence in support of operations in Borneo. Unfortunately shortly after arrival Lieutenant Seeger suffered a freefall parachuting accident, resulting in a broken ankle; he was relieved by Lieutenant Chris Roberts. 1 SBS moved to Tawau and based itself at Wallace Bay. From this advanced base they were able to patrol the waterways and recce areas close to the border. In particular they carried out a recce for the raid that was later implemented by 6 Troop of 40 Commando and led by Lieutenant Seeger, who had moved to that unit after recovering from his accident.'

2 SBS

'At its extreme western end, the border between Sarawak and Kalimantan runs along a high ridge to a point at the edge of a peninsular at Tanjon Datu. Approximately five miles from the point, in Sarawak, was the little harbour of Sematan which facilitated the export of bauxite from an opencast mine near to the town. About two miles offshore was a delightful little island sanctuary for turtles in the breeding season – Turtle Island. This was all a potentially vulnerable area and Sematan was garrisoned at that time by C Company 1/6th Gurkha Rifles. Of particular concern was the possibility of an enemy incursion by sea round the point of Tanjon Datu.

'In April/May '64, we were deployed to Sematan to support the Gurkhas and we set up an advanced base on Turtle Island. We then kept a covert observation post on Tanjon Datu. This all worked moderately well, however, it really all depended on good communication and sadly the A 41 VHF set operating in these conditions was not very satisfactory.

'The Royal Navy also put in an occasional appearance in the form of Coastal Minesweeper patrols and it was particularly helpful to have these ships close by.

Operating from one of the minesweepers, a small team was able to approach the shore by canoe, land and conceal their craft. They then checked out the area, which in this case showed signs of a past occupation but no enemy presence at that time. The team then withdrew to rendezvous with the minesweeper.'

Submarine Delivery

'On return to Singapore we continued to maintain our skills with jungle training but in particular we renewed our training with 6th Submarine Squadron, based nearby at *Terror*. The expectation was that, should the area of operations widen from that of more immediate concern in Borneo to that nearer to Malaya and Singapore, then it might necessary to mount small reconnaissance operations. The parent vessel for any such task is ideally the submarine. This can deliver a small team into the immediate area of operations by remaining underwater until the last moment and then only surface for a few minutes in order to release the SBS team in their canoes. This was the time-honoured method of operating from submarines but, although the drill had improved over the years, it still rendered the submarine vulnerable by forcing it to surface in waters where it would rather have remained submerged. So, as well as honing these drills, trials were begun to enable SBS teams to 'exit' from the submarine while it remained underwater.

'At that time the 6th Submarine Squadron consisted mostly of A Class submarines. In addition to having conveniently square buoyancy tanks, which were ideal for operating canoes from, these boats had originally been fitted with a gun, on the casing just forward of the conning tower. Access to the gun platform was via a separate 'Wet and Dry' chamber out of the pressure hull, which was also used as an escape route from the submarine, should that be necessary. By securing an inflatable, engine and part of their equipment outside the hull – say, on the gun platform or casing – it was possible to develop a technique that enabled the reconnaissance team to exit the submarine without it having to surface. This necessitated breathing compressed air from large bottles stored in the gun area and using a long hose with a demand valve to enable the team to reach the surface; the procedure was known as 'Goldfish'. At about the same time similar but more sophisticated procedures were being developed in the UK, in conjunction with the development of an underwater vehicle for transportation to and from the onshore target.'

Reconnaissance Operations

'Early in 1965, by which time 1 and 2 SBS had been amalgamated under my command, we were tasked to carry out a number of reconnaissance operations on potential targets. The team embarked in HMS *Ambush* (Lieutenant Commander C E T Baker RN) at *Terror* and moved up to the area of operations. During daylight a periscope reconnaissance of the island was carried out and panoramic photographs were taken through the periscope. That night *Ambush* surfaced approximately five miles off the island and launched a Gemini and four canoes. The Gemini was secured to the fin of the submarine and the canoes to the Gemini. *Ambush* dived and towed the Gemini and the canoes to within just over a mile of their target.

'The canoes proceeded inshore, landed and were concealed. Two of the team remained at the landing point to guard the canoes and the remainder moved off to check the target area. This revealed no enemy presence. On returning to the landing point the canoes were launched, rendezvoused with the Gemini and returned to the pick-up point with *Ambush*. In order to make contact with the submerged submarine, the Gemini lowered into the water a glorified football rattle, the 'clicker' being at one end of a five foot metal rod and the handle at the other. Turning the handle caused a clicking sound at the immersed end of the rod and this noise was picked up by the submarine's ASDIC, enabling it to home in on the sound and surface at the appropriate time.

'The recce party then came alongside and the craft and personnel re-embarked via the fore-hatch – the Gemini having to be deflated. The operation was completed by first light and *Ambush* made passage to return to Singapore.

'A further operation was later carried out and as usual a periscope recce was made in daylight. At about 0800 hrs five canoes were launched by the float off method. This involved rafting up in two groups on the casing and then the submarine diving gently and floating them off in the process – a very safe method for the canoes but of course it involved the submarine in coming to the surface. There was a slight breeze blowing but nothing untoward occurred. The five canoes were then divided into three teams.

'X Team, consisting of Colour Sergeant P Rook and Corporal D Humphries, landed just after 1000 hrs in order to check on a hut on the East side of the island; they concealed their canoes and tried to move along the shoreline; however, the going was very bad over the rocks and at times they had to enter the jungle. Just after midnight they returned to their canoe and at about 0200 hrs they attempted to launch but in doing so the canoe was caught by a wave and smashed on the rocks. They tried to pass a message to the submarine but failed and later that night a Gemini from the submarine tried to make contact but also failed. During the next day they moved via the jungle to an emergency pick up point and were picked up by Gemini at midnight. After collecting their canoe from the hiding place they returned to Ambush sometime after 0200 hrs.

'Meanwhile Y Team, consisting of Colour Sergeant Byrne, Sergeant Keogh and Marines Howe and Simpkins, had the task of covering X Team, establishing an Observation Point over the enemy hut and later carrying out a reconnaissance of the beach to check gradient and obstacles This all went smoothly and they were about to withdraw and rendezvous with the submarine by 0350 hrs.

'The third group, Z Team, consisting of Captain Mitchell, Corporal Woolvine and Marines Daniels and Silcock, had the task of checking on two other huts. Efforts to land the canoes on the rocks failed so, while the canoes lay offshore, Mitchell and Daniels swam ashore and moved through the jungle at the back of the shoreline to observe the huts. The going was difficult and it was not possible to get closer than about thirty yards from the huts. After noting very little enemy activity they returned to the landing point and made contact with their canoes. They then joined up with Y Team and finally returned to Ambush.

'The final part of this operation took place on the next night, after the usual daylight inspection of the area via the periscope of the submarine – an extremely useful and relatively secure way to finalise plans and check out the ground, even at a distance. The objective on this occasion was a river mouth, quite a large feature and one thought to be the home of possible raiding parties, whose target was on the Malayan coast. Three canoes were used on this occasion and were launched about four miles east of the river mouth at just after 0800 hrs. The approach to the shore was carried out very cautiously and the river entrance was not located until just before midnight. Here the canoes split, one to observe the offshore approaches, the second to cover and recce the north side of the river and the third to recce the river mouth. One canoe ventured about half a mile up the river to observe a hut but no enemy activity was noted. The operation was completed by about 0400 hrs when contact was made with *Ambush* and all three canoes were recovered.'

Surface Delivery

'For some weeks there had been evidence of minor incursions or harassment against the southern shores of Singapore and so it was decided to carry out a reconnaissance of possible target areas, operating this time from an inshore minesweeper, HMS *Camberford* (Lieutenant N E W Bush RN) with the Commander 6th Minesweeping Squadron (Commander J A B Thomas RN) embarked as the Naval Commander.

'Initial observations were carried out by the SBS from HMS *Greenford* on patrol during daylight. Some military presence was observed and as a result a reconnaissance was ordered by HQFARELF. Four canoes were released from an LCVP, tender to *Camberford.* They divided into two teams; P Team, consisting of Captain Mitchell. Colour Sergeant Rook, Corporal Humphries and Marine Simpkins, moved to the south west side of the island. They anchored in their respective positions just before 2200 hrs, particularly to observe any enemy reaction to illuminates to be fired from HMS *Picton* (Lieutenant Commander Leethes) at 2230 hrs. No reaction was seen so the team swam some lines of soundings to establish underwater gradients and kept the island under observation. Some, though very little, enemy movement was seen and the team moved away at about 0245 hrs.

'Q Team, with Sergeant Close, Corporal Woolvine and Marines Silcock and Daniels, moved to their launching position. Sergeant Close and Silcock left their canoe with Corporal Woolvine and swam ashore to the north east shore to take line of soundings opposite a hut. Close left Silcock about seventy yards from the shore and swam in to start a line of soundings. He heard dogs barking when he was about forty yards out and a man came out and shone a torch. He ducked twice to avoid the light and after removing the beach gradient line joined up with Silcock. The pair then tried to swim back to their canoe but the current was too strong for them to do this or for them to reach their emergency RV position, so the pair decided to swim back to base.

'P Team and the remainder of Q Team joined up at about 0300 hrs, then separated for a further search for Close and Silcock but, after having no luck, were picked up by *Camberford* at about 0400 hrs. Unknown to them, an alert observer on board *Picton* had seen the two men swimming at about 0330 hrs, about six miles from their objective and had recovered them. They were later transferred to *Camberford.*

'In all, the recces carried out by the SBS were inconclusive and insufficient evidence was collected to support any type of counter raid. President Soekarno was deposed in September '65 and, although Confrontation did not end for another twelve months, his demise caused some political restraint on these types of operation.'

The Brigade Commander, Brig Pat Willasey-Wilsey, transfers to HMS *Ambush* for a secret briefing

Recognition

The London Gazette of 30 September '66 published the award of the MBE to Captain Mitchell for 'distinguished' service in connection with his leadership during a number of operations in 1964/65, specifically citing the three operations of May, June and July '65 that have been described above. Sergeant Close was awarded the BEM for his part in five operations over a similar period and specifically for his part in the final operation launched from *Camberford.*

The citations had in each case referred specifically to the 'coolness, courage and leadership' of the recipients and a variation of the award was published some three years later in the London Gazette of 17th October '69 which recognised their 'gallantry' and provided for the wearing of a silver oak leaf on the medal ribbons.

Appendices

Appendix A

'Hearts and Minds'

The Director of Borneo Operations

> "This campaign for the 'Hearts and Minds' of the peoples of Sarawak and Sabah must be won. The success or failure of the military campaign depends on it.
>
> It can only be won by the enthusiasm and co-operation of the government servants, police officers and the men of the armed forces at grass roots level.
>
> Action is required now so that subversion in Malaysian Borneo is halted and so that the Security Forces can bring the military Campaign to an end.
>
> I depend on each of you."

W Walker

The Director of Borneo Operations. 15 April 1964

The Contribution of the Armed Forces

'The people among whom you work and live consider you to be representatives of their government.

'The greatest contribution that you can make to the winning of this campaign is daily contact with the civilian population.

'You must treat all Malaysians whom you meet as friends and with goodwill. A confident, firm and friendly attitude will help greatly. A smile and a greeting to those whom you meet, especially in their own language, serves to break the ice.

'You must not tolerate any misconduct in your units. A single act of misconduct or ill-discipline cancels out the effects of much good behaviour.

'Some Dos and Don'ts are outlined...'

Some Dos

1. Cooperate closely with Police and Government.
2. Give help in making footpaths and bridges.
3. Give help with boating and river problems.
4. Render first aid to civilians needing it.
5. Evacuate critically ill civilians by air and arrange for their return when cured.
6. Help in flood relief and in putting out fires.
7. Pass urgent messages over service radio nets.

8. Deliver letters to and from remote areas.
9. Treat civilian leaders with due respect.
10. Help and advise on rural development.
11. Demonstrate equipment and weapons to civilians.
12. Play games with locals and share hospitality.
13. Conduct evening education classes in Malay.
14. Learn to speak the local language.
15. Publicise the Police reward scheme.
16. Assist Government officers to get about their areas.
17. Distribute Government publications.
18. Help in driving wild animals off paddy crops.
19. Help in the killing of vermin.
20. Take an interest in local affairs.
21. Treat the civilians you meet as equals.
22. Respect the women of the country.
23. Drive carefully. Inconsiderate driving by drivers in service vehicles causes criticism by civilian road users.

Some Don'ts

1. Don't give offence by ignoring local customs or conventions.
2. Don't bathe or wash in the nude.
3. Don't shout at civilians. They hate that.
4. Don't interfere in religious affairs.
5. Don't take anything without paying for it.
6. Don't point with the forefinger at Asians. It is considered rude.

Finally

1. Do give all the help that you can that does not interfere with the military task.
2. Do go out of your way to find out what the local problems are and try to solve them [If you cannot, then ask advice of your superior].

*

The interpretation of Dos and Don'ts may appear to be clear cut and a simple question of common sense; in the relatively primitive society that existed in the forest areas of Sarawak the dividing line could be much less straight forward and could sometimes even be potentially contradictory:

Pat Gardner – OC B Company

Which Doctor?

'Our forward Troops did their best to look after the health of the local villagers and did much to improve their lot with some basic hygiene. Often the Medical Orderly, an ordinary Marine who had done short course of training, would have a 'surgery' of a score or so villagers. If they were seriously ill we would try to get them out to hospital.

'We all carried water sterilising tablets. A small white tablet sterilised a water bottle and about thirty minutes later a blue one was put in to take away the taste. A Medical Orderly confessed that when he hadn't a clue what was wrong with a 'patient' he had told him to take a white tablet and thirty minutes later to take a blue one. It apparently worked.

'There were some frightful frustrations as the witch doctors would insist on treating serious cases until they realised that they were going to fail and then, often too late, they turned them over to us. If the patient or victim died, the witch doctor would contend that the white man's medicine was no good. Tragically this happened to a child and I had a long session with the Headman who must have sorted the witch doctor out, as he never interfered again.'

Appendix B

Jungle Warfare

Rules exist for jungle operations and these were effectively taught to the comparatively few that had the opportunity to attend the courses at the Jungle Warfare School in Johore, or even the improvised courses arranged within units when operations allowed. Most simply learnt on the job, where, in any case, all honed their personal skills in the light of experience and developed their own capacity.

As we have seen in various accounts, even the golden rules are there for guidance and are to be broken advisedly, when appropriate or unavoidable. Use of tracks is a particular taboo that was probably most frequently broken, for reasons of speed, silence, undergrowth, contour, pursuit – tracking – or any combination of factors; in all cases the risk had to be recognised and assessed against the requirement.

For much of the time it was a Troop Commander's war; the two expositions that follow come from Troop Commanders at each end of the scale; the one from an experienced operator, who at one stage commanded an ad hoc company on operations; the other, with a whimsical touch, from a young officer then still under training and on his first attachment to an operational Commando. Both took part in cross-border (Claret) operations.

Seasoned Subaltern 1964/65

R A M Seeger, Lieutenant

'I very much enjoyed the jungle. Aesthetically it is excessive and overpowering and I prefer other wilderness areas. However it is very satisfying to operate in. If you are efficient, well organised and follow good procedures, you will fare well; if you are not and don't you won't!

'It is made for small patrol operating. Because of the closeness of vegetation you have to move in single file for good control. This is obviously easier with a four man patrol than say a cut down company of sixty or so men (which is what I took over the border when we were hitting the Indonesian bases). A large group also makes tracks and moves slowly.'

Movement

'You are very safe in the jungle (however small a group you are), providing you keep off tracks (obvious ambush sites), keep quiet (so no hacking of vegetation or talking) and keep moving. You are always in danger if you stop to basha up early and leave late the next day. An enemy following your trail can catch you up and hit you when you are relaxed or preoccupied with packing up and getting under way. What you did therefore if you decided to play it hard was to stop for your evening meal and then move on till it was dark and basha up. Likewise you packed up in the dark and moved off at first light stopping for breakfast somewhere further on down your route. A final refinement for a small group with para-hammocks (improvised hammocks made from old parachutes) was to basha up on the side of a steep slope. You could sleep comfortably in a hammock but any enemy would find it virtually impossible to get close without noise – especially in the dark. Movement by night in the jungle (without torches) was virtually impossible. It was too black. I tried it once and got nowhere.

'Jungle equipment soon becomes refined to the minimum as you want to carry as little as possible. You used dehydrated rations as water is rarely a problem. During the day you are permanently wet with sweat or rain and soon stink of the jungle. You don't notice this when you are in it, but outside it, your smell is very noticeable. Communication is by silent hand signals and whispers. Radio communications are often difficult.

'Helicopters give useful support but finding suitable and secure sites is not always easy. In Borneo we would use helicopters to move between our front line bases but would patrol out from these on foot. We seldom went out for more than a week. It wasn't necessary (you could get to most points in your area of responsibility in that time) and more than a week's food supply made your pack too heavy and bulky.

'Navigation was by dead reckoning. You walked on compass bearings and counted the paces. You could seldom see or recognise identifiable features. The maps were mostly blank sheets of paper with grid lines. Near your base there were features you could recognise and the maps had contour lines, so even if you were never entirely sure where you were while on patrol, providing you got back to the general area of your base you could always find your way back into it.

'I think on the whole we operated very efficiently. The Army had a Jungle Warfare school in Malaya which ran excellent courses. They were not only for British Forces and were attended by Americans and soldiers from other Asian armies. I was lucky enough to go on one of their courses and found it to be excellent value. Combining what I learnt there with what I had learnt in the SBS enabled me to develop some effective procedures. These I enforced for certain in the Recce Troop (my last command in 40 Commando) but also if my memory serves correctly, partially at least, in my company (D Company) and Rifle Troop (6 Troop).

'Tracks were rarely used and all communication was strictly limited to whispers and silent signals. My Recce Troop which worked in small patrols used hammocks

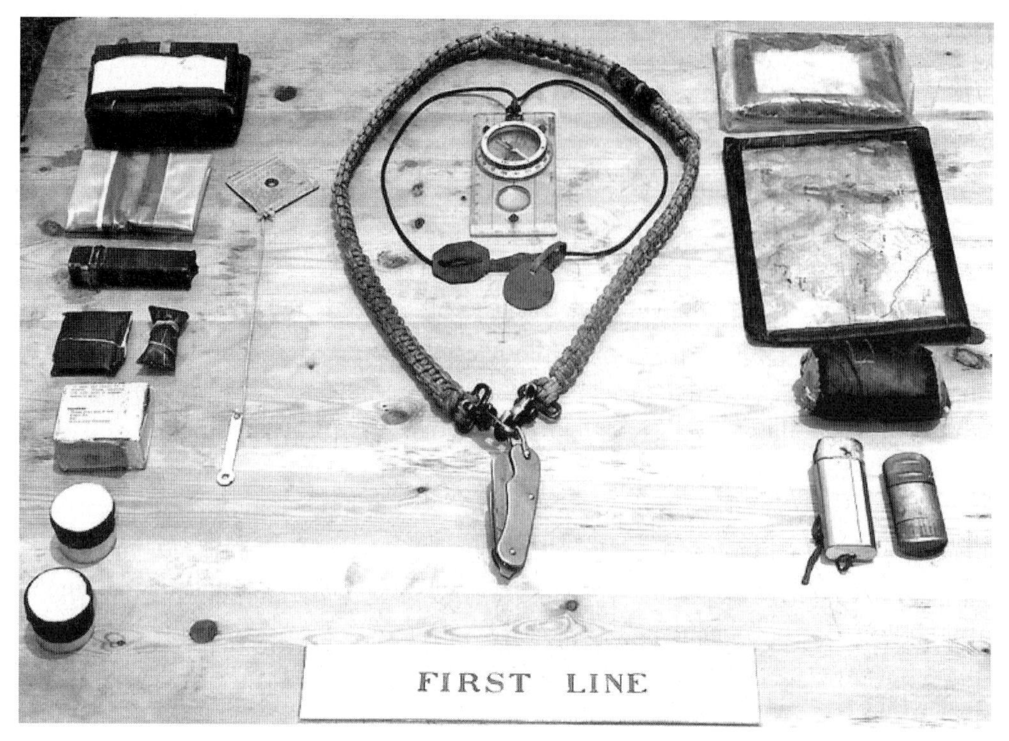

First Line gear

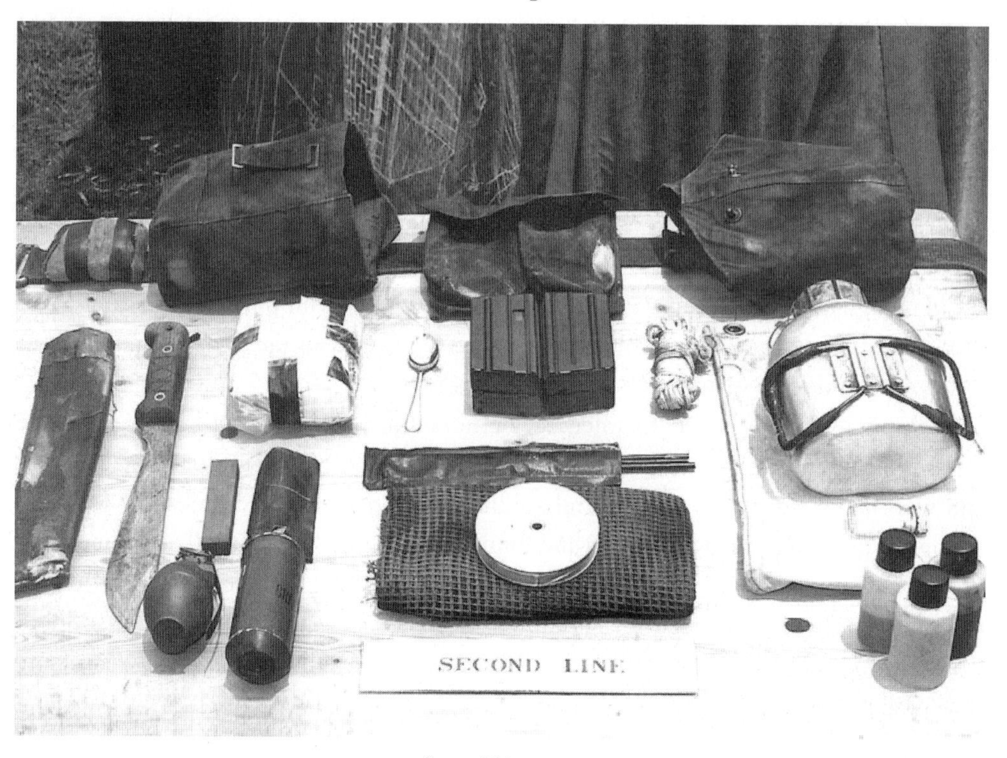

Second Line gear

Third Line gear

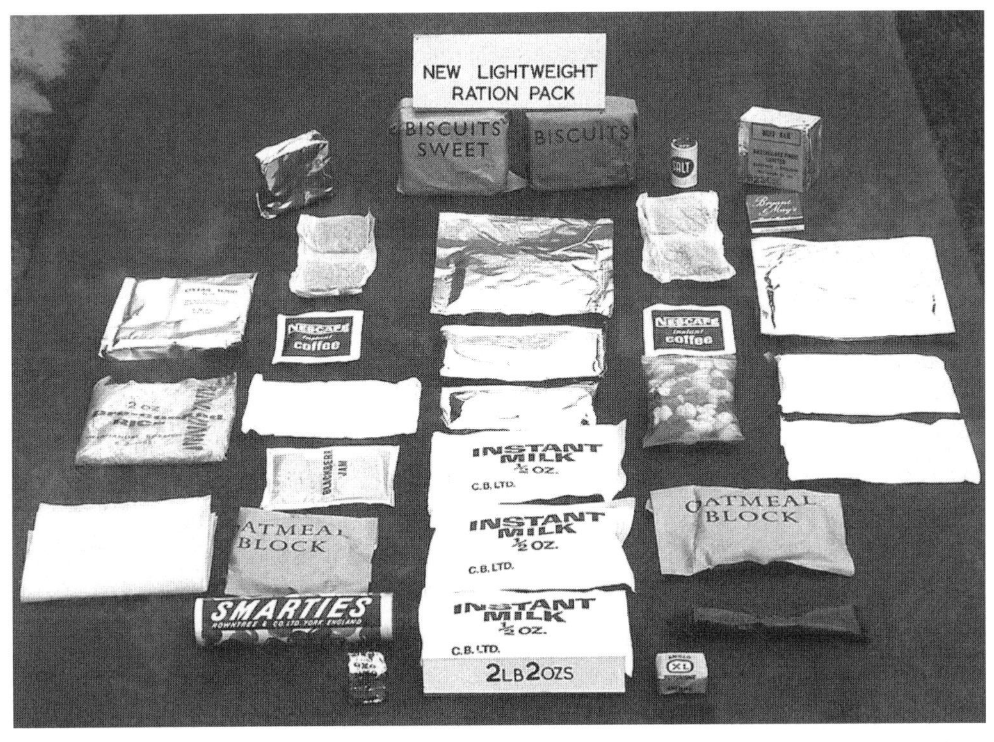

New Lightweight ration pack

and slept on the sides of steep hillsides or other such awkward ground. My Rifle Troop and company which operated in larger groups used para-cloth sleeping bags and slept on the ground in their defensive fire positions. These would be in a circle round my HQ basha where I was located with my radio operator and any other HQ personnel, e.g. Mortar and Artillery fire controllers (MFCs and FOOs) and Indigenous trackers/guides. To communicate and find our way around at night (to change over sentries or attend O groups) all positions were linked by thin cord.'

'Gear was personalised and cut to the absolute minimum. The dehydrated ration packs which were already lightweight and good were even further reduced. Cutting rarely occurred and never on the move. When we stopped for the night I would allow one to two minutes of cutting only (and done all together at the same time) to prepare our camp site. Swiss Army knife saw blades were invaluable here, as you could saw silently before or after the time allowed for chopping. Para-cloth tracksuits were used to sleep in and then your wet clothes put back on in the dark in time for a dawn move off or stand-to. We usually played the hard routine, moving off at dawn and keeping going till dusk, stopping later or before for breakfast and supper.

'Gear was organised into three lines. Essential survival items (map, compass, pills, emergency food etc) in your pockets, water and ammunition and other essential operating kit on your belt and the rest in your pack. Belts were made from airdrop straps with buckles so that they could not suddenly unclip and come off. Your pocket gear always stayed on your person as did whenever possible your belt kit. If you did take your belt kit off it was always within arm's reach. The same applied to your rifle – it was either in your hand or ready to pick up. OG (olive green) trousers and shirts were painted to achieve better camouflage and cam cream worn on the face and hands. Maps were unmarked and all waste gear carried out in plastic bags.'

Student Subaltern – 1964/65

Martin Read, Second Lieutenant

'My children have often referred to the Swinging Sixties, envious of the excitement I must have been part of – the young discovering their influence with the liberation of convention and behaviour. What was it like? How did it feel to be part of this? The answer is that I don't know – I wasn't there. I was undergoing a forced growing up process having one of the most challenging, life changing and exciting experiences of my life. I was with men, who like me, had chosen adventure – under the thin disguise of patriotism – to support a young federation of countries to achieve democracy and independence within a framework of broadly accepted behaviour that would allow societies to coexist in peace and relative harmony.'

Basic Training

'In the environment in which I was immersed as a twenty-year-old, success required not only the revival of basic human instincts that institutions and parenting had spent twenty years trying to suppress, but also their refinement. To foster, control and manage the reawakening of these basic instincts, we had spent two years undergoing an unforgiving regime of training that broke us down to expose the raw elements, only to reassemble them into a format that would last throughout our lifetime. The resulting character comprised a complex mix of determination, loyalty and reliability with motivation emanating from an embedded sense of pride, honour and tradition – conditions alien to the mediocrity that is now encouraged by all good peace loving Europeans. This was all wrapped up within an envelope of discipline to provide a lasting bond and commitment to Queen and Country and the certainty of moral conviction.

'Civilisation, as society is repeatedly reminded, is merely a veneer over human nature; it takes only a scratch to expose the raw and often brutal instincts of survival. Discipline is the keeper of Civilisation; without discipline the rules that bind society together to allow peaceful coexistence and constructive evolution will not hold, and the reversion to supremacy of human instincts takes effect with often disastrous consequences.

'Success throughout the Borneo Campaign required us to learn to live in total harmony with the natural environment – the jungle. We rediscovered and honed all those survival instincts – smell, hearing and even the instinct of 'gut feeling'; we accepted the aim, to actively seek out one's so called enemy and if necessary to be prepared to kill him. In such an environment the dangers of reawakening and refining these basic instincts of survival without an embedded allegiance to discipline, would have resulted in a lawless, ill disciplined and dangerous rabble, as is so often depicted in the other campaign that ran alongside Borneo – Vietnam. In the modern day we see the consequences of the reluctance to apply discipline on our screens as headline news, in the form of senseless vandalism and diminishing values. Success on the ground in Borneo emanated from a fine balance between discipline and the refined instincts of survival, to ensure that the veneer of civilisation that we were there to uphold was not sacrificed in the pursuit of our success.'

Jungle Outpost

'Operations in Borneo were undertaken on a three to four month turnaround. Once in Borneo units operated largely at Troop level, forming self contained well defended secure bases. They were our 'castles'. Within them we could 'hunker' down for extended periods if necessary, but they also provided secure bases from which to patrol. They were often collocated with villages, which enabled us to provide protection to the villagers, giving them confidence to resist any approaches from over the border, as well as allowing us to monitor movement effectively, developing a thorough understanding of the local terrain and hopefully to identify any incursions.

'Each encampment was self contained and a microcosm of society. Invariably on a hill, it had a complex system of defence. The first fifty to 100 metres would be cleared to provide clean arcs of fire. This area would be peppered with panjis – sharpened bamboo stakes angled downhill. Any undulation providing protection from defensive fire would be covered by a pipe bomb or Claymore mine which would be triggered electronically. In addition there would be a series of wire fences and entanglements, trip flares and other warning devices and booby traps. One or possibly two entries only, constantly manned with sentry points around the camp perimeter housed under mortar proof sangars. Within the encampment there would be facilities to meet daily requirements; latrines, water, a cook house, sleeping quarters, first aid and command centre.

'The preparation of water for showers, drinking and cooking was a well established affair. Water was drawn up from the nearest stream by pump and fed into a large flexible separation tank positioned normally at the highest point. Alum paste would be mixed in and allowed to settle for eight hours. This would then be gravity fed into a metal Braithwaite tank where chemical sterilisation would be added and allowed to rest for one hour before using.'

Surviving in the Jungle

'We were very good at living and surviving in the Jungle and became acclimatised surprisingly quickly to the hot and humid environment. Health precautions became automatic, with the process of treating water with Millbank bags and sterilisation tablets, the taking of paladrine tablets to prevent malaria and the treating of seams of clothing to prevent the various worms and bugs getting through. As a result we had few troubles from disease and illness, though we had to remain very wary.

'One early morning packing away my pack I heard a noise from within, to discover on inspection one of the biggest scorpions I have yet to see! Everything – including the scorpion – was jungle green, our vests, underpants, handkerchiefs, socks. We allowed ourselves flexibility in choosing our own webbing packs, most preferring the small '44 Pattern' pack and tailor-made ammunition and magazine pouches made up in Singapore. With the ready supply of water and minimal food requirements, we could undertake extended patrols of up to three weeks while remaining totally undetected.

'On such patrols we aimed to blend with the natural environment. There was no smoking, no use of toothpaste or soap. Cooking with hexamine was strictly limited. Communication along the patrol was by signs only, triggering well rehearsed procedures. As a result our senses became honed. No doubt if we had been dumped straight into a Singapore cocktail party, our odour would have created few friends, however in the jungle it blended in with the natural environment. It also removed the camouflage of other man made smells, and allowed us to smell our surroundings.

'I remember on my first return to Singapore being surprised at being able to smell the difference between a man and a woman at about twenty yards away which with the 'kytye' could have been useful! On a more serious note, I was stalked one night by a leopard. Virgin rainforest at night is pitch black. I was with a small group of four and on sentry duty, slightly removed from the other three who were bedded down. For about an hour I followed the movements of a leopard who circled me and my sleeping colleagues. I never saw him, I only smelt him. The following morning we picked up his tracks and he came within four yards of me, obviously smelt the others and moved on. It was one of the few occasions I have experienced fear.'

The Iban

'During my musings when on my own for long hours of watching and waiting, I often used to ponder on why the world was not ruled by Ibans! They are in the land of potential plenty – with not too long a venture out from their long house they have all the food they could possibly want – with little effort. So with the essentials taken care of, and leisure time in abundance they have time to think… or do they? As we all know if you have life too easy, you become lazy. You need stimulus; you need to have to struggle to trigger intellectual inquisitiveness. Not to the extremes of the Eskimo, who struggles all his waking hours and is the converse of the Iban, with no time to think beyond the demands of survival. Of course a balance is required; hence historically it is the global temperate zone that has spawned those civilisations that have refined and developed the human intellect.

'The Iban, though, is at home in the Jungle. We may congratulate ourselves that we managed pretty well, but compared with the lifelong experience of the Iban we were novices. Maps were pretty much non-existent, displaying tree symbols throughout, though the suggestion of a stream gave some reference to possible position. Hence each Troop would have attached a pair of Iban trackers, who would route find, read trails and listen to the jungle in ways which to us were uncanny. You might suggest that they were in touch with the spirit of the jungle and few among those who had worked with them would disagree. The one thing they did not understand however was the compass – they had never had a need for one.

'We were returning from a patrol to a temporary camp and I recognised that we were commencing a large loop back retracing our steps. Using our map I determined the rough bearing of a direct route and indicated the direction to my two trackers. They thought I was mad, but after some remonstrations proceeded. Within half an hour we hit the temporary camp – through luck more than accurate navigation – spot on. The Ibans were in awe – regarding me as a demigod. My basha was made for me, food cooked – I was even presented with a hat made out of monkey's fur and later with a very fine hand crafted jungle gollock – a long heavy knife essential for living in the jungle.

'Ibans are known particularly for their historic head hunting exploits; indeed in many longhouses shrunken heads were still in evidence, hanging from the rafters! Initially their willingness to support our efforts was reflected as an opportunity for them to reactivate an interest in their historic 'sport' by pursuing specific targets on the other side of the border. Proof was always required in order to claim any reward and to avoid the presentation of severed heads, they were eventually persuaded that an ear from the claimed victim would suffice. Whether it came from a severed head we never knew, though a sudden increase in their long house hanging decorations was noted.'

Roll of Honour

Chappell, R	RM 15686	Cpl	42 Cdo	L Company	20 February ’64
Clark, I C		Lt	42 Cdo	L Company	16 March ’66
Collins, T J	RM 20139	Mne	42 Cdo	L Company	16 March ’66
Davidson, P F	RM 17455	Sgt	42 Cdo	L Company	11 February ’65
Danells, P J G	RM 19528	Cpl	40 Cdo	B Company	4 November ’65
Deering, M A	RM 20642	Mne	40 Cdo	A Company	30 October ’64
Formoy, R D	RM 16883	Mne	42 Cdo	L Company	12 December ’62
Foster C W	RM 10369	Sgt	42 Cdo		13 March ’66
Gillingham, G J	RM 20270	Mne	42 Cdo	L Company	24 December ’62
Hind, J T O	RM 20875	Cpl	42 Cdo	K Company	13 April ’64
Jennings, R	RM 19233	Mne	42 Cdo	L Company	12 December ’62
Kierans, G	RM 16941	Mne	42 Cdo	L Company	12 December ’62
Macfarlane, W G	Ch/x 4743	Sgt	42 Cdo	L Company	12 December ’62
Marriott, M	RM 17999	Cpl	40 Cdo	B Company	1 January ’64
McRea, E	RM 17368	Mne	42 Cdo	K Company	13 April ’64
Powell, F S	RM 21017	Mne	42 Cdo	L Company	12 December ’62
Rolls, G		2nd Lt	42 Cdo	L Company	1 August ’63

The Governor of Sarawak, Sir Alexander Waddell, unveiling the Limbang Memorial in August 1963. Brigadier ‘Billy’ Barton, commanding 3rd Commando Brigade, can be seen on the left of the photograph.

Appendix D

Visitors

Derek Oakley – G3 Int

'Visitors are always a two-edged weapon. Whilst we are delighted that people should come and see what we are doing and see our problems at first hand, it must seem to them that sometimes we are inclined to ignore them. This apparent standoffish behaviour is only superficial, as there are usually more operationally essential tasks to perform at that particular moment. Underneath we realise the value of visitors.

'However it did come somewhat near to impossible recently when we had four Brigadiers, one Air Commodore and two Colonels visiting on the same day. The Brigade Commander himself took on these visits. Not to be outdone, the GSO 3 (Intelligence) carried out seven different briefings of visitors that day which included an Australian senator and a British MP. However to cap it all, a telephone call was received from the airport during the forenoon, saying that an Air Chief Marshal had arrived, this call soon saw the Brigade Major hurrying towards the airport, seven miles away. It is interesting to note that from reports we hear from the Indonesian radio Station just across the border, the Indonesian Army also have a crop of visitors!'

Pat Gardner – Company Commander

'One of the downsides of being located at Bau was that it was accessible by road from Kuching and the airport. This meant that if a visitor came out to Borneo, it was the easiest place for them to get to and obtain a feel of what was going on.

'I had a policy in the Company that we aimed to use visitors to our advantage. When the Director of Borneo Operations came round, I would brief him at Company HQ about what was going on and end up by saying that what we were really short of was sandbags. The outlying Troop Commanders would do the same until we were certain that he had hoisted this in. Then the message would be sent to the next Troop Commander to plug our next requirement which might have been corrugated iron sheeting. In no time at all sandbags and corrugated iron would be falling from the sky!

'Peter Thorneycroft came out as Defence Secretary; it was clear that he hadn't a clue what was going on, as he asked some strange questions such as "Do the Indonesians come over wearing uniforms?" Denis Healey as Shadow Defence Secretary was of a different calibre and one could only admire his grasp of the situation; I almost became a Labour supporter!

'The RAF sponsored a Press visit and I rather naively asked the Colonel what I could tell them. The rather unhelpful reply was "Nothing!" The RAF laid on an airdrop to show off their expertise; it proved to be a disaster with parachutes missing their target and ending up festooned in 200 foot trees – it was hard not to laugh at their discomfiture. I ended up sitting on a rock overlooking the border surrounded by journalists and chatting to them. One of them thanked me and said that it was the first time during his trip that he had something worthwhile; the payoff was that the Corps got some good publicity.

'An MP with the Commonwealth Parliamentary Group, Bernard Braine, who became the Father of the House and was knighted, arrived with his personal TV cameraman. It became clear that his only interest in us was to be photographed with one of his constituents against a jungle background. Much to his chagrin we had no one from Essex.

'Clare Hollingworth, a veteran and hard-bitten war correspondent, had written an article – in the *Observer*, I think – saying that there were not enough Troops in Borneo. After I had briefed her, she said "What you are saying is that there are not enough Troops for the tasks in hand." I replied that this was not the case and, with our ability to reinforce quickly using helicopters, we were strong enough on the ground. Before we left for the forward Troops, I had managed to warn them what they were up against and the Troop Commanders backed me up – the lady had made up her mind and wasn't to be confused by the facts.

'Most visitors were a delight, but they were time-consuming as they had to be briefed and led around, which was not always that convenient.

'In Labuan, where I later was G2 Ops on the staff of Commander Land Forces Borneo, another MP, Julian Critchley, made a fool of himself. He went swimming and took the un-seamanlike action of placing his clothes below the high water mark. He had a long swim and succeeded in getting himself stung by a jellyfish. He ended up in the Mess with his leg up and feeling very sorry for himself. Our blunt senior Naval Officer, a Captain, did not improve his morale by saying to him in a jovial way: "I think you are a complete nit; if I was one of your constituents, I would not vote for you!" It was, perhaps, a portent as he was to lose both his seat and his wife.'

Sunday – a Moveable Feast

'Our camp at Bau was on the edge of a beautiful, deep lake. I had some reservations about swimming in it as it had been part of a gold mine and the extraction process used cyanide. We had the water tested after which we bathed regularly and very refreshing it was.

'We hadn't been there very long before people from Headquarters in Kuching used to come out on a Sunday and were something of a curse, as they expected to use our camp and regarded us as their hosts. As we could never get the Chaplain on a Sunday I hatched a scheme for altering Sunday. We brought it forward a day each week. Thus when these 'swimmers' came out on Sunday they found it a working day, were asked their business and then couldn't hang around. It meant that we had the Padre on our Sunday and of course our Sundays came around more often! The Colonel never did work out what we were doing.'

Mick Reece – RM Aviator

'Reflecting the importance and reputation of the Sarawak detachment, inevitably we played host to countless visitors and took as routine visits which would normally throw a Naval Air Station into chaos for weeks.

The Captain General, HRH The Duke of Edinburgh visits 845 NAS, talking to two naval ratings with Captain Mick Reece (right)

'At the top of an illustrious list was Prince Philip, the Duke of Edinburgh, to Sibu. For reasons I can no longer recall, I was in charge and hosted the visit. Typically, three of our four Wessex were away on an extended Troop lift, the remaining Wessex was unserviceable and the Whirlwind was also dodgy. No matter, as is so often the case, the day was made by Prince Philip's excellent rapport with the maintenance ratings covered in sweat and grease endeavouring to restore the Wessex to serviceability, and a hilarious encounter with the Chawallah. Earlier, to his credit, Earl Jellicoe, the Minister for Defence, had made the long haul to Nanga Gaat.

'My 'Longest Day' fell on 9 October 1964 when the General Officer Commanding the Household Division, decided it would be a good idea before his imminent retirement to visit as many guardsmen as he could serving around the globe. Not surprisingly, the Guards Independent Parachute Company presented a particular challenge. My task was to fly him in what was a carefully co-ordinated operation to meet and speak, very briefly, to all the patrols scattered throughout the Third Division on that particular day.

'My abiding memory is landing on a reasonably large shingle bank in the midst of a fast flowing river. Naturally, there was no question of shutting down but nor was there any sight of the patrol. After what I suspect was a minute, but seemed an age at the time, I spotted the patrol wading up the river towards us. The water was over waist height and their rifles were raised above their heads. Only then did I permit the General to leave the aircraft and advance across the shingle bank. I then witnessed the magnificent spectacle of this soaking four man patrol gradually emerge from the river, place their rifles at the shoulder and take up their dressing in a single rank. And then, as the General approached, the Patrol Commander took an immaculate parade-ground pace forward, saluted and presented his patrol for inspection.

'The whole mission absorbed eight hours ten minutes of precious Wessex hours, not far short of one thousand miles, of which the last hour was at night returning from Nanga Gaat with the gallant General, not surprisingly, asleep in the copilot's seat. In slight mitigation to the General's main objective, wherever possible we combined these separate patrol RVs with a resupply. Nevertheless, with hindsight, I think it was remiss of us not to send an invoice. Knowing the Guards at the time, I suspect they would have paid in style!'

Martin Read – Troop Commander

'At the start of one patrol I was joined by two members of the US Army 'Green Berets' who were over to see how we 'did it'. As evening approached they became a bit agitated, asking when we were going to stop to prepare the helicopter landing pad for the evening supply of rations and mail. The concept of covert operations seemed difficult to grasp. On the second day they suggested that the men's morale would suffer if they did not get their mail from home and daily supplement of Coca-Cola. On the third day they cracked and left! We were out for another two weeks.'

Andrew Jackson – Company Signaller

'The larger huts were sometimes used for 'visitors' to the camp. During their visit they were usually invited to meet 'scorps'. This was a scorpion which was harmless as the Iban trackers at the location had pinched out the sting from its tail. He usually wandered around the camp on a piece of fine line for the Troops' entertainment. Great fun was had however when 'Scorps' was introduced into the visitors hut in the evening gloom. It was amazing how fast some incumbents moved – mosquito nets and all!'

Dick Sidwell – Company Commander

'We had a number of visitors from the Army. The Director of Army Training, General Laing, admitted he knew nothing about jungle warfare but disappointingly he also knew little about the equipment that was being used or what equipment was really needed.

He was closely followed by the Vice QMG, General Read, whose experience seemed to be entirely from service in Germany. The Director of Royal Artillery dropped in one day and we had difficulty in persuading him that one gun deployed on its own was a viable unit. I hope he left us with a changed opinion as we were very grateful for our 105mm on several occasions. He was taken aback when I told him that as a Naval Gunnery Officer I had trained a RM detachment on the 105mm gun and had carried out the hot weather trials on the 105 pack-howitzer for the Army, while serving with 45 Commando in Aden in 1960.

'We had a BBC TV crew with us for a few days – Fred the Sound and Fred the Camera – and they were keen to accompany a patrol, so I took them for a short walk through the local area. Their equipment was far too heavy and awkward to move through close country and they made a lot of noise, so we turned back fairly quickly. Later we had four Americans from Columbia TV and they interviewed some of our NCOs and Marines. I have never seen any results from these visits which were a great waste of our time and of helicopter space.

Captain Dick Sidwell shows the Director of Army Training round 'Park Lane', the accommodation in a longhouse at Pang Amo

'One afternoon, a three-man BBC TV crew arrived with Frankie Howard, Shirley Abicair – a very attractive Australian zither player and singer – and Al Coran, a brilliant illusionist. They gave a twenty minute show which was much appreciated. The TV crew wanted to film Frankie talking on the radio to a jungle patrol, but we were unable to make contact with the patrol so he was put through to Sergeant Bibbie in the mortar pit at the far end of our base. I am afraid Frankie was misled, but he was thrilled to think that he was talking to someone in the jungle even when Sergeant Bibbie said "The Marines were cutting through thick jungle towing their canoes behind them.'

The Commandant General, Lieutenant General Sir Malcolm Cartwright-Taylor
and Lieutenant Colonel Ian Gourlay negotiate a bamboo bridge
during his visit to 42 Commando

Appendix E

Air Dispatch

Phillips, Lance Corporal – HQ Company, 42 Commando

'During the past fifteen months, when I was a member of 4 Troop, I was often on the receiving end of air supply drops. We would be sitting, after a patrol, in our basha, when someone would shout "Air Drop – everybody out!" We would then watch the lumbering Hastings as it twisted and turned in and out of the hills. As it roared overhead, down would come our next week's supply of rations, beer and, we hoped, our mail. Most of us had wondered at one time or another, what it would be like to be doing the dropping rather than being dropped on.

'I soon got my chance when I joined HQ Company at Semengo camp a mere 300 yards from Kuching Airport; it is from here that all air drops are carried out. A quiet word in the ration storeman's ear and I found myself on a flight two weeks later.

'I was fortunate as this was not to be an ordinary air drop; we were to drop big bales of dannert wire, weighing 1,200 pounds each, to Malaysian Troops in the Third Division. This was to be done from a Beverley Freighter with its back door removed and there were to be two drops in all. The Beverley must be the ugliest aircraft ever built, especially when it has no doors; it amazes me how it ever leaves the ground.

'So at one o'clock on a rather wet and windy day Marine Hoddart and I arrived at the airport to find our Beverley. Inside we could see six very large bales of wire, complete with parachutes and securely chained to the floor on rollers ready to be pushed out.

'Just before we climbed in, I heard a member of the crew remark that they reckoned that they must have dropped enough wire to stretch along the 800 miles of the Sarawak/Indonesian border; I should think they were very nearly right too. A few minutes later we were airborne and crossing the Kuching River en route to the Third Division.

'The seating in a Beverley is in the upper fuselage running over the top of the main hold. To obtain a good view from the hatch I had to hang upside down securely strapped to one of the seats, because for obvious reasons we were not allowed down on the hold.

'After two hours flying over thick and seemingly impenetrable jungle, we arrived over our first dropping zone, a place called Belaga, which had a small Z cut from the jungle. As soon as it came in sight the bomb aimer up front gave the word 'go'. The team of dispatch men pulled out the chocks and pushed the first load into space; 1,200 pounds of dannert wire went plummeting down to earth without its parachute;

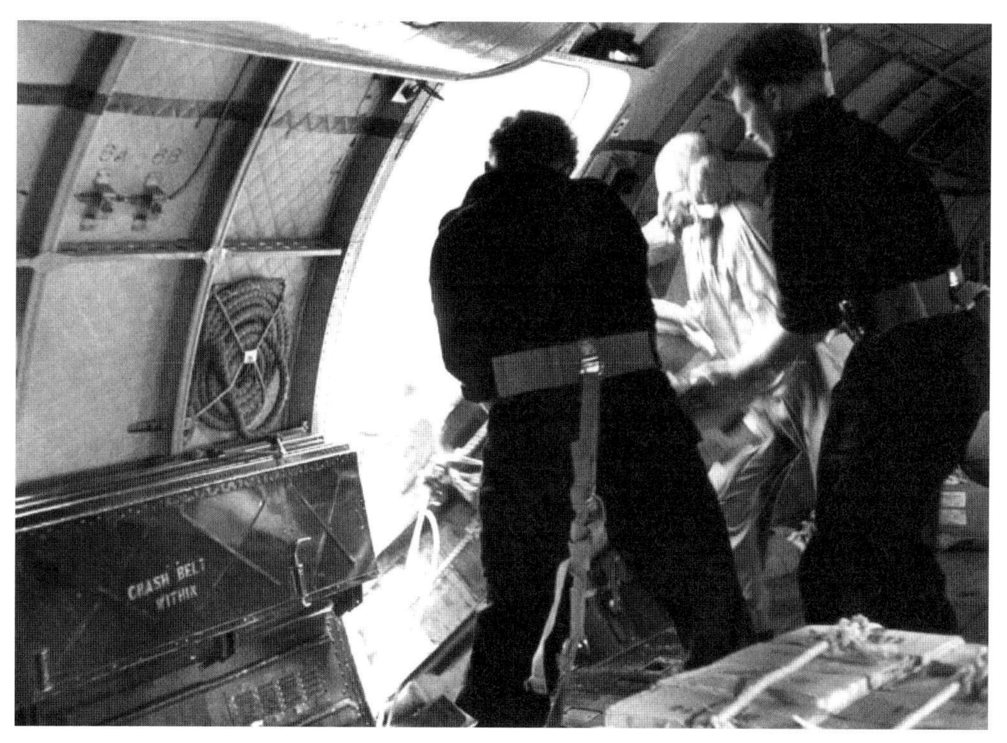

Dispatching air supplies from inside an RAF aircraft to up country locations

Air supplies dropping from an RAF Hastings. This was usually carried out at the larger locations, while helicopters were used for smaller ones.

the static line fixed to the 'chute and the fuselage had broken away, hence, I should imagine, one rather compressed coil of wire, which I would not have liked to unravel. The dispatchers thought this was a huge joke – they had obviously never had the job of untangling dannert wire. However, the next two drops at the location went off without a hitch.

'Our next dropping zone was a small Kampong situated in the jungle, the actual dropping zone being a small clearing alongside a river that ran nearby. On both sides of the river there were large hills and it seemed to me that the wing-tips were touching on either side. I had a good view of the Kampong from my window and was greeted by the sight of a hoard of 'chicos' waving at us. For them the sight of an aircraft dropping supplies must be quite an excitement. The air-drop completed we made our way back and two hours later landed at Kuching Airport. For me this had been a very interesting afternoon's flying.

'My appetite for flying had now been whetted, so I decided to try and get a flight in one of the 7th Recce Austers. Much to my surprise, two weeks later I was once again at the airport, climbing into an Auster, bound for Lundu. What a difference there is between a Beverley and the Auster. It is like comparing a bus with a fast car. I was quite convinced at the time that I could take over the controls because they looked so easy to operate; I have since been informed that it is harder than it looks.

'On arrival at Lundu, I threw out a large blue sack of mail to a group of waiting Gurkhas. Our next port of call was Sematan, where we landed and off-loaded more mail. We then took off from the runway to go on a coastal recce up to the northwest tip of Indonesia/Borneo. Having seen nothing, we headed back for Kuching. On the way back we spotted several small boats and a Navy minesweeper, all of which we flew round and had a close look at.'

'My curiosity had now been satisfied, for I had been on two interesting flights and had thoroughly enjoyed them.'

Appendix F

Afterthoughts

Terry Clarke, Fleet Chief Petty Officer

'In the years that followed, I served in 40 Commando, (though only for three weeks), 41 Commando, 43 Commando, 45 Commando, HQ 3 Commando Brigade, Commando Forces and CTCRM. I even found time to go back to the Royal Navy for short periods, on one occasion to serve aboard *Hermes*, when acting as a Commando Carrier!

'My final appointment was to CTCRM as the Fleet Chief, Practice Manager. Whilst there, I received a civilian job offer that was too good to refuse. So, I requested to leave the Service before completion of my current engagement. At the Commanding Officer's Table, the request with a supporting letter from my PMO was read out. The CO looked at the PMO and said, "This is a well written letter, Doctor". The Doctor nodded, to which the CO retorted, "You did not write this letter Doctor", then he pointed at me and said, "He did"! The CO however did agree to approve my request, on the condition that I attended the Officers' Mess for drinks prior to departing from CTCRM. This I did, as well as enjoying a Top Table lunch in the Sergeants Mess.

'In conclusion, I feel it appropriate to state that I am very proud of the fact that I served for most of my Service career with the Royal Marines and have always felt far more 'Marine' than 'Matelot'! I made many friends, with some of whom I still have contact, and retain my association with the Corps through the Commando Medical Branch of the RN Association.

Keith Wilkins, Colonel

'By early November 1964, I had completed my tour in 42 Commando and it was time for me and my family to return to the UK. Looking back on it now, I can say that it was probably one of the most stimulating periods in my Royal Marines career. There were the inevitable ups and downs and moments of sheer monotony, but I don't think that any of us forgot that we were involved in a real war, which had a habit of exploding on us at short notice – we had to remain alert and remember the lessons that we had learnt in training. There were the occasional mishaps, but as a unit, I feel that we faced up well to the challenges that were presented and made a valuable contribution to the overall success of the campaign.

Ian Moore, Colonel

'Those few short months in Sarawak, at the outset of the Confrontation, stay firmly in the mind. For me expectation was everything; I was essentially unblooded. Some three weeks after I left however, the village of Serabak was subjected, in the middle of the night, to five rounds of two inch mortar fire – happily inaccurate. About a week after that, the Troop under Sergeant Friel arrested two Chinese terrorists, trying to get back over the border, who confessed to being in that raid, which would have been followed by an attack had there been any coordination. So one's plans and fears were clearly not based upon chimera. I was touched to see in *The Globe & Laurel* that the Sarabak irregulars continued to be known as 'Lieutenant Moore's Own.' Sergeant Mackie, veteran of the Gumbang raid, had returned to 5 Troop, and took them over.'

Alan Hooper, Colonel

'As I embarked on board HMS *Albion* and enjoyed the unfailing hospitality of the Royal Navy for the four days back to Singapore, I reflected on the main lessons that I had learnt from this deployment.

'Uppermost in my mind was the excellent leadership at Senior NCO level exemplified at Gumbang. Sergeant Mackie and his team had been involved in four separate engagements, all at close range, and had come out on top each time – and without taking a single casualty in these actions. The Marines had been steadfast, shown good combat discipline, shot well and had gained in confidence with each engagement. The final contact when they faced an overwhelming larger force was a most impressive performance.

'This result was all built on mutual trust which, in turn, comes from the Royal Marines training. Officers, NCOs and Marines learn to trust each other at a very early stage so that in crises, it is a 'given.' This in turn leads to an 'empowered' approach stretching from the Commanding Officer to the Marine in the front line. Accordingly, I did not feel my Company Commander leaning on me and, in turn, I tried not to interfere too much with Sergeant Mackie. It was a lesson that I carried with me for the rest of my military career and tried to follow many years later when I became the Commanding Officer of 40 Commando.

'From this approach stemmed a reassuring calmness under pressure. It was particularly evident in the more experienced and older members of the Commando – a number of whom had served in the Second World War – and it rubbed off on the younger members. Years later, experience in Northern Ireland re-enforced my view that such an approach is achieved by the example of each generation passed down through the next. It helps if the military organisation is constantly in action (to date the Corps has only had one year without action since the end of the Second World War).'

Duncan Christie-Miller, Major

'It was the paradoxes that are the most vivid – never move at night, never use tracks! The minute details of life in the jungle also remain, down to: the need to know exactly where everything was located in your pack; the need to check everywhere for leeches; the lack of anything else but dark, green undergrowth and trees for hours on end; the smell of one's clothing and the stuff rubbed into the seams to keep bugs at bay; the need to fold your map so that it exactly fitted in the pocket on your left thigh; the speed with which it got dark and then the impenetrable darkness itself; the cries of unseen gibbons in the trees; the tedium of lying in ambush with absolutely nothing to do or to stimulate you; the pleasure of an unexpected helicopter lift back to base and the accompanying smell of AVGAS; the mildewed cigarette from a twenty-four hour ration pack; the pre-patrol check of each man to ensure that nothing rattled; the decreasing weight of your back pack as you ate the food and the reassuring fit of the webbing which almost embraced you as you slipped it on in the morning; the worn patch on the right hand magazine pouch where the SLR rifle rested; lastly the very comfortable and well designed jungle boots which slowly deteriorated and turned from green to pale albino in the process.

'And then there was Singapore – but that is another story!'